SAUSAGES
THE MAKING OF DOG SOLDIERS

BY JANINE PIPE

Encyclopocalypse Publications
www.encyclopocalypse.com

TABLE OF CONTENTS

As always to my loving husband and daughter.

To Neil, for making this movie in the first place and answering my endless questions along the way. Without his input, this would be nothing more than a long-ass love-letter.

To Mark, for accepting my garbled and excited pitch and being just as excited as I was. The support from Encyclopocalypse has been phenomenal.

To the memory of those involved who have since passed – Vic Bateman and Lisa Crawley.

Also, to Eddie Oswald

FOREWORD
BY JOE DANTE

Q. When is a war movie not a war movie?
A. When it's a werewolf movie.

Neil Marshall's *Dog Soldiers* (not to be confused with Robert Stone's novel "Dog Soldiers" that became the basis for the movie *Who'll Stop the Rain*), pits a squad of British soldiers on maneuvers in the Scottish Highlands against an unexpectedly dangerous enemy--a horde of werewolves. In its day this film didn't leave much of an imprint on US audiences[1], bypassing theatrical release in favor of premiering on the Sci Fi (now Syfy) channel where it languished among such lesser lights as *Sharktopus* and *Puppet Master vs. Demonic Toys*.

But it's time to bring *Dog Soldiers* out of the shadows, since it's one of the most assured directorial debuts since *Targets*.

After a luckluster DVD release from a source far from

---

1   Although Dogs didn't get a US theatrical release, Pathe were instrumental in its success in the UK.

the original negative, it's since been restored in 4K and awaits rediscovery as the major genre contribution it is.

All of us who have labored in this particular lupine vineyard have been confronted with the challenge of how to satisfy genre fans while bringing something new to the table and not simply imitating what has gone before.

During the 80s' what was new was the emergence of new kinds of special effects that galvanized a spate of lycanthropic favorites including *An American Werewolf in London* and *The Howling*. I can attest that one of the major hurdles making *The Howling* was its low budget and short schedule, which necessitated editing tricks designed to obscure the fact that the werewolf costumes weren't quite all there at the beginning of the shoot and indeed there was only one completed costume by the end. Through cutting we made it look like a whole pack of them. So I was pleased to see that one of the most accomplished aspects of *Dog Soldiers* is the editing. The glimpses we get of the wolves in action are convincing and impressionistic, which shows them off to best advantage. I was also happy to note some other borrowings from movies of mine, down to frequent cutaways to a soulful canine (the *real* dog soldier!).

During the six year gestation of the script, Marshall's template was the classic siege scenario familiar from *Rio Bravo* and *Assault on Precinct 13*, which focuses on building characters and suspense in a limited setting without coming off as claustrophobic. As he later proved with his remarkable Emmy-nominated turn as director of the "Game of Thrones" episode *Watchers on the Wall,* Marshall is a master of staging action in long takes with a firm sense of spatial integrity. And the last reel of *Dog*

Soldiers is a testament to this talent.

In addition, there's a lot of humor, a necessity in selling supernatural horror in a modern setting.

I say modern, but the fact is, although it plays like a new movie, *Dog Soldiers* is celebrating its 20th anniversary! (And how old does that make *me* feel, when *The Howling* is going on 40!!) I guess it just points up how popular these excursions into the lycanthropic continue to be, and the hold they have on the imaginations of generations of filmgoers who have kept werewolves in the public eye since 1935's *Werewolf of London.*

So, you're holding in your hands the first and only in-depth study of the making of Neil Marshall's latter-day classic, chronicling all the tsuris and second guessing that goes into any work of art. Since all movies are ultimately the sum total of hundreds of decisions made under duress, it's amazing when anything works, let alone rises above the fray. And now, although it's taken a bit of time, *Dog Soldiers* is assuming its rightful place near the top of the furry pile.

Joe Dante
The Howling, Gremlins and Explorers

INTRODUCTION
BY NEIL MARSHALL

If you'd told me 20 years ago that people would still be talking about *Dog Soldiers* in 2022, let alone writing books on the subject of its making, I'd have thought you quite mad. And yet, here we are, so what do I know?

Dog Soldiers' long incubation and realisation was the product of a lot of hard work by some incredibly talented people, and a couple of dogs. Its creation was fuelled by large amounts of alcohol, relentless and stubborn determination, and unfettered imagination. I didn't know what could be done, but better still I didn't know what couldn't be done. So I fundamentally wrote the movie I wanted to see with little, if any, consideration for the obstacles its relatively meagre budget might put in my way. I suspect it was this unbridled ambition, blended with dumbass naivety, that really threw a curveball at the British film industry of the late 90's, causing it to take 6 years to get financed, and ultimately not by them.

But I think now that the prolonged planning and development period actually did the film a big favour, not only improving the script through numerous rewrites, but also turning into a kind of creative pressure cooker that, by the time we finally went into production, burst open in an explosion of energy and imagination from every department. I can't thank enough all those lunatics who came along for the adventure and put their trust and talent in the hands of a debut feature film director and all-round Geordie. It would of rude of me to namecheck some and not all, but you all know who you are. The entire cast and crew should share and bask in the glory. It's well deserved!

And then there's the book! I've been a huge fan of 'Making of' documentaries and books all my life. I have an insatiable hunger to read about how other movies are made and the creative challenges other filmmakers face and overcome. I've always dreamed of someone writing a book about the making of one of my own movies, so I couldn't believe my luck when I pitched the idea to Janine and her publisher at Encyclopocalypse gave the green light. "Top Bosie!" as Kevin McKidd would often say during filming.

So thank the movie gods for Janine Pipe and her fellow passionate fanatics for making this particular dream come true.

Now, put the kettle on, make yourself a brew, put your feet up and enjoy!

Neil Marshall
2022

PROLOGUE

June/July 2002. My then fiancé now husband and I were in Corfu on holiday, celebrating the end of his final year of Law. The beer was cheap, and we were more than a little tipsy, sat in an outside bar, sun streaming. I think at some point there was some footy on, they'd constructed a large 'screen' out of a sheet and were projecting a no doubt illegal feed onto it. As the afternoon became evening, and the footy was long over, the barman put a movie on. The quality was god-awful because it was quite obviously a pirate copy. The footage was shaky and dark, and I was well on my way to drunksville but something about the soldiers on the sheet screen captivated me. I don't recall much else from that first viewing except for two things – Sean Pertwee's sausages and the name, *Dog Soldiers*.

A few years later, I rented the actual official DVD (or maybe even still VHS) from Blockbuster and properly fell in love with the movie. Fortuitously, I recognized the name of the director, realising he had a new movie out called *The Descent* (which quite frankly scared the shit out of me) and as luck would have it, it was playing at the local Cineworld.

And that was it. Two for two, both movies absolute

corkers, I knew I had found not only a couple of favourite features, but a favourite director.

The rest for me as they say, is history. I have watched *Dog Soldiers* more times than I should admit and own several varying copies. It has inspired and influenced my own writing and is the movie I cite the most in interviews.

When it dawned on me last year that we were fast approaching the 20th anniversary, firstly, I wept as that made me feel really old, but secondly, it filled me with excitement and determination. I wanted to do *something* to mark the occasion. At this point, I was a published author and had some non-fiction credits to my name, mainly interviews, but not a whole lot of experience in feature writing. Still, I pitched the idea of a celebratory retrospective of the movie to Fangoria and Scream Magazine. I can't begin to tell you how daunting it was reaching out to the people I had seen on my telly so many times. I had read and watched hundreds of interviews and interactions with Neil and Sean especially and they certainly seemed like cool guys but what if they turned me down? What if I talked to them and I made a tit out of myself (likely), or they turned out to be horrible (unlikely but would be heart-breaking). The result of course is obvious, and I can honestly say that each and every person I have communicated with who worked on the film in any capacity, has been a truly lovely human being. I expect a huge part of that is down to the fact that Neil has a strict 'No Dicks on Set' policy which really should be everyone's edict on life in general, but it is something he takes very seriously.

Once I had written those features, I knew I needed more and after conferring with Neil, as without his ongoing support, this would just be a just fan book, the idea for *Sausages* was born. I approached Encyclopocalypse Publications due to the awesome movie tie-ins they produce, knowing only they could make this dream come true. I could have been knocked back at the first hurdle. Thankfully though, Mark loved my garbled and over excitable pitch and said yes. The contract was sealed with blood and the promise of a first born. Special mention to Christian and Sean from the press here for being awesome too.

It has been an honour, a privilege and a dream come true to speak with the people involved in the making of *Dog Soldiers*. They say you should never meet your heroes or discover too much behind the scenes stuff about your favourite work as you'll only ever be disappointed. Well, I am testament to that being a fallacy as if anything, and I didn't even think it could be possible, I now love the film, and everyone involved with it even more.

Neil didn't just create a movie.

He created a family.

Long-lasting friendships and mutual respect between him and his cast and crew and with each other.

He has inspired people, made them want to write, direct, produce.

If you are reading this hoping for controversy, conspiracy theories, backstabbing on the set, I am not sorry to tell you that you'll be disappointed. There was none of that. What you see is what you get – a group of people made a brilliant movie who were 'bloody loving it'. I am also not interested in discovering if there were any tiffs. This book is a celebration. It is unabashedly biased but will hopefully serve as a peek behind the curtains and a delve into the mind of the creator.

Neil Marshall achieved something many had and continue to fail at - he made a good werewolf movie.

But *Dog Soldiers*, now in its 20th year, is so much more than just that.

CHAPTER
ONE

Sometimes, because a certain film or director becomes so popular, especially when it is a debut feature, you naively believe the path to success must have been relatively simple and quick.

The director has an idea.

They quickly write a script.

People *immediately* get on board and throw money at it.

They make the picture with ease and before long, it's being distributed for full theatrical release.

Critics love it, they have even more amazing ideas and now can do what they like with ridiculous budgets and a dream cast.

Tada!

But of course, it is never really that easy. Much like the hundreds of rejections Stephen King received before selling *Carrie*, Neil Marshall didn't come up with the idea for *Dog Soldiers* overnight and then just strike gold with casting and distribution. He didn't write the script in 2000 and shoot it in 2001. This had been years in the making with an absolute ton of knock-backs and disappointments along the way. He first drafted a pitch deck back in 1995, the full *first* script in 1996. By the time it came to shoot over in Luxembourg in March 2001, six long years later, he knew this story inside out, as did many of his long-standing friends who were there from the start, many being involved in some small way. It really was a friends and family affair.

So, where did it all begin?

Neil Marshall was born in May 1970 in Newcastle Upon Tyne in the UK. He knew from an early age he wanted to make movies. *Indiana Jones and the Raiders of the Lost Ark* and *Star Wars* were game changers for young Neil, especially after he watched the 'Making of' documentary that went alongside the Spielberg classic.

"So many of these films I saw as a child and in my early teens influenced me. It's the time where your future taste in movies is heavily affected. I watched horror movies for as long as I can remember, my dad would show me things like the old black and white Bride of Frankenstein, *and* Doctor Who *would have me hiding behind the sofa. As we got into the 80s, I started watching the then called Video Nasties and with the onslaught of VHS*

becoming more readily available, that led me to Zombie Flesh Eaters *and* I Spit on Your Grave, *grainy pirate videos. 1975 through the late 80s was my time period.* Alien, The Thing, The Shining *all of those are my favourites."*

Neil Marshall

Neil's sister, Sue, adds:

"He never wavered from his dream path, never had a paper-round or Saturday job or even bar work, nothing to distract him from his goal. He and his school buddies used to run around doing all their own stunts with film cameras and homemade guns."

Sue Kayall

He was unashamedly a geek, devouring comic books and watching as many movies as he could, learning from the masters. His love of genre features was heavily shaped by the likes of early Peter Jackson (*Brain Dead* – *"I kick ass for the Lord!"* -, *Bad Taste* and *Meet The Feebles*), Sam Rami, Joe Dante and John Landis. He still cites John Carpenter as one of his main influences, particularly for *Dog Soldiers*.

And not just horror stuff, *Unforgiven* and *Rio Bravo* also made an impact, as was did western which involved a siege scenario, and *Assault on Precinct 13*.

> **"If you just love movies enough, you can make a good one."**
> **Quentin Tarantino – *Pulp Fiction***

But let's not get ahead of ourselves. Neil attended Newcastle Polytechnic studying film. This was not the same as film school, more of a generic course but did enable him to learn a lot of theory and more importantly make a student movie. And whilst all the others were the usual kind of arty-farty type endeavours one usually expects from students, Neil's was of course about zombies and aptly called *Brain Death*.

Newcastle Poly was also where he met Keith Bell, who was in the year below. They formed a friendship, bonding over their love of *The Evil Dead* and worked on each other's projects, Neil as an editor. Learning this skill has been instrumental in not only being able to cut his own films, but in knowing what is needed as a director. He has often said why do three takes when you can get all you need in two and has stated that every director should know the process of editing. After graduation, they came back together to work on a movie *Killing Time* in 1998. Neil co-wrote and edited, and Keith was production manager, along with some of their other mates including Sam McCurdy. The idea behind this project being that if in theory *anyone* can make a movie, even a mobster/assassin/crime/thriller, why not them? It wasn't the best experience; a shit ton of things went wrong including an attempted mugging on the set, but they did it. They made a feature. And that's often how you learn, right, from practice and through your mistakes.

Keith had moved up to Scotland for work with the BBC. One day he received a phone call from a very excited Neil, who had an idea to pitch to him. They met up in Glasgow and Neil spills the beans. He has this idea for a crazy soldier siege story where the squaddies are fighting a bunch of werewolves. Keith loved the idea and Neil's obvious enthusiasm and said immediately, *"Yes, let's do it!"*

After a spot of hiking and a few too many pints in The Slaughtered Lamb, Keith decided they should have a contract. He will produce the movie; Neil will write the script and direct. They signed it in blood, or rather a biro on a soggy napkin. It might not have held up in a court of law, but just like any respectable crossroad demon, they were men of their word with souls to collect. Or a movie to make.

On one of those many trips hiking around the Scottish Highlands, back in the days of giant Ordinance Survey maps that never ever folded back up correctly, they came across a location that would have made a perfect setting if the film had ended up being made there. Neil needed to make a mark on the map so he could tell people where it was. He looked at the legend at the bottom of the page in order to work out the coordinates. Along with the legend, was a tiny box giving an example of how exactly to work out those coordinates if you weren't an everyday rambler or scout. And wouldn't you know, out of the whole of this map which was almost as big as he was, the tiny box giving an example showed the exact spot they discovered and wanted to mark. Welcome, to the Twilight Zone…

Over the next few years, Neil wrote (and re-wrote and re-wrote) the script. It was an intriguing story – *Saving Private Ryan* but with werewolves instead of Germans is a description he often uses. It was full of military jargon, testosterone and monster-fighting action scenes, the dialogue heavily laden with talk of girls and footy. A real post-pub laddish film with some good old British humour to boot.

Once he'd reached the stage where he was semi-confident the plot worked and the characters were believable, Neil shared the script with his good friend, Ian Flemming. Yes, that really is his name. Ian recalls visiting Neil at Pinewood Studios whilst *The Descent* was shooting, and the security guard refusing to let him in as he was convinced Ian was using fake ID. Because if you were inventing a persona, you'd obviously use the name of the author and not the cool, suave 007 moniker everyone knows. They'd also met at the Polytechnic and Neil even lived with Ian from time to time. They'd also been working together, Neil editing some projects Ian was involved with. Horror wasn't really Ian's forte, but he had screen-writing experience and Neil wanted his friend's honest opinion. He was also very excited about it. Therefore, Ian was both interested and wanted to support his friend. Something that crops up time and time again is how infectious Neil's enthusiasm is. He makes you feel like you not only want but *need* to be a part of whatever he's doing. Ian took the script with him on the hour or so train ride to work and started reading. By the time he reached his stop, he wasn't quite finished, and recalls walking through the town with his nose buried in the papers, you know like you see on the telly and think that no one in real life ever does it. He quickly finished it once he reached their building, Neil ready with the coffee as always. I think it is fair to deduce from this that although Ian might not have been a big horror fan, he really enjoyed Neil's writing and characterisation. He could tell an intriguing story. Ian and his wife Belinda were there through the whole sometimes painful experience of witnessing their talented friend have such an amazing idea but just struggle to find the right people to make it and finance it.

Coincidentally, although now in Surry rather than the

North-East, Ian still has to take the train sometimes into London and there is an army barracks (Pirbright) not too far from him. He still often hears the squaddies talking about how much they enjoy *Dog Soldiers*, and it always makes him smile and feel a sense of pride.

Neil never gave up. Ian states it was his sense of confidence, without being arrogant, and stubborn determination that got him through those years of being constantly let down, disappointed and left on the side by people who were just not interested in being part of a genre feature. There was a real sense of snobbery in regard to horror despite the British film industry being steeped in horror history with Hammer Film Production and Amicus Productions and then the minor boom in the 80s thanks to features such as the almighty *Hellraiser*. But in the mid to late 90s, no one wanted to touch horror with a bargepole. So, what the hell did Neil have to do to get this damn thing green-lit in the absence of a Monkey's Paw or a Wishmaster?

CHAPTER
TWO
PRE PRODUCTION

Okay where were we? Ah yes, we have a script, one which would be rewritten almost twenty times mind you, but still a script which people seemed to like.

Next step, money.

Oh dear.

> *"Everyone who ever made a low-budget film was influenced by* **Night of the Living Dead***"*
> **John Carpenter** – *Halloween*

The late 90's was not exactly a time synonymous with British horror. This new wave would come thick and fast and bring about a resurgence within the industry but at the time most of the executives and distributors were looking for the next *Notting Hill* or *Lock, Stock and Two Smoking Barrels*, not some lads running around with guns fighting werewolves. That would be ludicrous...

Edgar Wright had similar issues with getting *Shaun of*

the Dead greenlit. I bet there were a lot of people with egg on their face once both *Dog Soldiers* and the first of the Cornetto Trilogy did so well *blows raspberries*.

Neil and Keith were knocked back and turned down by every single studio in the UK.

No one wanted to touch it. Not only did people not believe a British horror film was viable at the time, but they also thought the script was far too ambitious for a first-time feature. Thankfully, Neil wasn't deterred by this. Remember that dogged determination? And yes, that is a pun, thank you, Ian Flemming. Neil's friend, not *that* one, I've already explained this!

They did manage to pique the interest of Vic Bateman from the Victor Film Company (VFC) who was a London based sales agent and saw something in Neil and his relentless drive. Vic and Allistair Waddell were instrumental in bringing Neil's vision to fruition. VFC also brought in well-respected producer, Christopher Figg. Christopher had made a name for himself in the 80s and early 90s with movies such as *Hellraiser* (the original, second and third) so he had horror chops. Christopher in turn would not only end up suggesting Kevin McKidd, whom he had worked with on *Trainspotting* and believed had great potential, but he also brought in the Noel Gay Motion Picture Company and another producer, Tom Reeve. Tom at the time had been busy making movies out in Luxembourg including *Tale of the Mummy* in 1998 starring none of than Sean Pertwee (on three, hum the theme tune for It's a Small World with me…)

Around this time, Neil began chatting with Dave Bonneywell, shown on the next page with fellow SFX wizard, Pete Hawkins after a fake-blood explosion. What a cool job.

Dave and Pete

He had met Dave via creature designer Bob Keen, who at the time ran Image Animation, one of the biggest make-up effects companies in the world. Dave was tasked with designing the wolves and even made a small model made based on some of the sketches Neil and Keith's mate, Simon Lang, had drawn for them years ago. That would be the basic concept for the graceful look his wolves would embody, which was so different from what had come before.

Wolf concept art by Colin Lang

As well as the maquette, Dave painted an updated

version of the wolf, something that would have fit perfectly in a Slaine story in 2000AD.

Original wolf artwork by Dave Bonneywell

Potential investors were also starting to ask exactly what experience Neil was bringing to the table, to prove he was indeed capable of directing such an ambitious debut feature. Sure, he'd done stuff at film school and had worked as a writer/editor and jack of all trades on *Killing Time* but what about direction? He needed something to show those controlling the purse strings he was up to the task. Managing to secure some cash from one of the local art funds, he and an old buddy got some camo gear and ran around in the woods for a bit making a cheap as chips teaser trailer for *Dog Soldiers*. He also shot a short film called *Combat* which is an extra on the UK DVD. This 10-minute production would have no dialogue and miniscule budget (they couldn't afford to pay the extras so put some money behind the bar. In the two days it took to shoot, many, many beers were sunk). Ian Flemming was involved (the friend!) and brought in Leslie Simpson and Craig Conway, who will re-appear later. The crew was made up of friends and colleagues including Director of Photography Sam McCurdy and several others who would end up on *Dog Soldiers*. They all had a blast making it and it turned out even better than they'd hoped. *Now* they had something to prove they could indeed make this movie.

But they still needed more. Much more. They needed financial backing and plenty of it. Vic and Allistair from VFC ended up heading to the American Film Market with the script, the wolf maquette and bucket load of hope. They just so happened to strike up conversation with a millionaire spinach tycoon by the name of David E Allen. Allen owned a film company called Kissmet but hadn't really got started on anything at the time. However, he was hankering to make a werewolf movie. Serendipity again. Allen had money but wanted werewolves and there was Vic and Allistar with a werewolf movie needing money! He agreed to partially finance the movie and take on a role as producer.

Things had taken a very positive turn, but it wasn't ready to go quite yet.

Many different locations, including the Isle of Man and even Canada, were scouted. They were mainly looking for somewhere that would offer a tax break as well as having a visual similarity to the Scottish Highlands. Then, they stumbled across Luxembourg and Tom Reeve. Not only would it offer forests reminiscent of Scotland, but they would also have access to a studio. Combine that with a crew of camera and tech guys who knew their stuff and had all been through compulsory military training and the very much-needed tax break, and they finally had a breakthrough. The wooded areas were perfect, with much of the location belonging to the Duke of Luxembourg's estate. But they'd need to build the cottage where most of the action would take place from scratch – welcome Simon Bowles to the party! Neil interviewed several set designers but when he met Simon, they instantly clicked. Despite his lack of experience (Simon had been an Art Director but not a Production Designer), there was something about him that Neil warmed to, and he saw the potential. Again, like so many others, they have gone on to work together on numerous other projects and remain fast friends.

Set building

Neil recalls a moment where he and Simon were driving around Luxembourg looking for suitable locations for filming, when they happened upon a strange sight. Passing by a field, they noticed around twenty seemingly ordinary people, i.e. not clad in hooded robes or brandishing pitchforks, standing in the middle of the greenery. At the centre of the congregation, stood a huge crucifix, around twenty foot tall. As they drove past, getting serious *Wicker Man* vibes, things got more sinister, as the entire group turned and stared at them. If there had been music playing, there would have been a scratch across the record as it screeched to a stop. Neil and Simon might have been there to shoot a horror movie, but they didn't much fancy becoming a part of one if these field dwellers were looking for a someone to string up onto or into the crucifix. Therefore, they made the only sensible decision available and got the hell outta there!!! As well as a very clear vision of the setting, Neil was adamant about one other thing – his monsters would be practical, and all effects would be in camera. This was a creature-feature, very much a job for SFX and make-up, not CGI. They didn't have the budget for it even if they had wanted to use enhanced computer graphics, but it was never an option.

> "An American Werewolf in London *has the best transformation scene but a very animalistic looking wolf. Then* The Howling *has amazing creatures, but you hardly ever see them. I wanted mine to be hyper real, a combination of wolf and human. A hybrid, bipedal seven-foot monster. In my mind, there was only ever one man for the job – Bob Keen. And something we agreed on from the start was that we wanted big, kick-arse creatures."*
>
> Neil Marshall

Bob Keen and Dave Bonneywell brought with them an expert team who were young, enthusiastic and eager to get their teeth into the work.

Cue Pete Hawkins, Mat O'Toole, Justin Pitkethly, Anthony Parker and Lisa Crawley. They designed all sorts of props and instruments to bring the magic of Neil's mind to life.

Mat and Dave testing stuff in the workshop

"I think cinema, movies, and magic have always been closely associated. The very earliest people who made film were magicians."
Francis Ford Coppola – *The Godfather*

And it really was very much a collaborative process. Much as it has come up time and time again in conversation with the cast, Neil was also fully on board with *anyone* involved in the feature making suggestions on little tweaks here and there, and the massively important creature design was no different.

> *"In the final design I presented the wolves had really long fingers and talons which Neil loved and that's how we started to build them. But then I got the final script! The werewolves were grabbing things using weapons (including shooting a gun!), punching through walls and doors etc and I realised that there was no way they'd do any of that with these humungous fingers and claws. I remember phoning Neil and asking just how in love with the idea he was and asked if we could ditch it for something more practical to which he agreed."*

Dave Bonneywell

As someone who loves practical in-camera effects in horror movies, I have been blown away by the sheer talent these guys have. All too often, the general viewer watches a movie without a thought to the SFX process. I have always been impressed, but now having spoken to most of the original team, I take my hat off to anyone who works in prosthetics and special effects make up. Utterly fantastic.

Now, what's a good creature-feature, soldier-siege movie without an atmospheric soundtrack? Certain film and TV scores are just iconic; think of the theme for *Halloween* or the opening credits of *The X-Files*. Christopher Figg suggested composer Mark Thomas, whom he had worked with before on a production called *House* (starring Kelly Macdonald who'd worked with Kevin McKidd on *Trainspotting*. They'd go on to star in *Brave* together too). Mark was not only a well-respected orchestral composer but had played violin on several film scores himself including *Highlander*. Mark pitched a score to Neil that he'd composed for the teaser trailer Neil made with his old pal, and he was in – another piece of the puzzle sorted. Let's hope it's not a Lament Configuration puzzle…

Mark says Neil was very easy to work with, not only liking him straight away, but finding him motivational and inspiring as well as being multi-talented. He realised early on, that traditional folk melodies seemed to resonate with Neil and bring the right tone to the piece. Since Neil was a Geordie, Mark researched folk songs from the North-East and found one entitled *Lyke-wake Dirge*. He wove parts of that into the score, particularly towards the end as it carries such an emotional component. Something else I'm convinced had some influence, was the score from John Carpenter's *The Thing*. There is a particular melody playing when the men are gathered outside in the snow and MacReady burns Bennings. Listen to that and tell me it doesn't remind you of parts of Mark's haunting music.

> **"A film is, or should be, more like music than like fiction. It should be a progression of moods and feelings. The theme, what's behind the emotion, the meaning, all that comes later."**
> **Stanley Kubrick – *A Clockwork Orange***

CHAPTER
THREE
CASTING

Imagine Jason Statham as Cooper.

Simon Pegg as Spoon.

Jason Isaacs as Wells.

Can you even do that?

Because I can't.

Now, I'm not a total idiot, and I realise that if those original castings had remained in place, we'd never know anything different.

They are all hugely talented and successful actors.

But, to think I, I mean *all* the fans, would have been deprived Kev's accent, Darren's boxing skills, and all of Sean's brilliance, is just too much to bear.

Therefore, let's take a look at how people got involved, along with the help of Jeremy Zimmerman from Zimmerman Casting.

SERGEANT HARRY G. WELLS

Neil had seen Jason Isaacs in a TV show called *Civvies* and thought he would be a perfect fit for Wells. He sent the script to Jason's agent who passed it on for him to read through, which doesn't always happen. Many, many people are thwarted at this very first stage. However, Jason read it and thought it was great. There was a problem though. He was completely tied up in many, many projects including of course becoming

Lucius Malfoy. However, Jason knew Sean Pertwee from *Event Horizon* and thought it would be ideal for him (give that man a round of applause). He gave Sean the script and of course, being the awesome fella he is, he enjoyed the writing and the concept so much, he agreed to meet with Neil. Seeing the enduring passion this man had for the project and how well he knew all the intricate ins and outs, Sean felt engaged by that contagious enthusiasm. So much so, he even told Neil to use his name if needed to try and get other people on board.

Sean does recall not really knowing what the hell it was all about though. At first, he'd thought it was something to do with aliens, but he liked Neil's confidence and positive attitude enough that the actual foe didn't matter.

Despite it taking almost two years to get to the point of being able to say, *"Let's make a movie!"*, Sean kept his word and took the part of Sergeant Harry G. Wells. And that sense of respect and loyalty between Neil and Sean has lasted way longer than just one shoot. They went on to work together on *Doomsday* and *The Reckoning*. He was offered the role of the husband at the start of *The Descent* also but had been unable to take the part due to prior commitments.

That sense of loyalty, camaraderie, respect and trust shines through time and time again with Neil and the actors he continues to cast and crew he chooses to work with. He has created a family who will oftentimes drop everything if they can to work with him. Neil has said that as a filmmaker, he likes creating these groups of people that love each other and it is evident from everyone you speak with.

PRIVATE LAWRENCE COOPER

Next was Jason Statham, not yet big-time but having impressed Neil in *Lock, Stock and Two Smoking Barrels*. Jason actually agreed to the part of Cooper but at some point, still in the limbo between casting and production, he was offered the role in *Ghosts of Mars* by one of Neil's own main influences, John Carpenter. It was actually Neil himself who told Jason to take the part, citing you don't turn down a Carpenter movie. It is interesting to note that there were no hard feelings afterwards and the pair have met sporadically since at various premieres and events and always get along well.

After Jason left the project, Christopher Figg suggested Kevin McKidd for the role. Although he hadn't played that sort of character before and was most well-known for Tommy in *Trainspotting* at that time, Christopher felt it would suit him and he had the potential. I'll buy Mr Figg a beer if I ever meet him as Kev is utterly perfect as Cooper.

Kev's agent wasn't sure it was the right sort of project for him to be associated with (that horror snobbery rearing its ugly head again) but luckily, he vetoed her opinion, having thought the script was just the right balance of action and very British comedy.

Obviously being set in Scotland was another huge draw. He met with Neil, liked him immediately and that was that. Woo hoo!

CAPTAIN RICHARD RYAN

Neil approached Liam Cunningham's agent for the role of arsehole, plummy Brit, Captain Ryan. Having read an older version of the script, Liam actually passed on it at first, as he just felt it was lacking something.

Then, around nine months or so later, a revised version turned up and he decided to take another look, just in case. This time Neil had gone away and added a vital element – humour. Liam felt it was now more coherent and very funny, dripping with comedy. He loved this version and said, *"Sign me up!"* right away.

PRIVATE PHIL WITHERSPOON

Can you imagine Simon Pegg in the role of Spoon? Although I'm a huge fan of his, right back from *Spaced* which is also where Neil noticed his star potential, it pains me to think of anyone but Darren Morfitt in this role.

Neil did actually meet with Simon, who was flattered and liked the script very much. There was just one small issue.

I'll let someone else explain that teeny-weeny problem.

"Neil offered Simon a part and when I heard about that I forbade him from doing it as we were writing Shaun *at the time and I didn't want him to be in a UK horror movie just before ours."*

Edgar Wright – *Shaun of the Dead*

It's a dog-eat-dog world this movie malarky. Of course, Neil supported Simon fully, and Edgar was impressed by his loyalty. There are actually many uncanny parallels to both bringing the film to fruition and in the features themselves. For a deeper dive into *Shaun of the Dead*, you should definitely read *You've Got Red On You* by Clark Collis.

After a successful audition, Darren Morfitt ended up being perfectly cast as Spoon. With previous boxing and on-scene military experience, and just the right sort of 'bloody loving it' attitude, Darren made his character completely gung-ho but in a way that you just warm to him rather than think he is a careless twat. He is an extremely well-loved character.

CORPORAL BRUCE CAMPBELL

Thomas Lockyear's character pays homage to The Evil Dead in a very open way – no Easter Egg here, just out there for all to see.

Thomas auditioned in the usual way via Zimmerman Casting and had a fair bit of acting experience behind him, albeit it mainly TV.

PRIVATE JOE KIRKLEY

Chris Robson also auditioned to play Joe. He'd had a little experience playing a German soldier in *Band of Brothers* and of course was a fellow North-East chap.

PRIVATE TERRY MILBURN

The part of the vomiting cavalier, Terry, went to Leslie Simpson, who Neil had previously worked with in *Combat* and had known since then he wanted Les to be in his werewolf movie. There was an official audition, but Neil was certain he wanted Les in the film in some capacity. As with many of the other members of the cast and crew, they would go on to work together again in the future too.

MEGAN

Neil remembers seeing Emma Cleasby way back in the 90s in Newcastle's answer to *Grange Hill*, one of my favourite TV shows from my teens, *Byker Grove*. He has wanted her to be in *Combat*, yet again after an introduction from Ian Flemming, but she was unavailable at the time. He didn't give up hope of working with her and was thrilled when she was able to join the cast as Megan.

Although Emma was approached to speak with, she is no longer acting and has stepped away from the spotlight. She is busy with her family and wished us luck with the project. We wish her all the best for her future also, no matter the time of the month...

THE CAMPERS

DAVID - Having worked with fellow North-eastern actor Craig Conway yet again on *Combat* via an introduction by yup, you guessed it, Ian Flemming, Neil asked if he wanted to audition for the role of Terry. However, Craig's agent passed on the script and set him up with a 2-year theatre contract instead.

Later he received a call from Neil asking if he wanted a small part at the start of the movie and if so, could he fly out that evening? The original actor, Casper Berry, had been delayed in Las Vegas (he was a professional poker player!) and couldn't get back in time. Of course, Craig jumped at the chance and pretended to be sick to get away for the weekend.

He refers to the opening scene playing the male camper, as his Drew Barrymore moment, à la *Scream*.

SARAH – Tina Landini was cast as the female camper after Neil had seen some of her previous TV work. She auditioned via a video through Zimmerman casting and of course was selected.

Although *Sausages* is a celebration of *Dog Soldiers*, it would be remiss of us not to mention a very sad accident that occurred after Tina returned to the UK. She was unfortunately involved in a serious road traffic collision and badly injured. All of the cast and crew had nothing but lovely things to say about her and how tragic the event was. Everyone continues to wish her and her family well.

Heeeeeeeeere's Ben!

THE WEREWOLVES

Neil went to the Pineapple Dance Studios in London to recruit Bryn Walters who had appeared in *Cats* and Brian Claxton Payne.

Their physique and movement were perfect for the look of the wolves Neil had envisioned. The third performer was an actual stuntman, Ben Wright who has gone on to work for some major players such as Marvel, DC and *James Bond*.

43

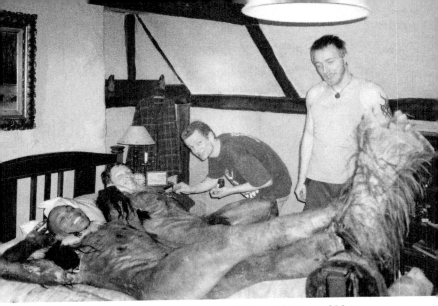

They're not that scary – Bryn and Brian with Dave and Mat

CHAPTER
FOUR
THE MOVIE

We now have a cast raring to go. The actors showed up a few days before filming started and got kitted out with costumes, visited the hair and make-up people to make sure they had military acceptable barnets and to practice the scars etc.

Wells went 10 rounds with Captain Hook

And speaking of scars, if you ever wondered why Wells has that very unique blemish on his cheek and what the story is behind it, well you'll have to keep wondering! Sean asked for it specifically and called it his 'bottle scar'.

But there is no elaborate tale as to why other than Sean says it was inspired by a guy he knew of.

The cast also got some time for training and a bit of rehearsal. Mainly this calm before the storm was for them to bond and create some electricity between them so their ensemble performance would seem more authentic since they were portraying such a tight knit group of friends. And it certainly comes across that way on screen.

Just three lads hanging out

There was a youngish and extremely multi-national crew ready to show what they could do.

The whole gang

And an eager director who knew this story inside and out, having spent the last five years writing and re-writing and pitching it to people.

But it was still Neil's first-time shouting action. He remembers being incredibly nervous on that morning. Generally, he would be on set ready for 8am, aiming to start turning over (filming) within the first hour. Whilst some movies will have continuous days and wrap an hour earlier instead of stopping for a designated lunch hour, they did tend to break for in the middle of the day and finish around 8pm.

That's 12-hour days.

> *"It's hard work making movies. It's like being a doctor: you work long hours, very hard hours, and it's emotional, tense work. If you don't really love it, then it ain't worth it."*
>
> **George Lucas** - *Star Wars*

They aimed to get around thirty-five to forty set-ups per day. For the people who didn't go to film school *raises own hand*, 'set-ups' are where you move the camera to a different location for another scene/shot. 'Takes' are what the camera captures within the same set-up. Clear as mud?

The very first scene involves Craig Conway and Tina Landini, a young couple camping in the Scottish Highlands.

Sarah has bought David a solid silver letter opener (affectionally referred to as Excalibur on set), to say well done for a promotion at work. We don't know what exactly, but she does say, *"What my writer, lost for words?"* so he is perhaps an author or journalist? Soon the couple are enjoying some alone time, and during some snogging, David's hand begins to travel down to Sarah's bright orange trousers. There is a great moment where he unzips them but once he's finished, the sound continues. A very different zipper is being slowly undone by unknown persons - the tent opening, which as all horror fans know is never ever a good sign.

Craig after Tina gets it

48

We get a quick taste of action without anything solid being given away. All sorts of growling and the tent shaking about. Poor Sarah is dragged out and very clearly attacked by something due to the amount of blood shown in the tent and splashed onto David. His fingers attempt to reach for the letter opener, but it's too late.

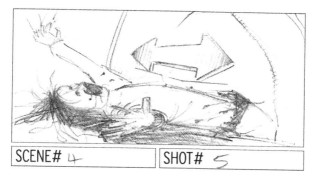

SCENE# 4   SHOT# 5

We get one final shot of his terrified face, frozen in shock and of the full moon and BAM the title card appears. Neil has said he really doesn't like it, that it looks cheap and nasty, similar to something he could have made when he was just a kid running about with a Super 8 camera. Things like that were usually sent to him for approval first, but by the time he got to see this, it was too late, and he was stuck.

An early Title Treatment hand-painted by Neil Marshall

It's the kind of opening scene that gives you just a teaser of what is about to happen, if you went into the movie with no prior knowledge as to the theme or what the soldiers would be encountering. It sets it up perfectly to know this will be bloody, there will be jump scares and don't be at all surprised when the character you have bonded with is suddenly ripped away from you, literally.

But let's talk a little more about the making of that first scene.

Craig and Tina had only met the night before and had been introduced by Neil suggesting they do a bit of rehearsing. So, as you can imagine, they got to know each other pretty well and practicing your snogging in front of your director doesn't sound at all awkward!

First off, the scene was actually filmed inside the studio location.

The SFX guys had rigged up a special tube to spurt David with Sarahs' blood which was actually tomato puree and the whole area smelt like pizza topping for days. By not giving Craig an exact cue as to when the blood was coming, the look of surprise on his face when he gets covered in Mariana sauce is actually authentic.

Matt on location

Mat O'Toole (special makeup effects artist) actually dragged Tina out of the tent, acting as the off-scene attacker and in the midst of this realised if he continued to just pull at her, she would likely snag her back on a rogue piece of wood. So being a gentleman and caring person, he sort of grabbed at her waist, lifting her up. This resulted in her straddling him in a slightly compromising position. But at least she didn't scratch her back.

2 HOURS EARLIER – NORTH WALES

Less than three minutes in and we are now in Wales, two hours before the scene in the tent according to the digital subtitle. It's dark, cold, and a man is running through the woods. A flare goes up into the sky, he looks panicked. We see shadows of people chasing him, but thankfully for now, they look like just normal men, oh and a dog. The musical score reflects this chase perfectly, the tempo rising as the man starts to fight with this unknown enemy. A few quick punches are thrown, and he even manages to lob a torch at one of them. Then, smack and he's down with a gun to his head. But it's okay, we soon learn these men are soldiers, nothing to worry about. He also has nothing to worry about with that gun. Obviously, it wouldn't have been loaded with live ammo but this one didn't even have blanks. The reason why? It's missing the magazine. But that was only picked up on after the film had wrapped.

The solider on the run is of course the wonderful Kevin McKidd, who looks pretty cool here laying in a few punches, right? He seems the type of guy who can do a few choreographed stunts, has a good physique etc. He wouldn't be the type of wally to injure himself on the first morning of training, that's right training. Not even during a fantastic fight scene or anything. Oh no, wait a moment…

> *"We flew out to Luxembourg and were doing some pre-training with a military advisor. This was Day One. He was giving us this tactical advice like how to create cover when you dive out of the helicopter, how to make a perimeter etc. and I was really into it. Anyway, I managed to fall over and forgot I was wearing this huge utility belt and I landed on a metal canteen and broke my rib. Day one! I didn't tell anyone though as I thought I was going to get sent home, so I spent a week wincing in pain. Then when I thought there was enough in the can that they couldn't fire me, I told Neil I kind of broke my rib…"*
>
> Kev McKidd

That's how committed Kev was already to this feature. Balls of British steel.

Training time

52

Back to Wales…

The other soldiers in this scene were some of the crew from Luxembourg. Grips, camera operators, all sorts. This was because Luxembourg still had National Service where young men had to join the military after school and therefore had basic training under their belts. This would come in useful for a few different scenes especially since there was nowhere near enough money in the budget for a second unit or stunt actors. The dog here was also a pain as it was a Luxembourg breed of Alsatian which happens to be incredibly placid and wouldn't act aggressively or bark like Neil wanted. The sounds had to be added in post.

We learn Private Cooper has evaded capture for 22hrs and 47 minutes and is to go straight to the top of the class. Except for one thing of course. Toffee-nose Captain Ryan wants him to finish the job. And by that, he means shoot the dog.

What a way to introduce your villain! We all know that there is often a rule with horror fans, particularly within the world of prose, that an author can do whatever the hell they want with their human characters, just don't mess with the animals. I distinctly recall watching this scene and thinking, don't do it, Cooper! And of course, he doesn't, but Ryan does, cementing the fact he is pure evil and deserves nothing but hatred and contempt now throughout the entire movie. The cocky little jaunt of the head just before he pulls the trigger sums up Ryan in one swift movement. As does Cooper's incandescent with rage reaction, we get our first taste that he is a soldier and therefore a man who is trained to kill, but not without reason. Cooper has a conscience and immediately becomes someone we warm to and want to know more about.

Ian Flemming told me that Neil imbued Cooper with many of his own qualities of character - loyalty, confidence, chivalry and a sense of moral justice. Perhaps this is why he is such a well-rounded and instantly likeable character.

So just like that Cooper fails selection for this elite group and is RTU'd (Return to Unit) back to his squad and thank god as we know what would have happened to him otherwise.

Cue another title screen – 4 weeks later, Scottish Highlands.

4 WEEKS LATER – THE HIGHLANDS OF SCOTLAND

The ariel shots were actually taken over the Highlands once principal filming had wrapped despite the rest of the feature being shot in Luxembourg. We are also treated to one of my favourite and I think most iconic pieces of music - the theme tune.

Composer Mark Thomas stated the role of the music here was to announce the epic nature of what we were about to see. It sets the tone perfectly, alerting the viewer they are about to embark on an adventure, whilst also imbuing the soldiers with a sense of bravery and camaraderie. Mark adds Neil's very specific musical direction allowed for an excellent collaborative relationship.

Remember again, this was a movie on a shoestring. There were no stunt doubles. The guys who you now see jump out of the helicopter were in fact the crew again and stunt co-ordinators.

SCENE# 24   SHOT# 1

Sergeant Wells delivers the first piece of dialogue, immediately setting the scene. *"I want a good, clean disposal,"* he shouts over the whirring blades of the chopper, *"I want a secure landing zone. Go, go, go, go, go!"*

Our actual cast then run down the hill and get into position, fully kitted up but with one obvious tell-tale item to show the eagle-eyed watcher this isn't anything too serious – the yellow on the end of the guns shows they're for firing blanks – this is an exercise.

Now I was lucky enough to be an army cadet back in the 90's as a teen, and this bit really rang true as I recalled some of the exercises we took part in. Covered in camo paint at night in one of the local parks, we probably scared the crap out of innocent dog-walkers. It was basically playing hide and seek with plastic rifles, AKA bloody good fun.

We get a glance at each of them, the six ordinary squaddies who would win us over, rip out our hearts and still leave us craving for more twenty years later. Six regular Joe's, including one actual Joe of course.

Wells (a rather rugged looking Sean, minus the horrific moustache he arrived with, instead resplendent with that bottle scar he asked for) confirms our man with morals had indeed been RTU'd, calling out, *"Cooper, I want a position and bearing, I want to be on the move in three minutes."*

Cooper in turn reinforces this is the man in charge by replying, *"On it, Sarge."*

Next, we get almost exactly the three minutes sarge has requested of introductory banter.

Anyone with experience of the forces or emergency services will recognise it. The casual piss-taking that only occurs once a familiarity has been established. You can call someone a twater without any offence if they know you have their back. Being an ex-police officer, every time I hear this interaction, it puts a smile on my face. This shit-talking takes me back to nightshifts where you'd drive around for hours with your partner, bored out of your mind because it's a Tuesday and no one is holding up banks at 3am on a Tuesday. Even all the late-night pissheads had passed out. You'd end up having ludicrous conversations as tedium and exhaustion sets in and you realise, you're on your seventh night in a row and can't remember the last time you actually saw your spouse. Military and emergency services personnel need that gallows humour to survive.

Although Neil hadn't served himself, both his father and grandfather were in the army and he grew up listening to their stories and understanding the way of life and importantly to ensure authentic dialogue, the jargon. His familiarity with the life of a soldier shines through.

Joe lets us know with his sulky looking face that he's not happy about being there. He'll follow orders as usual, but he will be preoccupied. You see whilst they're in the back of beyond, it's the biggest match of his life – England V Germany, man. Full on footy war.

Right away Wells sets the tone, this might be just an exercise, but they are going to treat it seriously.

> **WELLS:** *"Now as of this moment as far as we are concerned, we are 50k behind enemy lines. Now if we do happen to make the contact... I expect nothing less than gratuitous violence from the lot of you. Because we are firing blanks doesn't mean we have to be thinking nice thoughts. So, remember you put the fire down right, you get stuck in, you kick their fucking teeth out or I guarantee you, Joe, they will be having your bollocks for breakfast, Sunshine."*

And there you go; the sarge has laid down the law

but not in a shouty-aggressive fashion. We already understand he is going to be a leader the others respect and obey without cowering in fear of reprimand.

Spoon forgetting his watch is less of a pawn to show he's a bit slap dash and careless and more a device in which to show Wells in a fatherly light. Not 'just' their boss and leader, he genuinely cares about his lads. So, he gives Spoon his nice and shiny but doesn't mean it's worth shit watch, whilst he quips, *"Well I'll count, won't I?"* when asked what he'll do. A nice nod to his namesake H G Wells' book *The Time Machine* there too.

This short conversation between Wells and Cooper demonstrates the trust the Sergeant has in his Private, who very much seems to be his right-hand man and someone who the other lads are happy to take orders from. Despite being far younger than Wells (Kev was 27 at time of filming to Sean's 36) there is an obvious brotherly, best-mate type bond between them. This doesn't appear to bother Campbell who as a Corporal would actually be second in command due to rank.

The rabbit's foot keyring on Cooper's compass indicates he's feeling down on his luck after the incident with Ryan and also refers to a deleted scene where he has been having a spot of woman trouble. Included on the DVD extras, it features Cooper showing Wells a series of polaroid photos. They start with him and his girlfriend on a date. A second man joins them, none other than Director of Photography Sam McCurdy and as the photos progress, Sam nicks Cooper's lady and the last photo depicts Kev looking thoroughly pissed off on his own whilst Sam has got the girl.

Poor Coop.

WELLS acknowledges SPOON'S signal as he and

COOPER continue chatting.

> WELLS
>
> ...Any new developments with
> your lass?

> COOPER
>
> You mean the lads haven't
> told you yet? Oh, this is a
> peach.
>> (He shows him three
>> polaroid's)
> A picture's supposed to tell
> a thousand stories, right?
> Not these. Courtesy of
> Spoon.

WELLS looks at the three photos' one by one. The first shows COOPER sitting happily with his girlfriend in a pub giving cheers to the camera.

The second shows COOPER with his girlfriend, only now there's another man sitting beside her, and she clearly has eyes for him. The last shows COOPER sitting alone, looking utterly rejected.

> WELLS
>> (wincing)
> Ooh, nasty.... Annie's the
> best thing that could've
> happened to someone like me.
> It doesn't bear thinking
> about new but I used to be
> just like you lot, full of
> beans and talking bollocks,
> itching for a fight. Now,
> I'd sooner curl up with her

59

> in front of the telly.
>
> SPOON gives the ALL-CLEAR and they move off.

It is also our first subtle hint at legends, folklore and such. If Cooper is willing to believe in or at least have an open mind regarding talisman, what else might he be willing to take into consideration?

Wells lets him know the squad wouldn't be the same without him, saying, *"Listen, the only people that go looking for trouble are kamikazes, glory boys and full-on fucking fuckwits. Take my advice, son. Be patient."*

Mark Thomas underscores here perfectly, something else which we are treated to time and time again throughout the film. It never detracts from the speech, merely enhances the emotion, and enriches the scene. He knew how important it was to infer sub-text but never impinge on the dialogue.

And just like that, a tad over the three minutes Sarge wanted, they are on the move and start tabbing with Spoony on point and Terry and Joe, tail-end Charlies. This was six pages of dialogue when they still hardly knew one another, second only in length to a later scene inside the farmhouse which was eight pages. That's a way to either break or bond your actors straight away and thankfully for them, Neil and us, it was the latter.

Again, the iconic theme tune begins to play as the lads track across the Highlands, some beautiful scenery and cows filling in the few seconds. This was a pick-up shot filmed by producer Keith Bell acting as a second unit. Look at me sounding like I know what the frig I'm talking about…

What that means to anyone such as me who hasn't worked on a movie, is that this scene was filmed after the shots with the main cast. Although there are Highland cattle adding to the authenticity, this was actually still in Luxembourg. So that's not the actors, again just people from the crew filling in as extras.

The next scene shows the lads having a quick refs break. This only lasts for a couple of minutes but it one of my favourite parts of the entire movie. *This* is how to do a lore drop, an Info Dump 101. Cooper recounts the story from the beginning to the squad, telling them how once in a while, people go missing, whilst character building and slowly raising the stakes.

> *"Just last month, a young couple were hiking through these woods. They set up camp somewhere near here. During the night something happened. Mountain Rescue team found the remains of the camp a couple of days later, the tent was ripped to shreds and there was blood everywhere. Paper said it was a monster like the Beast of Bodmin Moor. Locals claimed it was an escaped lunatic. But no one's been caught, so nothing could be proved either way. Every year, more and more people come through here, every once in a while, they don't come back. No trace, no bodies. Just disappear. And never seen again."*

That one speech tells us the campers from the start were not the first to meet their maker in this fashion and the authorities are aware that something is amiss. Of course, the lads all scoff at such tosh, except poor old Terry, who is the only one actually looking at Cooper as he recounts the tale. Spoon tries to make him jump by lobbing a bit of twig his way. This seems to set Terry up as the baby of the group, still very much a part but the one they like to tease and who is quite easily spooked. Les Simpson portrays the wide-eyed schoolboy look very well.

The Beast of Bodmin Moor is of course a very real big cat legend from Cornwall and growing up in Somerset, one I was very aware of.

Off they go once more with an added touch of whistle while you work. This scene was a bugger to film as the guys kept getting out of tune or out of time and sync. We are given a glimpse at just exactly who the lads are up against on this harmless exercise. Yes, as Bruce said earlier, it is Special Forces you plonker, and if you too were thinking there was no way Neil would hire Liam Cunningham just for the first scene then you'd be correct and now *you* can go straight to the top of the class also.

Captain Ryan is in the woods, watching them, stealthily.

Shifty bastard

We cut away next to what is possibly my all-time favourite scene of the entire movie. It's an iconic one that people remember, but often gets listed behind those with more action and comedy. For me, this is where I fell in love with these characters. This is where I became fully invested, where I wanted them *all* to survive and could even imagine being part of that troop. As I watch this scene twenty years later, these six men feel very much like old friends.

It's now night-time and the lads have set up camp. There's nothing ambitious, no stroke of ingenuity to this. It is simply an old-fashioned campfire story and by golly does it work. It actually was a ghost story in the original draft too, but Neil changed it to be more relevant to military life and anecdotal whilst still allowing a touch of mysticism. Although the setting looks perfect, it was actually a last-minute spot as the original location was deemed too muddy. It ended up being far closer to a road than they would have liked but thankfully that isn't apparent.

We start with Cooper asking each of the lads what frightens them, a thought-provoking topic of conversation although meant in good spirit.

Bruce – *The self-destructive nature of the human condition* (indicating Bruce has a contemplative nature and is possibly a deep-thinker)

Spoon – *Castration* (every male's worst fear, confirmed by the rest of the squad readily agreeing whilst likely squirming slightly)

Joe – *Only-one-thing guaranteed-to-put-the-shits-up-me... A penalty shoot-out* (this man lives and breathes for football)

Terry – *Watching a penalty shoot-out. With Joe* (the youngest of the group but still one of the lads and enjoys injecting a touch of humour when he isn't shitting himself)

Cooper – *Spiders. And women. And spider-women* (primal fear on all three accounts also demonstrating a push against toxic masculinity by being brave enough to admit to not liking creepy crawlies and 'man enough' to show a tender side that just needs to find the right woman).

Terry then wants to know what scares the sarge, who replies with the ever endearing, *"The thought of never seeing my wife again scares the shit out of me."* Again, this short exchange gives us the character development we need to feel for these guys, to recognise we do not want them to just be cannon fodder.

Wells has a wife; Cooper just needs the right woman to catch spiders for him. This humanises them, shows they are not solely mouthy, macho army men. They are people with hopes, fears and families. An important part of any story is evoking emotion, having feelings about the characters. You do not have to like them; they do not have to be relatable. But if they can make you feel anything, even contempt, the writer/director has done their job.

We then get what should have been an award-winning monologue from Sean. As well as listening to his beautiful voice (there is a reason Mr. Pertwee is not *just* an actor but also does wonderful commentaries and voice-overs), I love the facial expressions of the rest of the squad as they listen to the story. Terry in particular looks to be catching flies...

The Eddie Oswald speech is complete and utter perfection.

Sean recalls being stunned (and losing a bet) that Neil kept it in its entirety after the edits, stating that horror and action movies never have more than fleeting moments of pure monologue.

His speech is exactly 2 minutes and 55 seconds and is recited with such conviction, it gives me the feels each and every single time. I and all the fans out there, including Robert Englund, are bloody glad Neil not only wrote it, but kept it in.

> **WELLS:** *"Nah, there's one thing actually in particular that I'll remember 'til the day that I die.*
>
> *Yeah, it's back in '91 just before my unit was flown out to Kuwait to mop up the last pockets of resistance.*
>
> *Me and this young fella called Eddie Oswald decided to go and get a tattoo done to commemorate our first trip into the desert."*

BRUCE: *"I…I remember Eddie. He was a…he was a stocky hard case with a broken nose and bong eye, yeah?"*

WELLS: *"Yeah, that's him. Good looking fellow. Big hit with the ladies.*

Anyway…me and Eddie, we went and had a few drinks. We had a lot of drinks. And we went down to the tattoo parlour, and I got a desert rat done.

And Eddie being Eddie wanted something with a bit more meaning. And being a bit of a believer, he said that his soul still belonged to God.

But his flesh, well his flesh was way beyond redemption. It was up to Satan to save his skin.

So he got this fucking great laughing Devil tattooed right on his arse.

Anyway, about six days later we were making a regular sweep along the Iraqi border.

And Eddie…poor fucker, triggered an anti-tank mine.

Yeah, we all saw it happen. I mean he was on point.

White, blinding lightening flash and a fucking deafening crack and by the time we picked ourselves up off the deck, Eddie was…he was gone.

Just bits and pieces of him.

It's all that remained.

This big fucking red circle. 100 meters

I'll tell you something lads, it really puts things in perspective when you have to scoop your mate up with a shovel and stick him in a bin bag.

Anyway, the thing that really did our nuts in that day was when you...came across a bit you recognized.

Bit of ear.

Toe.

A nose.

A tooth.

The thing that really freaked us out that day was when Left-Hand Charlie found a bit of Eddie with a tattoo on. I mean everything else was burnt to a crisp.

Covered in claret.

All mushed up, pulped up.

Not this bit. This bit was perfect. And there's old Nick. Chortling his fucking arsehole off at us.

So, you could say that Eddie was right. That Satan did indeed save his skin. Just not all of it.

Or you could say that Eddie was just unlucky. Either way...it taught me to keep a very open mind.

Boom. Boom.

Anyway...Eddie Oswald."

It's a soliloquy fit for an Oscar and oft compared to Quint's speech in *Jaws* about the USS Indianapolis and Sean ran through his lines in their entirety around five times.

Give that man a clap.

And it's not far off the original script.

                    WELLS
          I don't know about that. The
          thought of never seeing my
          wife again scares the shit
          out of me. And those little
          things that make the skin
          crawl and the hair stand up
          on the back of your neck...

As WELLS speaks for the first time, all eyes
turn to him and the group hang on his every
word.

                    JOE
          What, you mean like Spoon?

                    WELLS
          Close, but no, I mean those
          inexplicable occurrences
          that could be something
          extraordinary or may be
          nothing special, but the
          only thing that you can be
          certain of is that you'll
          never to know for sure.
          There's this one thing in
          particular that will stay
          with me as long as I live...
          Back in '91, just before
          my unit was flown into
          Kuwait to clean out the
          last pockets of resistance,
          me and one of the squad,
          a young lad called Eddie
          Oswald got, ourselves
          tattooed to commemorate our
          first trip to the desert.

                    BRUCE
          Shit. I remember Eddie.

                      68

Stocky hard-case with a
broken nose and a bong eye?

                WELLS
That's him. So we have a
few drinks and we go for
these tattoo's.. I went
first, got the Desert Rat
on my arm. Eddie though
wanted something a bit more
meaningful, at least to
him, and being a bit of a
believer, he said his soul
may belong to God, but his
flesh was beyond redemption
and it was up to Satan to
save his skin. So he got
this picture of a laughing
Devil tattooed on his arse.
    (Beat)
Six days later we were in
the desert making a sweep
along the Iraqi border when
Eddie triggered an anti-
tank mine. We all saw it
happen, he was on point.
There was a bright flash
and this deafening crack
and by the time we'd picked
ourselves off the deck
he was gone. Bits of him
littered the ground for a
hundred feet in this big
circle. It really gives you
perspective when you've got
to scoop the remains of your
friend up with a shovel and
put them in a bag. For the
most part it's just random

pieces of unidentified
flesh, but every so often
you find something that you
recognise and that really
does your head in. Well one
thing that did everybody's
head in that day was when
Left Hand Charlie found the
piece of him with the tattoo
on, totally undamaged by
the explosion and Old Nick
still chortling his arse off
at us. Everything else was
burnt to a crisp or covered
in blood, but not this one
bit, this was good as new.
So... from one point of view
you could say the devil did
save his skin, just not all
of it. Or you could say it
was pure chance and Eddie
was unlucky. You take your
pick, but it convinced me to
keep an open mind.

There is a long pause, then...

                    TERRY
          I want to change my answer.
          The Sarge scares the shit
          out of me.

I won't add too much other than Eddie makes an
appearance in Neil's work since it is a well-known fact
rather than a hidden extra. But can you name them all?

The Descent – the name Oswald appears on an old
miner's helmet

The Descent Part 2 – this is NOT one of Neil's movies,

70

he neither wrote nor directed it but it is a direct sequel to the first and there is indeed a character called Ed Oswald played by Michael J. Reynolds.

Doomsday - Oswald Enterprises is the company that builds the wall. Their logo appears in several places in the movie.

Centurian – Neil's cameo character at the end is called Osvaldus.

The Reckoning – character called Edwin Oswald played by Callum Goulden.

The Seasoning House – directed by Paul Hyett and starring Sean Pertwee, this movie has a cameo by a guy called Eddie Oswald in the credits…and of course, it's Neil, again.

After this brilliant and thought-provoking moment, Spoon breaks the sombre mood by beginning to tell a joke about a man walking into a bar with a little dog on his shoulder when-

BOOOOOOOOOOOOOOOOOOMMMMMMMMMM!!!!!

It's a dead flying fucking cow. The guys react with a mixture of incredulity, laughter at the absurdity, annoyance at the inconvenience and just a bit of fear from poor 'You're firing blanks, man' Terry who gets a decent coating of blood on his kit.

If you thought the reaction was pretty realistic, that's because it was! Obviously, the guys knew it was coming, it was in the script, and you can't exactly hide a massive fake dead cow. But it was Christopher Figg who suggested that instead of pushing it off at a certain cue when the cast were expecting it, push it off a few minutes beforehand and catch them by surprise which they did, and it worked!

Wells refuses to break radio silence (did you notice how quick Joe was to suggest Bruce call it in, so he'd be able to find out the footy score!) and decides to post a watch instead, two on. four off. As he says, *"Unbelievable."*

In a deleted scene shown on the UK DVD, Joe actually suggests they eat the cow – *"Alright lads, how'd you like your steak done?"* whilst the disgusted Wells retorts, *"You bunch of dirty, bloody savages. You lot make me sick."* Ultimately Neil chose not to use the scene which I think is the right choice, they hadn't exactly been stranded for days à la *Lord of the Flies* or *Yellowjackets*, so it would be unlikely they'd start salivating at the smell of burning cow flesh. Still out of the frying pan, onto the fire…

There should have been another extra scene in the Special Forces camp where we see one of the soldiers wearing glasses.

EXT. RYAN'S CAMP - NIGHT

There are several bivouac's, bergens and bits
of kit stacked around as a SOLDIER (wearing
wire-framed spectacles) stands watch. RYAN,
anxious and unable to sleep, approaches the
watch...

RYAN

Anything?

SOLDIER

All clear, sir. Just...

RYAN

Go on.

SOLDIER

I've done many watches like
this and you get this sense,
like you are being watched.

There is silence. No birds. No sound.

Neil states there wasn't an abundance of extras over in
Luxembourg that fit the bill for playing the SAS guys,
and although they did grab a few scenes, the actors
looked way too young and un-soldier like, so it was
ultimately cut. Also, you wouldn't have been able to be
in Special Forces if you wore glasses so…

Shifty bastard Captain Ryan pops up after a quick visual
reminding us not only that it's night-time but there is
very much a full moon watching over proceedings
(these shots were added during post-production back
in the UK). He is back with his binoculars, and we get

some night-vision shots (filmed on Sam McCurdy's camcorder) but wait, something else is watching *him*, something that sees in black and white. For the first time, Ryan looks slightly concerned, his head whipping from side to side as he tries to determine if there is indeed something else out there. He certainly won't like not being 100% in control at this point. The music sets in again, tempo building along with something animalistic – the sound of panting as something moves quickly towards him. We follow its POV for a moment and when it reaches Ryan, it emits a sort of growl/ grunt. The music hits a crescendo and we see and hear the blood splatter onto the rock. All of a sudden, things don't look good for our antagonist.

But there is no time to cheer, I mean worry about Captain Twatter.

It's now morning and we are back with the lads, Spoony having discovered where the cow fell off the ledge and interrupted his joke. Why *did* that man in the pub have the small dog? I guess we'll never know.

Wells is not looking for trouble, he's, *"Just looking and it's on the way,"* he informs Cooper, and sure enough as the troop make their way to the fold, they discover more breadcrumbs. Along with geeky cinephile in-jokes, there are lots of fairy-tale references dotted throughout the narrative too. Breadcrumbs of course comes from *Hansel and Gretel*.

There's no dialogue nor need for it in these few short moments, the score is beautiful, and we see Wells lead the lads with mere hand gestures and signals.

Despite there not being enough money in the kitty to send the cast off to bootcamp, they had been able to get a chap in from the Foreign Legion just to give them the basics and how to handle the weapons, that kind of thing during rehearsals. Sean already had experience with this from several previous features too including *Bodyguards* and his familiarity is obvious. Again, this simple portrayal of the rest of the squad just knowing what he wants and following without question demonstrates their trust in his lead and their loyalty to their leader.

As an aside, it would appear Neil and Liam have a similar relationship and way of communicating when working together. According to Liam, whilst they were filming pivotal scenes in the famous *Game of Thrones* episode *Blackwater* – which was Neil's TV debut – Liam was on board a huge ship and couldn't hear what Neil needed to say to him. Instead of wasting valuable time running backwards and forwards, they developed a sign language where they could just wave at each other and know what was needed. It somewhat baffled the rest of the crew but got the job done!

In another deleted scene, there was a short sequence before they reach the compromised-to-fuck charnel house that was basecamp for the Special Forces boys, where Terry steps in some lovely looking entrails and they also discover a pair of spectacles. This was meant to be the remains of the team they were up against on this harmless little exercise.

```
TERRY, standing atop a boulder, looks up as
another flare arcs up into the sky. Gaining
his bearings, he jumps from the rock to the
ground below. But instead of hearing his boots
```

impact on the firm ground, he hears a mushy, squelching sound, like jumping into strawberry jam.

Slowly, cringingly, he looks down at his feet to see he's standing in a heap of entrails with the odd dog tag catching the light!

                    TERRY
            Ahhh Jesus. Sarge!
            Saaaaaarrrrgggge!

Quickly, the others come to his aid and stop dead, eyes wide as they see what he's standing in.

                    TERRY
            What the fuck is this?
            Don't tell me it's more cow
            because I think I'm going to
            puke.

Things are starting to look a bit iffy as Wells stabs a chunk of meat with his knife and deduces, "*Natural causes my arse.*"

And then a distress flare goes up into the sky.

Now what?

Before we find out, there is a transitory clip of the lads walking through the beautiful scenery, which was a bloody nightmare condition wise to act and film in.

Often, they were almost at a 90-degree angle, and when it got muddy, everyone was slipping and sliding all over the place.

Fun times for the grips and camera operators I'd imagine!

Steep, wet and muddy – perfect location

Next, we get to see exactly what the guys have come across. It looks like a basecamp but as the camera pans around, we see no sign of life. Fleeting glimpses of destroyed equipment, blood dripping and eugh, what the frig is that on the ground?

There are several things which make a feature stand out from the crowd, enable it to become memorable and not just fade away or get mixed up with hundreds of other similar works. Neil's ability to create not only relatable but actually likeable characters is one, but his quotable dialogue is often the reason credited for why this film has such a high re-watchabililty factor.

Poor Terry is stood in some dodgy looking entrails cut from the earlier mentioned deleted scene. Despite the obvious carnage, Wells remains calm and practical, highlighting for us again that he is the only member asides from Bruce to have seen action on the front line. He tells them to ditch their bergens (those giant and damn heavy backpacks), they've got casualties to locate. And then he delivers one of my personal all-time favourite lines.

"We are now up against live hostile targets. So, if Little Red Riding Hood should show up with a bazooka and a bad attitude, I expect you to chin the bitch."

How could you not love that speech?

According to Sean, this was the day when things really started coming together for the more seasoned actors, something of a breakthrough where they just knew this was something special, despite the heavy rain and shitty conditions.

Bruce poses the question where the hell are all the bodies as the group salvage what weapons are left and useable, Cooper noting they must have been hit hard and fast as the magazines are all full. Wells instructs Bruce to get on the radio and organise an immediate emergency airlift when-

Arghhhhh!!!

CONTACT!

Captain Ryan pops up from the midst of the rubble and scares the shite out of everyone before meekly asking, *"Help me."*

Cooper recognises him straight away and in testament to his character, rushes straight over to try to help despite their previous interaction ending acrimoniously.

"Do not tell me you fucking know him," says Wells.

"Captain Ryan, Special Ops," replies Cooper.

Now the rest of the team know who this bastard is.

Bruce is desperately trying to get through on the radio whilst Cooper (foreshadowing some expert medical procedures from the future Dr. Owen Hunt on *Grey's Anatomy*) and Wells attempt to patch up Ryan who now looks like he, *"Took on Jack the Ripper and came last."*

Neil confirms that by this point, his intricately detailed shot-list went out the window and they often let the actors just play the scene. After several rehearsals they clearly knew what they were doing, so the crew just spent the time covering the scene with three different angles and letting the cast run with it.

Ryan is clearly in pain and shock, not showing that he in turn recognises Cooper yet, but saying they need to get out of there and that there was only supposed to be one. Someone either can't count or didn't do their homework properly. Either way they should go straight to the *bottom* of the class.

It'll all be fine and dandy in a bit though as they're getting an airlift out of there, right, they'll soon all be home with a nice cuppa and a hot woman – expect Cooper as he's scared. But wait, Bruce is seeming a little agitated – he can't get a signal

"This is Spearhead to Control, does anyone copy?"

Terry bless him (looking as per most of the time like he's about to crap himself) asks, *"Didn't you check it?"*

Wells gets Terry to look around, suggesting the team must have had their own comms kit whilst asking Cooper what the hell Ryan was even doing there. They know they were up against Special Forces but as Cooper notes, if Ryan was part of their exercise, he isn't advertising – no cap badge, no insignia, only tags.

On that note, have you ever looked closely at the squad's own insignia badge? There's a spot of foreshadowing right there. Neil designed the wolf with the spear in its head and gave one of the patches to composer Mark Thomas' son, Tristam, who was so flattered and inspired by Neil and his generosity, that he went on to work in directing himself.

Cooper has noticed they're packing all kinds of weird shit – tranquilizer darts, nets. Not exactly your everyday run of the mill kit for an ordinary exercise one might presume and as Cooper says, *"Less like a special ops mission, more like a fucking safari."*

Terry finds their radio and there is jubilation and wait – oh shit. It along with the rest of the camp has been ripped to pieces. Useless. Bin it.

Ryan is still incoherent, insisting they need to get out of there before they come back. *"They tore them to pieces, in front of my eyes!"* Whoever they are, our lads don't want to be there when they come back…

Poor old Spoony has been desperately trying to get Wells' attention, tapping on his watch with Wells ignoring him. This time he disregards the *"Not now, Spoon!"* by informing his sergeant that in about half an hour it will be getting dark. This isn't a sign of insubordinate behaviour, more informing us Spoon is thinking ahead, noting they need to get somewhere safer whilst they can still see and alerting us to the time. We realise they need to get the hell out of Dodge and pronto.

Bruce is still fiddling with the radio, having now taken it apart to check the circuits and finds a transmitter inside.

"Why would they bug our radio?"

Spoon provides us with one of Neil's nerd-alert quotes

here. And that's not me being rude, nerds are the best. I should know, I married one. But you'll only 'get' this is you're a Trekkie.

"It's the Kobayashi Maru test. They've fixed it so we can't fucking win."

The Kobayashi Maru is a training exercise in the fictional Stat Trek universe designed to test the characters of Starfleet Academy cadets in a no-win scenario. This particular line is from *Star Trek II – The Wrath of Khan*. So now you know.

It would be pretty cool to have a nerd-alert bingo or drinking game. I did wonder about a drinking game for every time Sean says fuck, but do not want to be responsible for all the massive liver failures…

Wells however tries to maintain at least the semblance of calm and tells them it was probably some joker didn't want Joe to hear the footy scores. He then ensures they have all ditched the useless SA80s and are carrying live rounds. Shit just got real.

Rain!

You can occasionally make out the echo of rain here over the dialogue and underscore. Filming conditions for the outside shots were miserable but Kev McKidd says he never heard anyone complaining, and if anything, although being wet and cold wasn't ideal as an actor, it helped to put them in the mindset of a soldier and amplified the grittiness of the situation. And of course, us Brits are used to the rain even if we do like to have a moan about it.

Ryan cheerily informs them that despite now having live rounds, *"It won't make a difference, they won't die."* Way to build morale, Sir. Well of course they won't, you need silver bullets not regular ammo. But more on that later.

Wells doesn't like this and tells Ryan so.

"Now you just shut up like a good gentleman. You are scaring my lads."

Sean says he made sure to sneak this *Zulu* reference in and was glad it made the cut, but I would imagine Neil loved it. It was his version of Colour Sergeant Bourne's, *"Be quiet* now *will you, there's a* good gentleman, *you'll upset the lads."*

Being a seasoned veteran, I asked Sean if he adlibbed much or stuck to the script. He recalls it being very collaborative and that once he got to know Wells and the pentameter of his speech, he would sneak the odd swear word in since he has, *"a propensity to say fuck a lot."* I knew I liked him. He adds it was always within the perimeters of Neil's words though. As well as adding more F-Bombs, there are more bits that Sean improv-ed in the heat of the moment which we will look at later.

Suddenly we hear howling, maybe screaming? It has been suggested this could be the Uath family changing ready for when we get to see them shortly since the sun is going down. The noise is extremely guttural, like a wild animal trapped and fighting for its life, willing to chew off its own leg to get out but is actually Neil's old pal Ian Flemming who practically threw up a lung after making that horrendous noise one day in a sound booth. It does sound great though.

As Terry says, *"Oh shit."*

Indeed, my son.

Wells is quick to instruct, *"Aright lads, grab what you can. Head for the tree line. We are moving, let's go!"*

And we are off, frantic, percussive music and quick camera shots adding to the immediacy of the situation as they start to move through the trees. There was plenty of this running about and bearing in mind it was in the thick, slippery mud, it was no wonder they were all physically exhausted after a long day shooting. Kev says they would get back to the hotel, shower off all the mud and blood and head to the bar where they all drank a lot whilst bonding and having a laugh, just as squaddies do in real life and many of the emergency services. I recall attending Super Friday when I was a response officer in the police. We had just come off a seven-day week of 10pm-7am shifts, finishing at 7am IF you were lucky and could hand straight over to the day shift. So, by 7am Friday we were all knackered and would go home, shower get a quick kip or a run if you were hardcore and then be in the pub by Midday at the latest. Some of those Friday afternoon/evenings were legendary and others I can't even recall a thing beside a killer hangover the next morning. But we did it and it was the best, so much fun to just have a laugh with the people you had to trust with your life on a daily basis. We'd all seen some shit and there was so much we couldn't talk about even with our other halves.

Sean recalls the bar closing one time, but they weren't ready to call it a night, so they got a load of beers and sat down by the lift shaft, drinking, chatting, bonding and becoming brothers. Kev refers to his time on set as a True Bromance and it shows.

Anyway, back to the action. Wells asks for some rear-guard action which Bruce is quick to volunteer for, Spoony is on point and off they go! Just before dragging Terry off with them, Wells reminds Bruce, *"Remember, no heroics."*

Sean also decided to add, *"Right lads, let's 'ave it through the long grass, double time, go!"* which his co-star Ray Winstone says in *Love, Honour and Obey*. He admits he doesn't know what it is supposed to mean but it sounded right at the time. And it did!

That beautiful music plays as the lads rush through the long grass, well trees and then stops.

We know something is about to go down.

The atmosphere builds.

The next part is really quite tense. We know it's a horror movie and by the very nature of the beast, there will be casualties. But because Neil has very quickly and cleverly enamoured us with these soldiers, we are in no way ready to lose one of them. Bruce is the next most experienced after Wells. Although he doesn't mention having seen action, he recalls knowing Eddie Oswald who we know died in Kuwait in 1991 and after all he is a Corporal therefore second in command in rank despite Wells' closeness to Cooper.

Neil teases us for a moment, we get a close up on Thomas Lockyer, some shots of the trees blowing in the wind, he's in place ready with his gun and then – a howl. Despite his experience he looks anxious, as he should be since he was in no way expecting live and hostile enemies on a routine exercise in Scotland. Who the fuck is out there and what keeps making that noise? Wells has heard it too, allowing Sean to show off how natural he looks with a firearm.

It's fairly quiet and then something crosses blurrily into frame, accompanied with some percussion and we see Bruce load the MP5 and ban- no, not bang, nothing.

It's jammed.

Defective.

He takes out the mag, checks it, reloads and ba- nothing again.

Shit! He now knows there is something out there just waiting to pounce, and his gun is as good as a chocolate teapot. He makes a run for it, dumping the gun and rushing through the trees looking disorientated and frantic. He knows something is coming, we know something is coming and the music gets faster and faster, the handheld camera more and more shaky until...

BAM!

He impales himself right through the chest on a nasty branch stuck out from one of the trees. In the original script, he was meant to be so frantic that he runs straight off a cliff edge and falls to his death.

That would have been too costly in both time and money to execute, so Ash Williams—I mean Bruce Campbell— ends up looking like one of Vlad's victims, a stake through the heart vampire style.

The blood dripping down out of his mouth looks great too, as he slowly looks down and sees he has become one with nature – literally.

That must have smarted

The 'death blood' itself was made in the SFX workshop since there was so much needed, but any 'mouth blood' used was Pigs Might Fly, which apparently tastes quite nice (confirmed by Les Simpson) but has a very Spoon-like side effect – it might 'give you the shits.'

Quick shot back to Wells looking cool as a cucumber just before Bruce is ripped off the branch which is now painted red. Sean does an awesome little tilt with the gun here which I love, and he is pretty proud of. Whilst never appearing smug, he is happy to confirm he was very comfortable with the firearms. They may have been 'boys with toys' but I think Sean looks bad-ass as always.

You may have gleaned from this so far that I am a huge fan of all these guys, but Sean in particular is someone I've been in awe of for years. I was so nervous the first-time I spoke with him I was almost sick, but he immediately put me at ease and along with all of the others, was just genuine, down-to-earth and lovely to talk to. Kev confirmed he was also star-struck the first time he met Sean, as he was a big fan of his dad!

Anyway, the camera circles around Wells and he suddenly spots some blood on the floor. As he crouches down to look, we see the shape of something huge and hairy in the trees, growling and ready to launch itself at our protagonist.

I remember my heart being in my throat at this point and even now having seen the film so many times that I can almost visualise each scene without needing to put it on, I still feel a mild rise of my pulse. We might only be 30 minutes in, but we are by no means ready to have another death so soon and don't you dare kill off our leader, our father figure, the lovely Sean!

No apologies for fan-girling.

Wells fires off a few shots and we hear a slight whimper. Presuming Neil is going to stick to the lore, we know these bullets won't kill the beast, but we are hopeful for our lads that these monsters might at least sustain an injury.

He does a couple of commando rolls and almost lands on top of the bloody remains of Bruce. RIP Corporal Campell.

And now we get treated to another one of the film's most iconic moments – a still blurry creature reaches out and claws Wells across the abs, ripping open his stomach and exposing his guts.

SCENE# 34 / (unde)   SHOT# 33

If you can cast your mind back to the prologue, where I hung my head in shame admitting my first viewing of this film was on a shitty pirate on holiday after a few too many beers, well THIS was the scene that stuck with me until I rented the DVD and watched it again. It was that cool movie with Sean Pertwee's sausages. Sounds a bit dodgy unless you know. And ever since we saw this back in 2002, if me or my husband has a really bad stomach pain, we'll hold our bellies and say, "My guts."

Sausages!

Moving on, Wells is now on the floor looking like he's dropped a full English on his lap, thank God Cooper rushes in and gets a few shots in before they can finish Wells off. Of course, the wounded sergeant immediately tells Cooper to get lost, he's binned, done for and Cooper should save himself.

"You said 'No heroics', you bloody hypocrite," admonishes Cooper, *"where's Bruce?"*

"He's all over there," answers Wells, another of Sean's improv-ed lines. *"They fucking tore him apart. Now you listen to me and piss off. That's an order!"*

Of course. Cooper is loyal to a fault and does no such thing replying instead, *"You can take your orders and shove 'em up your arse!"*

"Jesus. My guts are out, Coop."

"Well we'll just put 'em back in again."

"They're not gonna fucking fit!"

"Of course they'll fit, man."

This exchange is so legendary, I have it on a t-shirt which both Sean and Kev loved.

WITHIN STAND OF YOUNG PINES - DUSK

WELLS rolls under a fallen tree and comes face
to face with Bruce, twisted and torn, his dead
face streaked with blood. But WELLS hasn't
time to stop. He gets to his feet on the other
side just as a hairy, muscular, clawed hand
reaches under the fallen tree missing him by
a fraction of an inch! Running blindly on
through the trees a second shape lunges out
at him. WELLS is caught in the midriff and
thrust against a tree where he slumps, dazed
and winded to the ground, looking down to see
his own intestines spill from the slash across
his belly and spill out into his lap. In shock
he looks up as the creature rushes in for the
kill!

Suddenly the moment is shattered as the creature
is struck broadside by a savage burst of
machine gun fire! The bullets riddle its flesh
and send it flying away into the undergrowth.
Stunned, WELLS turns in the direction of the
incoming fire... It's COOPER.

COOPER swoops down to aid his friend, picking
up WELLS' rifle and slinging it over his
shoulder. He takes out a field hypo full of
PAINKILLER and injects it into WELLS leg!

                    WELLS
          Cooper get the hell out of
          here! I can't move like
          this, I'm binned mate!

                    COOPER
          You said no heroics ya
          bloody hypocrite! Where's
          Bruce?!

                    WELLS
          They got him and they tore
          him apart! And the same
          thing's going to happen to
          you if you don't piss off!
          That's an order Cooper!

There is more movement in the trees and COOPER
opens fire!

                    COOPER
          You can take your orders and
          shove them up your arse!

                    WELLS
          My guts are out!

                    COOPER
          Well put them back in again!

COOPER picks up a handful of WELLS intestines
and passes them to him!

                    WELLS
               (panicking)
          They don't fit!

                    COOPER
          They've got to fit! Here!
          Now come on!

There are sounds of snarling and movement
closing in all around as WELLS stuffs his
intestines back in, holds them in one hand and
holds onto COOPER with the other!

Together they stand up, spinning around,
covering all angles as they back away, covering
their own rapid retreat as best they can!

Sean's pouch

Now, let's talk about those guts…

Sean recalls being sat eating lunch with the group, still in full kit as there wasn't exactly a budget for numerous costume changes and there would be this 'pong' as he put it, which in the end they worked out was coming from him – his sausages were 'on the turn'. I know enough to realise that being an actor isn't all awards ceremonies and red-carpet events but for some reason the thought of Sean wandering around with a little pouch made out of gaffer tape to carry his now rotting sausage guts in just makes me laugh every time I try to imagine it.

Anyway, Cooper has shoved Wells' guts back in (see they *did* fucking fit, man!) and they're back off running again through the treeline.

Here there are some great shots flipping between the squad and the wolves which we still only really see in shadow but very much now understand exactly what they are capable of. The shouts, gunfire and music are perfectly in beat with the images, and we just want our lads to get the hell out of there. Although the scene is quite dark, you can differentiate between human or wolf POV as the wolves see in black and white. They are all shooting and shouting (Target!) even Wells, despite his guts hanging out but this is desperate times, desperate measures. However, in the end, I wholeheartedly agree with Cooper who yells, *"Just fucking leg it!"* At the end of the day, it seems to be the most sensible suggestion.

Besides being extremely tiring and slipping over in the mud countless times, the cast had a lot of fun here running around shooting guns. Poor old Liam was feeling a bit left out so he was allowed an MP5 and blanks to he too could whizz about pretending to be in *Apocalypse Now* for a bit.

Suddenly the music changes just ever so slightly and what is this? Behold, a vision appears in the mist – headlights…it's a vehicle! Spoony spots it first, being closest to the edge and alerts the others, *"Lads! On me! On me!"*

They race down the hill with the lights coming closer, it's a Land Rover and it's coming right at them. Spoony runs out in front of it and the bloody thing just stops before it runs him over. I remember thinking for just a millisecond, bloody hell, this director isn't going to kill off another one with a non-wolf death so quickly after the trauma of Bruce is he, but thankfully of course, he didn't, and I could rest. For a moment at least.

SCENE# 4 1   SHOT#   2

There is a sticker on the Land Rover which says, 'Let's go off road.' This is a lovely salute to *The Fast Show* and in particular to *The Off-Roaders* which is fabulous. Trolls!

A woman jumps out of the vehicle and shouts, *"Get in!"* which they comply with quickly and without question, I mean, any human has to be better than whatever they are facing out there and now they have no one but two injured men, one being their beloved leader. Besides they have guns, and she has…an awesome hat? There will only be trouble if they are from Denwell Burn (give yourself a clap on the back if you get that reference.)

Cooper jumps in the passenger seat, the rest in the back, Joe now supporting Wells.

This part was meant to be filmed outside but due to dire weather conditions – it was snowing! – which would ruin continuity, they actually shot this scene inside the barn with the crew surrounding it to shake it as if it was moving.

Chilling in the barn with snow outside before the van scene

There was a lot of that kind of oh shit, now *this* has happened, but Neil and the others always found a way to make it work and it was always a team effort. Again, he constantly enthused others with his positive attitude and a bit of snow wasn't going to deter them.

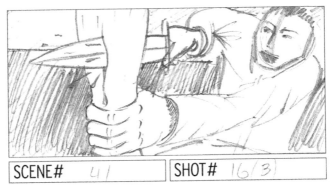

SCENE# 41   SHOT# 16/3

The werewolf arm that shoots through the roof was of the SFX guys, Pete Hawkins and there are some great sound effects here with the wolves howling and scratching on the side of the vehicle and when Joe shivs it and the knife goes through the gristle and bone.

Pete doubling as a stunt wolf arm

To draw out some tension, the wheels of the Land Rover are stuck in the mud and the mysterious lady can't get it to move. Cooper is helping, giving some pointers – try reverse – whilst the others are panicking in the back and trying to avoid the claws hanging from the roof getting too grabby and ripping into anyone else. The music amplifies the immediacy and all of a sudden, the wheels shift out of the mud and they're off, minus a scary non-squaddie arm thank God. There's an ominous howl and then we are back in the vehicle, Cooper checking on casualties.

The others suddenly notice someone missing in all the chaos that has ensued – where's Bruce?

"Bruce is gone, ah fuck it," replies Wells as the sad music that never fails to bring a lump to my throat echoes in the background. They are a man down, but although the immediate threat seems to be over, they still need to get to safety and tend to the wounded. There is simply no time to mourn.

Cooper remembers his manners and thanks the mysterious saviour.

"What happened?" she asks, and it seems like a pretty standard question since it is highly unlikely, she runs into groups of squaddies armed to their teeth on a daily basis.

"What happened? We were attacked. By huge, fucking, howling things that's what!" answers Spoon, succinctly summarising for her.

Well, she did ask!

As she explains, they were lucky she found them, having heard the commotion the night before. There is also the first of a fleeting glimmer of recognition between her and Ryan. That's Captain Ryan who not too long ago was at death's door but is now back to looking shifty and sitting pretty. Hmm. More on this later.

Dr. Hunt, I mean Cooper, is worried about Wells and Ryan, they need immediate medical attention and she explains there is only one farm in this glen but luckily, the owners are friends so that's handy and off they go.

The sombre music continues as the vehicle makes its way

to the farm, parking in front of an old cottage. Now if they had indeed been able to film in Scotland or somewhere similar, there may well have been a structure they could use. Instead, Simon Bowles' construction team built the exterior of the farmhouse from scratch. Since the only parts of the cottage that would be in shot were the front and one side, that was all that was actually built.

Scaffolding

"When you have no money, you need invention."

John Carpenter – *Halloween*

The Cottage

All of the interior scenes would be filmed in the studio on a purpose-built set.

Coming into this project as a huge fan but complete novice when it comes to filmmaking, this kind of thing is both fascinating and jaw-dropping. These realistic structures and sets get made? But they are so incredibly detailed and believable, it looks like it has been inhabited for years.

Cosy

Mind-blowing. The amount of time and talent involved is staggering, and I can see what Neil saw in Simon at that interview back in London.

The woman knocks on the door as the men cover her and each other, but it seems no one is home. Odd? Or not...

Cooper is undeterred however, thinking of the sarge and getting those wounds dressed, so he and Spoon carefully make their way inside to clear the building. If you notice Cooper nudging the door open carefully with his foot, that's another John Wayne thing. There are so many bits like this, it could almost be a soldiers-versus-monsters western. Thankfully the lights are still on and the MP5s have lights on them, so they don't need to try and balance a gun and a torch like Mulder and Scully perfected. There's even still a fire burning in the hearth. Cooper checks downstairs as Spoon makes his way up, *"Little pigs, little pigs, we've come to nick your video."*

As I said before, there are lots of fairy-tale reference throughout the movie and of course this is in relation to *The Three Little Pigs* as well as the famous scene from *The Shining*.

Neil wears his influences on his sleeve whether it be subtle hints to well-known dialogue from Jack Torrance as above, cinematic choices or plot points or even the positioning of a character. There are many salutes to John Carpenter's *The Thing*. The chopper at the start, wanting to shoot the dog. Being set in the middle of nowhere. Explosions, radio not working. The ultimate bleak yet heroic ending. Some scenes are a deliberate tribute to the people and movies who inspired him, others more subconscious but one thing is for certain. Neil Marshall's debut feature is imbued with his love of the genre.

> *"I steal from every movie ever made."*
> **Quentin Tarantino**

Back to the cottage. Let's just hope since this structure is made of bricks so the big bad wolf can't blow it down no matter how hard he, or indeed they, huff and puff. Of course, that doesn't mean that it won't blow up, but that's for much later. Brothers Grimm aside, we are now in an actual cottage in the woods and Cooper makes his way into the kitchen, where the table is nicely laid, and something is still simmering away on the stove. This is a nod to *Goldilocks and the Three Bears* of course. An interesting theory that's been seen on the interweb is that Kev was chosen for Cooper since he is blond and is in fact the only one with fair hair and therefore, he is the Goldilocks character. This was debunked by Neil though. Chris Robson actually has quite light hair although they shaved it off. Whatever happened here, it happened quickly, like Roanoke and the place is as empty as the Mary Celeste…or is it?

Suddenly there's a sound from what looks like a cupboard or pantry, a whining. It could be a dog but judging by what we've just seen outside it could be anything. Cooper approaches with caution and his hand slowly stretches toward the camera as the scratching increases and the music builds and something leaps out and…

Thank fuck for that, it's an actual dog, a lovely Border Collie in fact who are usually very well behaved and easy to train. I know as I had one growing up – Milo had a beautiful temperament and let both me and the cats boss him around and dress him up. However, it would seem that's not always the case as there are actually two different Collies used during filming since the first had to be fired! He was a lovely boy but with fuck all respect for on-set etiquette since as soon as Neil called, *"Action!"* he'd run off the set, the very opposite of his script. Which I actually find really funny. What's that old adage, never work with kids or animals…

Sam

We already suspect from the start of the film when Cooper refuses to kill the dog that he has an affinity to them and sure enough, this is confirmed as he immediately pets the animal and shakes a paw. If we didn't already love Cooper, we sure as hell do now. Thankfully Kev also loves dogs, and this is apparent as he is very comfortable with Sam. Yes, the dog's called Sam too. I'm not talking about the incredibly talented Mr McCurdy. Besides, *that* Sam nicked Cooper's girlfriend in that deleted scene, remember?

He heads back out to tell the rest of the squad it's all clear, the mysterious female seemingly blankly staring into space. Or is she listening for something? Regardless, she heads straight in and the others follow.

Just before Joe walks through the door, he asks what everyone is thinking.

"What the fuck happened back there, Cooper?"

Inquiring minds need to know, but Cooper doesn't... yet.

"I dunno, mate," he replies. *"But she might have some answers."* He scans the perimeter once more and then heads inside as Spoon is coming down the stairs, stating the upper level is also all clear.

"Where the hell are we now?" is a repetition of Spoon's comment when they first start tabbing after the helicopter scene. *"Home, sweet home."*

Our cast move into the kitchen where Spoon starts to put a field dressing on the sarge. Wells is looking like he's knocking on heaven's door, yet Ryan appears as if he's never been sick a day in his life. Suspicious? Not if you know your lore. Neil did extensive research to ensure the mythos he chose was traditional. He states

The Book of Werewolves – An Account of Terrible Superstition by Sabine Baring-Gould was the definitive tome he frequently referred to. I'd concur and throw *Blood and Rain* by Glenn Rolfe and *Wolf Land* by Jonathan Janz into the mix also as two of the best fictional werewolf novels I've come across.

Cooper asks if there is a telephone – of course, there isn't – whilst Joe takes the pan off the stove, declaring, *"It's still hot, lads."*

The woman is appalled, exclaiming they can't just help themselves. Is she a stickler for etiquette and manners or does she know the chef has been using Hannibal Lecter's cookbook again? Interestingly although Cooper does not eat the soup, Kev went on to play Kolnas in *Hannibal Rising* and eats Hannibal's little sister, Misha, which is one of a catalyst of events leading to one of literatures most famous fictional cannibals. Neil also went on to direct an episode of the TV series *Hannibal*, entitled *The Great Red Dragon*.

Dinner for five

Either way, Joe ignores her because he is of course chin-strapped and starving. For those of you without military training, that means he's knackered, hanging on by the strap of his helmet. It's that extra layer of authenticity of dialogue that Neil is so good at. Although according to a friend of mine (thanks, Conrad) from the police who is also ex-forces, to be 100% accurate the movie would have needed to use another certain expletive a lot more. I'll leave that one to your imagination and see you next Tuesday…

Spoon confirms it's the training and that they never waste an opportunity to eat as he douses Wells' guts with medical alcohol and does his best to patch up what he can for now.

Cooper tells them to get it down their necks, whilst spinning what looks like a sort of egg. Neil says this is another nod to supernatural lore. The egg is in fact a saltshaker and of course, salt is known to ward off demons and witches when sprinkled around you in a protective circle.

Joe and Terry begin to eat, and Terry asks, *"Top grub, what is it?"*

"Dunno, mate," Joe replies, *"tastes like pork."*

Mmm, pork. Wait a minute. Actual pork, like the three little piggies or a rather more acquired taste, harder to come by 'long-pig' type of pork? Long-pig as most horror nerds will know is a pseudo name for people. People pottage. Won't see that on *Master Chef: The Professionals…*

Cooper isn't distracted though – he still wants to know where the nearest phone or population centre is. That's a town to you and me.

And here we do get a confirmed fairy-tale nod, as our mysterious woman, looking like she is off to spend the night with the Eskimo's, takes off her fur flapper hat and shakes out those curls. She might not be blond or have hair to the ground like Rapunzel but that was a deliberate, scripted move. It also gets her noticed by the men, especially Cooper. At least she isn't a Spider-Woman. In one of the deleted scenes, Spoon asks Terry and Joe what they think of her. Terry says she's not his type whereas Spoon says there is only one type. Joe questions why she would want the runt of the litter when she could have the cream of the crop? The scene wouldn't have given any more context to the story or depth to the characters so I'm not sorry it didn't make the cut. But these are young, and we presume single, men full of testosterone and adrenaline. It is very likely they would comment on her appearance and Emma is a very attractive lady.

She tells him Fort William is the nearest town but it's at least a four-hour drive. But that's fine, they need to get the wounded looked at properly, no matter how far they have to go. So. Cooper suggests they leave right away. No time like the present, right? She seems okay with this, at this point not giving off any suspicious vibes other than just who the hell is she? But she doesn't seem hostile, has transport and knows the roads. Right now, that's all they need.

Cooper may only be a Private, but he is now very much in charge with Bruce gone and Wells injured. And Kev too seems to happily sink his teeth into the quasi-lead role for now. Les Simpson described this as 'acting like it's a bodily function'. What he means by that, was that Kev was born to do this. He never seemed like he had to work at acting, it just came naturally. As natural as a bodily function. To clarify, Les isn't saying Kev's acting is crap. He is saying Kev's acting comes across as naturally as taking a crap. Oh whatever, it is a huge compliment anyway, lol.

The others never question the chain of command, he seems to know what he's doing, and they implicitly trust him. He instructs Joe to look after the sarge whilst he and Spoon go and bring the vehicle up to the door. Terry oversees watching Ryan, showcasing that even though he is injured, Cooper doesn't trust him one bit. Shifty bastard.

Out step Cooper and Spoon into the night. It's deadly quiet, just an owl hooting in the distance. However, they sense something is a cropper and Coop lights one of the magnesium flares to see better. And ah crap, the engine has been ripped apart, the vehicle is completely buggered. What could have done that?

Ah…

Oh dear.

We see *them* in the tree line, silhouetted against the darkness, just visible from the light of the moon and the flare. Hot steamy breath rising. They look huge, bipedal for sure. And they are not looking to make friends.

Spoon cocks his gun but Cooper orders, *"Don't shoot."*

And then adds the brilliant, *"Don't stare back,"* thinking of regular dogs and dominant eye contact I guess but Spoon replies with, and I would have to agree, *"I can't help it."*

Cooper then hurls the flare onto the floor, shouting, *"Go!"* and fires into the petrol tank so the vehicle explodes.

BOOOOOOOOOOOOOOOOOOMMMMMMMMM!!!!!

This was an actual on-set explosion too, not a model and was way more spectacular than they were expecting. It looks awesome on screen too, another round of applause to the stunt and effects teams.

The wolves and SFX team making sure they look cool enough on the screens

They rush back inside where the others were waiting

to load Wells in and make a hasty exit. That puts the kybosh on that plan.

We see the fiery remains of the car and then bang; the door is being pushed and those giant fucking howling things are trying to get in! Cooper, Joe and Spoon push back against it and try and keep whatever wants in, out.

The wolf arm that comes through the door and the lads are desperately trying to push back, was actually another one of the SFX guys, Mat O'Toole. He says there was a wedge in the doorframe so they couldn't actually slam his arm, but it still looks like he should have asked for danger money. I'm not sure why but hearing Coop shouting, *"Fuck off!"* as they finally get the arm out, and just before he shoots the gun through the letter box, always makes me chuckle, same as later when Wells is telling one to, *"Go away!"*

Meanwhile poor old sarge is looking a bit peaky and Sam, as we now know the dog is called, can smell dinner. Strangely enough many fans thought that in this scene, Sam was pulling at Sean's sausages and that there was a lovely yummy looking tug of war with his intestines going on. Maybe that's what they wanted to believe was happening? Because I don't think it's that hard to see it is actually just the bloody field bandages that Spoon has hastily applied to try and put Wells back together again like some sort of camo wearing Humpty-Dumpty. Sausage, bandage or sausage-bandage, it must still bloody hurt and he is trying to get the dog to piss off whilst Ryan just sits all lurky-like on the stairs. Watching. Again, it has been speculated that Sam reacts to the smell of the blood and offal emanating from Wells as he is likely used to being fed leftovers from the family meals. Hmm, human scraps. My favourite.

Poor old sarge is still lying there looking distinctly off-colour and pleading for someone to get the dog off him. Ryan glares menacingly and for one horrible moment I thought we might get the second animal death of the feature, incurring the wrath of many and ending Neil's career in one fell swoop. Which would be ironic as he actually adores dogs.

Ryan even picks up and the gun and then-

BLEUGH...

Terry saves the day by puking all over him.

Hurrah!

Throughout the writing of this book, I have been honoured to have been able to speak with most of the cast and crew. They have all been wonderful to communicate with, each being generous with their time and my endless questions and fan-girling. Les Simpson is now over in Australia somewhere in the outback where the spiders have their own Utes to drive around in and he has to crank up the interweb each morning. He is also a bit of a joker and likes to tease me. The first time I asked him about this scene he told me this.

> *"Hmm how many times did I puke on Liam, well it's not as easy as you think. By the third or fourth take I was struggling to produce anymore vomit. I'd had a big lunch that day to make sure my stomach was full and the first couple of times I just shoved my fingers down my throat and yoink. There was the master shot, the close up and the landing on Liam's head. So he got my lunch about 4 times."*
>
> Les Simpson

Now I'm not an idiot but I also don't know exactly

how method some people go with their acting or how hardcore Neil was. After I responded with something akin to, *"Oh erm thanks?"* he relented and admitted he was pulling my leg, which he now does on a regular basis, the bugger. Anyway, it was actually some sort of cold vegetable soup, standard for the vomit-gag but he really did get Liam with it around four times as it was *necessary*. Whether or not it was remains unknown but Les does reiterate what a good sport Liam was about the whole scenario.

Hey at least it got Sam off sarge's sausages.

"Bloody charming that is."

Ryan rears up at Terry, who in my opinion is precariously close to the antlers on the wall and he looks like a schoolboy about to be scolded by the scary headmaster. Joe comes to his rescue and Ryan sensibly decides to use the bathroom instead, traipsing up the wooden steps as if going off to the firing squad.

Cooper calls up after him, *"We need to talk, Ryan."*

He replies with, *"Well it doesn't look like I'm going anywhere, does it?"*

And with that, Cooper slips right back into leader mode and gets the show on the road.

"Joe, Spoon, looks like we're staying, you know what to do. I want a secure perimeter with a clear view of fire but give them something inviting, right?"

The quick ruffle of Terry's hair from Joe again just shows that they look after and care for one another and it was the same for the cast.

"We all just got along. We were like brothers. There was nothing made up or false. We could annoy one another and then carry on."

Kev McKidd

Cooper makes sure Terry is okay.

"I've got a real craving for a kebab," he replies, reminiscent of many a Friday night out on the town.

Cooper tells him to find as many pots and pans as he can, fill them with water and keep them on the boil since they have limited ammunition, adding then just a throwaway line but one that I love, *"Terry, while you're at it, stick the kettle on. We could all do with a brew."* It's just so archetypally British but also as we know, they're all chin-strapped and need some nourishment too. Again, it was exactly the same in the police, any kind of briefing, you had to make sure you had a brew. But isn't that just UK sentimentality to a tea (geddit?).

Terry puts the gas on the cooker ready as Spoon starts securing the kitchen. There is a wonderful moment where he is moving some sort of dresser and asks Terry to help and he gets behind it right in the way and no help whatsoever. A really small piece of filler that only lasts moments but never fails to make me chuckle, especially when Spoon says, *"Nah, you fool."* Terry really is the *"Don't tell him your name, Pike,"* member of the team (that's a *Dad's Army* reference for anyone not over 40 and British reading this which starred amongst many other illustrious actors, one Bill Pertwee, first cousin once removed of our lovely Sean).

Meanwhile the woman, who is very comfortable with Sam and vice versa, is still in the entryway along with poor old Wells and Cooper.

She asks now, *"You came here because of them, right?"* looking hopefully at Cooper who is now reassessing the sarge.

"I don't have a fucking clue who they are, and right now, I don't really care," he replies. Because at the end of the day, they are soldiers who are facing an enemy and who that enemy is doesn't really matter aside from the fact they are hostile and extremely dangerous.

"So this wasn't a rescue mission, nah, guess not," our mystery saviour replies, making us wonder what exactly this woman knows, clearly more than she is letting on right now, that's for sure.

But for a fleeting moment, she looks almost sad. Wistful.

Spoon comes past and hands Cooper the back door key which he attaches to the compass with the lucky rabbit's foot. It's not much of a talisman yet, Coop, I'd ask for my money back if I were you. Spoon reports they're still moving about but they're keeping a distance, and Cooper suggests hopefully that maybe they've had enough for the night.

"Hardly likely", scoffs our lady, *"they're smart, you've seen what they can do! They're working as a team, looking for a weakness, a way in."*

Cooper points out he isn't going to try and second guess whatever's out there – they're the enemy, it's that simple.

"This is no ordinary enemy," she states, as the music rises and we cut to Ryan, in the bathroom having cleared off Terry's little present. He looks into the mirror which seems like it could do with a wipe. There is nothing overt here, no yellow eyes or sprouting hair yet, just the slight canine incline of the head. Subtle yet unnerving.

Back in the kitchen, Spoon delivers his *Zulu* speech...

"Know what this reminds me of? Rourke's Drift. One hundred men of Harlech, making a desperate stand against ten thousand Zulu warriors. Outnumbered, surrounded, staring death in the face, not flinching for a moment. Balls of British steel."

The company sent over to Rourke's Drift were the 24th Regiment of Foot – the South Wales Borderers. There is a piece of music used in *Zulu* called Men of Harlech which is a very important song for Welsh regiments and Mark Thomas interwove some of it into the score since it underpinned the feeling of the calm before the storm.

Spoon's speech is followed by Joe's rather more down-to-earth, *"You're bloody loving this, aren't you? It's totally bone."*

If you haven't figured out bone by now, it is another squaddie term, meaning bollocks. Not very good.

Joe sits back down whilst Spoon breaks the glass on the window, pointing the gun through, resplendent with the cheeky little look he is now synonymous with.

Although not exactly a surprising action, you don't want glass in the way when you're trying to shoot your gun, this reminds me of Garry near the start of *The Thing* when he shoots at The Norwegian. And bizarrely, Garry was played by Donald Moffat which isn't massively different to Darren Morfitt...cue *The Twilight Zone* theme tune. Whilst all of the characters are loved by the fans for different reasons, Spoon is one who is named time and time again as a favourite and I feel it's because you get exactly what you see with him. Every single member of the cast and crew have said what a blast they had on the set, some even stating it was the most fun they'd ever had making a film, but Darren in particular has always struck me as having way too much of a good time.

> *"I was 'bloody loving this'! I'd been in things before where they had wanted you to look cool, but they always gave shitty costumes and dialogue and make up. I remember thinking 'finally make up that makes you look better instead of worse'. It was a total buzz shooting the movie, we all got one really well and would shoot all day and party all night. It was awesome for us that were less experienced to learn from Liam and Kevin and Sean."*
>
> Darren Morfitt

Back to the hallway with our lady (don't worry, we learn her name immanently), Cooper and a decidedly iffy looking sarge.

Neil cleverly uses authentic dialogue between the characters to info dump and lore drop with expert execution, the casual viewer probably doesn't even know they are being Spoon-fed pertinent material.

"What are we talking about here, wolves?" Cooper asks.

"Not entirely wolf, nor all human, but something in between." comes the reply.

Hmm.

We know what they're up against, *she* seems to know too, but what will this very practical soldier think? He does have a rabbit's foot so maybe it will be easy to convince him of what's out there?

No of course it isn't, and I bloody love Coop's response.

"Wolf-men, you're having a laugh, right? I might be nuts but I'm no fruitcake."

This line was actually taken directly from that third-year student zombie movie, *Brain Death*, Neil made all those years ago at Newcastle Polytechnic, with a character called Cooper no less.

Cooper's blasé response clearly disappoints her. Although it should have been expected, she seems to have been labouring under some sort of false hope that just maybe the men were there to help her in some way. Cooper's emphatic response has all but dashed that now.

"Just don't be an arse-hole," she adds, plopping herself down onto the stairs.

Despite the fact he appears to be fading rapidly, Wells manages to sneak in a cute little remark here which again always makes me chuckle even though the sarge is starting to resemble something straight out of the Black Death period.

"I like your new girlfriend, Coop."

Cheeky bugger.

"How are you feeling?" asks Cooper, checking his vitals since it looks as if he could drop dead at any given moment.

Sean looking a bit squiffy

Next comes another example of where Sean expertly added a couple more lines to his scripted dialogue, managing to inject just that touch of comedy into a dire situation. Gallows humour is a very real coping mechanism within the forces. When you have seen some of the sights, read some of the files and dealt with some of the scourge of the earth that we have, you have to be able to release that somehow. Taking the piss out of your colleagues and seemingly making light of events such as this allows you to cope with the atrocities and stressful situations.

"Touch of gas," he chokes out, all whilst looking like he's about to cark it. *"That and the fact that various body parts are trying to vacate the premises, fucking awful."*

Back to the lads in the kitchen and dutiful Terry has indeed made a cuppa but suddenly we get one of those quick movements both on screen and with the music and Spoon fires off a few more rounds than the short, controlled bursts he's been told.

We finally find out the mysterious curly locked lass is in fact called Megan and there is a 'blink and you'll miss it' moment here where she announces, *"And I know how to kill"* - before she is cut off by Wells gasping with pain. Was she about to tell Cooper how to kill the wolves? Could the entire scenario that follows have been avoided if Wells hadn't cried out right then or if Cooper had said, *"Sorry, love, can you repeat that, please?"* But they don't hear, of course.

There is definitely some ambiguity regarding Megan's character and motives but her attitude so far – agreeing to drive them away before they find the ruined car – and the titbits of information as to what exactly is out there, along with this, seem to at least suggest that she hasn't

117

just simply led the lads to the house as an entrée. Still, she remains to this day one of the most elusive members of the cast, surrounded by speculation.

With the sarge leaking like a sieve, Cooper asks Megan to find some whisky and superglue whilst he helps Wells up the stairs. Another adlibbed line here from Sean, *"Come on, Coop, up the wooden hill."* Sean attributes this turn of phrase to his wife Jackie, and it is certainly one I was familiar with, having heard it many a bedtime from my own parents and grandparents growing up in Somerset.

We also see he is indeed leaking as he leaves blood drops on each stair. He asks Cooper where they're going, his second in command simply replying that he doesn't want to know…

We head back to Spoon, Terry and Joe, each searching through the downstairs of the cottage for weapons. Terry's face with the unplugged electric knife never fails to bring a smile to my own and the triumph on Spoon's as he discovers a sword in the ottoman in the lounge is priceless – top bollocks or even Top Bosie as Kev McKidd might have said. If you have followed Kev's career, you will know one of his more coveted roles was as the voices of Lord and Young MacGuffin in *Brave*. When I announced to my 12-year-old daughter I was writing this book, she really couldn't have cared less. Her first question was had any of the cast worked on *Stranger Things* and her second was did any of them know Tom Holland? The Sony *Spider-man* actor not the writer and director *Fright Night*. Standard for a pre-tween girl. Seemingly unimpressed as I reeled off the remarkable IMDB entries for Sean, Liam and Kev, we suddenly came across something that she in fact did care about – because Merida is one of our favourite princesses. Anyway, the MacGuffins are famous for basically speaking gobbledygook and it appears making words up is somewhat of a forte of Kev's.

> *"One day we were just running around in rehearsals having all this fun and I just called out, 'Top bosie!'"*

Kev McKidd

Instead of being like *'you what?'*, it seemed to stick and soon the rest of the cast were joining in, and it became the word of the film. He says it never meant anything expect he'd been having a great time when it just came out, so it became a substitute for any word that meant great.

Anyway, back the film.

This leads us in to one of the best and most talked about scenes of the movie. It's now well known that Sean did in fact take method acting very seriously as was perhaps more than a little sozzled. But Kev has remained suspiciously low-key about it over the years. Guilty conscience, maybe? Let's look at the scene and then get some answers straight from the horses' mouths.

First off, the superglue fact is true, and I can also attest to it sticking your damn fingers together although in a false nail situation not in the fields of Vietnam.

In the original script, this scene had Cooper and Megan sewing the sarge up but at some point, prior to the shoot, Bob Keen had mentioned in passing a story about superglue and the Vietnam war. Being a history buff and loving any extra little details, Neil amended the scene and swapped out stiches for superglue as it was funnier and had real military connotations.

As Cooper and Megan begin the arduous task of gluing the sarge back together, he is guzzling whiskey having already taken a shit ton of painkillers.

The script called for drunk acting which Sean knew he could do. However why not take it up a notch and to be really authentic, have some brandy for real. This is obviously usually frowned upon since it would be highly unprofessional to turn up to the shoot sozzled. However, Sean was a professional and because he had sought permission from Neil, Christopher Figg and informed Kev, it was allowed. Neil by this point had been in the bar with Sean a few times and knew he could handle his drink, so he wasn't *too* concerned.

"How are you feeling, sarge?" Cooper asks, wrestling the whiskey and then gun out of Wells' hand.

"Absolutely fucking top fucking bollocks," comes the reply.

He manages another cheeky swig of firewater before Megan removes it again, questioning if he should be chasing painkillers with drink. To be fair, as Coop says, he's earned it. Too bloody right he has!

We are then treated to some top-notch, hit the nail right on the head pissed up rambling which is hilarious, and we have all been guilty of at least once. I know for certain I am an incoherent and happy drunk and have told many a casual acquaintance that I love them after a few too many pints so this scene although comedic is also bang on the money.

Here are some of his lines, make sure you say them in a slurred fashion, perhaps adding the odd giggle.

Is it your birthday, Coop? Is it my birthday hey hey?!

I'd see any one of them marrying my sister…if I had one.

I tell you what I love him. I love you. Like a mate that I love.

Cooper! Knock me out. Hit me!

No, you fucking pussy hit me p…

At this point you can hear the impact of Kev's knuckles on Sean's nose. I don't care what anyone says about the noise being added in later, that was real.

So, what does Mr Method Actor have to say on the matter?

> *"Filming was going really well, I took Neil aside and said look, Wells is turning into a lycanthrope. He's had enough morphine to kill an elephant and now a bottle of scotch, no one can do that, he'd be off his maracas. I can do drunk acting but how do you feel about experimenting with some Martell brandy. And he went, okay. So I told Kev and Chris Figg. We were meant to keep it under tabs legally but the amount I consumed it was hard to keep anything quiet. I still to this day don't know if it was a missed blow by Kev or slightly on purpose. I think I annoyed him so much, all that you pussy was improv. I just recall a blinding white light, seeing blood all over the SFX guys and just giggling to myself. They were all asking are you alright mate and I just thought it was fake blood, but no, Kev had clocked me right on the nose."*

Sean Pertwee

To be fair, Sean has told this story time and time again, it was even the first interaction I had with him on Twitter and what sparked the seed of an idea for this book. But what about Kev, what's his rebuttal? Surely, he didn't really mean to hit him? Only a short time before he had been almost too nervous to talk to Sean since he was such a big *Doctor Who* fan. Maybe his fist just slipped?

> *"He was definitely annoying me that day he just wouldn't shut up and we were trying to concentrate and get the scene done and he was being all method like hit me hit me so there was a part of me that was like alright you really want me to? But I didn't mean to hit him, I think I caught his nose? I did not intend to break his nose, but I definitely intended to hit him to shut him up. Basically, my aim was too good. I love Sean, hope he's not still mad at me about that. He deserved it and he was egging me on to hit him, but I never meant to actually hurt him. He was all like come on come on do it properly and I was like really okay, so he was definitely asking for it, literally asking me to and I obliged, I had to."*
> Kev McKidd

So, there we have it.

And I think that everyone would agree, he deserved it. We love you, Sean!

I also asked Neil what was going through his mind at the time.

> *"Like the others, I didn't even notice Kev had actually hit Sean until I saw the blood. My first thought was of course, is everyone okay? But that was very quickly followed by, did we get the shot?"*
> Neil Marshall

Luckily for Sean's nose, they did get the shot.

Of course, I left out another very important detail here.

Sausages.

Another of Sean's improv lines, obviously because of

not only the way his guts looked but also due to the fact they were actually made of sausages, and he was pissed and rambling. It's such an iconic line, one that fans still randomly shout at him and just works perfectly for the title of this book. However, I can't take any credit, it was all down to Neil making the suggestion, Sean approving and my editor Mark agreeing.

                    COOPER
              (turns to WELLS)
         How you feeling Sarge?

                    WELLS
              (drawling)
         Absolutely arseholed unless
         I'm seriously mistaken.

                    MEGAN
         You sure he should be
         chasing painkillers with
         whisky?

                    COOPER
         He can take it. He's earned
         it.

                    WELLS
         How come I'm pissed then?
         It's not your birthday is
         it?!

                    COOPER
         No, it's much better than
         that.

                    WELLS
         It's my birthday?!

                    COOPER
         Not exactly. Believe me,
         you'll thank us for it come

morning.

                    WELLS
I'll thank you now... for
coming back for me Coop.

                    COOPER
You would have done the same
thing.

                    WELLS
        (lapsing into
        melancholy)
Yeah? Then why couldn't I
save Bruce?

COOPER removes WELLS blood-soaked dressing and
begins trying to stick the open cut together,
but his hands are shaking with adrenaline.

                    WELLS
        (to MEGAN)
Do you know... this man is
my best mate in the whole
world. I mean, the other
guys in the squad are top
blokes, and any one of them
would be welcome to marry
my sister, if I had one.
But this man here, is the
salt of the fuckin earth. A
better mate, no one could
ask for. I can honestly say
that I love him... like a
mate... who I love.

                    MEGAN
Would you two like to be
alone?

                    WELLS
          Ahhh! Somebody better get
          stuck in soon before I sober
          up and start to feel this!

COOPER can't control his shaking.

                    COOPER
          Shit!

                    MEGAN
          Here. Take this.

She passes him the lamp and snatches the tube
of GLUE!

                    COOPER
          It's the adrenaline, I...

                    MEGAN
          Here. I'll stick. You...
          bond.

INT. DOWNSTAIRS - NIGHT

Moving from room to room, we pass TERRY, JOE,
RYAN sitting on a chair looking guilty, and
finally SPOON, staring out into the darkness
while listening to the muffled cries from
upstairs.

INT. BEDROOM - NIGHT

WELLS has passed out and is snoring loudly as
COOPER and MEGAN continue.

But what else is going on whilst Megan and Cooper are

knee-deep in the sarge's insides? Well, Spoon and Joe are keeping watch and Terry is having a tidy up. Between making a lovely brew and cleaning the place, he'd have made a lovely househusband one day...

Neil uses the next few moments whilst Wells is unconscious and not pissing Cooper off to allow Megan to relay some information. She tells him she is a zoologist who heard the stories of the missing campers, went looking and found evidence. That was two years ago which gives us a vague timeframe. Cooper is still not entirely convinced David Kessler is running amok outside but Megan is serious and suggests before the end of the night, he'll change his mind and accept that werewolves are as real as they are.

We are then treated to the terrifying sight of Spoon attempting some LARPing and making like he's Sir Lancelot swinging the sword around as Cooper asks, *"Everyone tooled up?"* and he responds, *"To the nines."* I just love this little moment, the genuine look of 'oh yeah' on Spoon's face before Cooper takes it away like he's a toddler with a sharp stick and says, *"You'll have your fucking eye out with that, man,"* Makes me snicker every time.

They head back into the kitchen and whilst Megan rinses her bloody hands, Cooper tells the lads that they will stay and fight, no more running.

Any questions?

Joe answers for them all saying, *"Just the one, Coop, exactly what is it we are fighting against?"*

Cooper defers to Megan who answers – lycanthropes.

Ever wondered where the word lycanthropy actually originates from? Well, that would be Greek Mythology, specifically, Lycaon, King of Arcadia. Allegedly, Lycaon wanted to test Zeus' omniscience, as one does. So he roasted one of his sons (he did have over fifty so…) and fed the child to Zeus to see if he would know – also another cannibal reference! Of course, Zeus did know and not being fond of eating children (they gave him terrible gas) he punished Lycaon by turning him into a wolf. Hence, lycanthropy. Not the best origin story but not the worst either.

As much as I love werewolves, they have always been my favourite creature, I feel Joe's response here after Cooper explains *"That's werewolves to you and me,"* of *"You taking the piss?"* is what 99% of people would at first think. Because no one in their right mind is going to just accept *The Company of Wolves* are running around outside, right?

Except unless you are good, old Spoony. It makes perfect sense to him, he's on board and ready to kick some hairy arse. Joe throws in a bit of mythos here – full moon, silver bullets, even the old 'eyebrows that join in the middle' which was in fact a sign of evidence back in the dark ages akin to a witch's mark which was likely just a skin defect. If you haven't read about the Werewolf Witch Trials in Germany in the late Middle Ages, you should. Fascinating and terrifying and that's what people were willing to believe, not the poor accused.

In 1521, inquisitors appointed by the Pope presided over several trials of alleged werewolfery. Two shepherds, Pierre Burgot and Michel Verdun, confessed to making a pact with the Devil in exchange for food: meeting with a man in black who gave them an ointment that turned them into werewolves, then attending midnight witch gatherings and hunting and eating children. Both were convicted and burned at the stake, along with a third who refused to confess

www.history.com/news/
werewolf-trials-europe-witches

Whilst Megan does her best to convince Joe, telling him how she's tracked and studied these creatures, Cooper is reloading one of the magazines. You can also see here if you look quickly his fingers are slightly stuck together due to the damned super-glue. Been there, done that…

This is a good scene for Megan. Right now, she holds all the cards as the only one who truly knows what they're up against. Knowledge is power. She informs the squad at least fifteen people have been not only killed but ripped apart, leaving but blood over the last couple of years. Joe looks increasingly unhappy with this news whilst Spoon confirms he's sold and ready to whoop some werewolf butt. Cooper seems to be on the fence, the practical military training likely acting as a barrier to completely accepting this fantastical information. Still as he says it doesn't really matter whether the cast of *The Howling* are out there or whether they've just *'escaped from the local nuthouse and forgotten to shave or trim their nails.'* Whatever is out there, they are the enemy. And that is that.

We get a lovely Ryan moment (he's still there lurking

ominously, remember) after Cooper has relayed all the relevant call-signs. That's names to you and me. We had call signs and collar numbers in the police. It's easier to distinguish on the radio and you quickly get used to being addressed as a number. I was PC 2352, call-sign DC36E, part of Team 5 Response, Wilts Pol. Loads of stuff gets shortened or nicknamed in the services, much like a lot of professions, I guess. Calling comms (the call-handlers who answer 999 calls and assign jobs to officers, known on the radio as QJ in Wiltshire) to let them know, "QJ, show 2352 state 11," was always a favourite. Status 11 meant you were going off duty.

Megan asks about Ryan, Cooper informing her the captain is not part of their squad and his being there is hazy at best.

"If I could tell you, I would," begins Ryan, pausing for just enough beats to raise the tension and make you wonder what he's going to add. *"But I'm just a soldier. Like you."*

Um, oh no you didn't! You are not like the others you shifty, dog-killing psycho! Luckily Cooper knows his game.

"No stripes. No insignia. A suit in a uniform does not make a solder. He's with Special Ops."

Take that, Ryan.

Cooper goes on to explain to Megan Ryan's unit were ripped to shreds last night and somehow, he was the sole survivor. Which is not at all suspicious or sketchy.

Whilst Ryan tries to pull rank and be menacing, stating he doubts he needs their help anymore; Cooper looks at a photo on the fireplace depicting what looks like a mother and father and three grown up children. And because this film is full of awesome in-jokes, gags and the occasional Blue Peter type prop, the family is actually made up of crew:

Left to right -
Mat O'Toole - Creature FX
Helene Coker - 3rd Assistant Director
Ralph Eisenmann - 2nd Assistant Director
Christina Shaffer - Art Director
Edward Wiessenhaan - Special Effects

Megan informs Cooper they are the Uaths (which is actually Olde Irish for horror) – and the family have lived in this glen for centuries. So where exactly are they then, huh?

Cooper has been growing ever more wary of Ryan, not just due to him being shady as fuck, but because that aside from looking pale enough to star in *Carry On Screaming* (a favourite childhood movie of both Neil and myself – "Frying tonight!" – more on this later) he seems to be fighting fit and sitting pretty despite being at death's door not that long ago.

I also love Ryan's answer, he really is an arrogant bastard and seemingly unflappable, *"I have a strong constitution."*

"You're not bloody kidding."

Yeah, what Joe said!

Cooper wants to see his wounds, something Ryan doesn't seem too keen on, to the extent he draws a gun on Cooper. Despite all those soldiers surrounding him, tooled up to the nines, it's Megan that shows us a few years before Rapunzel in *Tangled* that frying pans make excellent tools for knocking weapons out of hands and clocking someone around the noggin. There's an awesome little woo hoo moment when Cooper throws Ryan's gun to Spoon and he catches it one-handed like a boss. I've always loved that moment, a bit like when an awesome guitarist does that thing when they spin the instrument 360 degrees around them, and it looks cool as shit.

I asked Darren about it.

> *"The scene where Kev throws the pistol, he was close enough to just pass it originally, but I suggested to throw it, so it turns in mid-air as it'll look better. We practiced a few times and ended up doing this, throwing instead of passing and it looks great. It was wicked having that freedom and encouragement from Neil to play around and try things. There was a real open vibe and if he didn't like it, he'd just tell you."*

> Darren Morfitt

Anyway, with Big-Man Joe holding onto Ryan's arms, Cooper is able to get a look at Ryan's wounds and lo and behold, they have healed up nicely. No gaping flesh, no leaking blood. Just smooth skin. It comes as no surprise to the viewer as I would presume everyone knows their lore – IF you are lucky enough to actually survive a werewolf attack, you will become one, no ifs or buts – but it is a mindfuck for the characters.

Cooper ripping the tea towel to tie him up might look pretty cool in the final edit but check out the blooper reel on the UK DVD and you'll get to see a moment of Kev facing a cotton nemesis.

Of course, I gave him a chance to defend himself against the infallible piece of cloth –

> "Basically, the tea towel was meant to rigged so that when I picked it up, it would easily rip so I could tie Liam up. But I must have picked up the wrong one, so it was pretty embarrassing. There I was meant to be all hard-arse and I couldn't rip the damn thing; it wasn't a good look for me. We ended up referring to it as the kryptonite tea towel."
>
> Kev McKidd

As they're tying him up, Megan asks if they're going to torture him, with a glint of glee in her eye. She has no love for the captain. Cooper replies he doesn't know, what would she do? There is the briefest glance between her and Ryan before she answers, *"I'd torture him."* Atta girl.

Suddenly the power shuts off. A well-known, well-used trope in many a movie and a nod to *Aliens* in particular here but also to implicitly remind us these are intelligent beings who are playing to their advantages.

Those bloody animals have shut down the generator – why, Terry, well because they can see in the dark and you are afraid of it (I bet Terry actually was, bless him).

Joe of course hits the nail right on the head proclaiming, *"This is a pile of rancid shit."*

Yes, Joe, yes, it is.

Cooper says he's beginning to believe Megan and we get a fleeting glimpse of movement from out of the window - one of the foe making a run for it.

"This is it," cries Cooper. *"Mark your targets and preserve your ammo. Three round bursts. We've only got one stun grenade apiece so only use it if absolutely necessary."*

The shot of the men with their guns stood with the window in the background is a quick salute to *The Wild Bunch*. The music is rising again, building up along with the tension. We can feel the enormity of the situation, our senses on high alert. We want these guys to be okay but also, we know what's out there. Neil has ensured we give a crap, and we are genuinely worried for our lads. There are just a few seconds here where the men are in shadow and it's not that easy to see what's happening. I have read several reviews where people criticise this, even though it is mere moments and not a pivotal scene. As I have already pointed out countless times, this book is a celebration of my all-time favourite film. It has allowed me to deep dive into the creative process, from the genesis of an idea to the final product. I have been able to talk to and get to know the cast and crew, hear hilarious behind the scenes stories and learn why certain decisions were made. Everything about this book is completely and utterly biased because I bloody love *Dog Soldiers* and all the people involved. The fact that on occasion some scenes are a little dark never bothered me, I always took it on face value that it was night-time and Neil was allowing us to see and hear what we needed.

I'll get off my soapbox now.

In the original pitch deck, there was mention of an attraction between Cooper and Megan and there are certainly some shots where they are stood quite close which could be interpreted that way. Fans have also speculated some flirting between her and Spoon. There's a lot that could be said about this. Sex and horror often go hand-in-hand, there is even a well-known theory that people crave sexual interaction if they have experienced a near death situation as the very basis of intercourse is to make new life which is in turn the antithesis to dying. No one really knows how they might react in this sort of situation with all that adrenaline and testosterone flying about. Ryan certainly either picks up on some vibes or merely chooses to make the situation uncomfortable, quipping, *"Still chasing that first kiss, Cooper?"* which is cute since the score accompanying the exchange between Megan and Cooper is inspired by *The Sound of Music*. Almost a nice Disney moment for them!

Cooper doesn't rise to it though, simply stating they won't be there for Ryan since he isn't there for them. There's another one of 'those looks' between the captain and Megan, indicating what, prior knowledge of each other's existence? There was a little more meat to the bones in the script (much to Neil's chagrin), but most was edited out.

INT. KITCHEN - NIGHT

RYAN sits, bound to the chair, with MEGAN holding SAM close, hugging the warmth and safety of the fire.

> RYAN
> I knew you weren't dead
> Megan.

> MEGAN
> That's all you have to say
> to me? You left me to die
> out there Ryan.

> RYAN
> There were extraordinary
> circumstances to consider.

> MEGAN
> Right.
> (sarcastic)
> I can see you've already
> worked your charms on Cooper
> and his men.

> RYAN
> What's going to happen to
> me, Megan?

> MEGAN
> You really want to know?

> RYAN
> Yes I do.

> MEGAN
> Why don't you just wait and
> see what happens.

Enraged and frustrated, RYAN throws himself into the back of the chair.

The musical tempo rises and then…

Quiet.

Quiet in a horror movie is never good.

Next comes around four minutes of pure unadulterated action filled batshit crazy heart stopping fun, something I'd suggest now that Neil is renowned for and executes so well.

I really enjoy watching this sequence of events but on that early second watch (since I couldn't recall much from the first time) I really did wonder if Neil was going to break my heart and cause me to shout expletives at the telly on several occasions.

It starts with Spoon in the hallway by the stairs, chewing on that gum like Violet Beauregarde, looking in front of and behind him since he has both exits to keep an eye on. We see one of the doorhandles begin to move. He slowly raises the gun, even stopping chewing momentarily and looks through the sight on weapon at the door. They both begin to bang and rattle now, and we get another fleeting glimpse of something rushing past the window on the back exit. The something is growling and it's getting closer and easier to hear. He edges towards the door and…puts the chain on obviously 'cause that'll keep 'em out!

Joe is in the living room with the shotgun. Glass smashes as we hear, "*Contact!*" and he starts firing bullets at the beast. The impact does seem to have a mild affect, we see them being hit, flailing about and that emitting that awful whining sound, but it is seemingly unlikely they are going to obey his instructions as he shouts, *"DIE!"*

Still, the thought is there.

A quick black and white POV of Terry in the kitchen brings forth our next enemy and as usual the poor lad looks petrified. But good on him, he doesn't freeze or run, and his training seems to kick in as he fires at the monster who has smashed the glass on this window too. Cooper rushes to his side apparently ignoring his own instruction of three short, controlled bursts as he lays into the figure in the window. I sometimes think back to the original casting of Jason Statham during these action scenes and whilst we all know he can kick arse and look cool doing it, I honestly feel Kev brought more of a caring presence to the screen that allowed him to become a beloved hero without dominating the other characters.

Back to Spoon in the hallway and he fires a sea of bullets out of the little window in the door but bugger he's out of ammo and needs to reload the magazine. There's a wolf right outside, pressing against the door so when he gets the bullets in his hand, the door bumps him, and he drops it just out of reach. The noises radiating from the creatures at this point are quite spectacular too.

The whining from outside the kitchen window where Cooper and Terry have been firing seems to suggest that one is at the very least pissed off for now, and Cooper gives Terry a lovely little reassuring pat on the arm. Again, these tiny probably often over-looked details, which it doesn't really matter if you don't pick up on or not, make this movie so much more than Soldiers Versus Monsters for me. Cooper giving that pat on the back, that show of affection and encouragement is what makes a great team and that is evident from both the characters and the cast. As Kev has said, it was a lovefest, a real bromance and at the end of the day, those actors were like brothers.

SCENE# 68   SHOT# 2 (B) W

He grabs one of the pans of boiling water and rushes out to help Spoon, pouring it through the hole onto the wolf. Spoon then takes the now empty pan off Cooper and starts battering the wolf through the window (a lovely bit of improv from Darren which Neil and Kev thought worked perfectly in the moment) perhaps foreshadowing their final showdown later.

We are back in the living room with Joe and the pump

action shotgun, and this does look pretty cool for those who like some badarse action. There are some awesome camera shots cutting between Joe and the wolf in the window. As he gets closer, likely hoping to kill it at that range (if only the shells were silver), the wolf grabs the gun out of his hand. He quickly dives to the side onto the ground as the gun goes off but is thrown back inside. It would seem werewolves don't have particularly dextrous fingers. He decides to use his grenade, lobbing it out the window to the well-recognised call of, *"Fire in the hole!"* and BANG we get a nice little explosion.

Terry is still firing away in the kitchen, with both Ryan and Megan looking slightly nervous.

Joe backs himself against a window as he attempts to reload the shotgun, each shell seemingly taking an extraordinary amount of time to load

There's an awesome quick shot (which doubles as Kev's audition for the next Marvel superhero) as the chain on the door starts rattling and he slides across the floor slamming his boots against it before wedging the gun. Kev said it was moments like this that made them feel like real action heroes and he certainly looked the part here.

Joe is still reloading those shotgun shells and one of the wolves' notices through the open window and legs it – where is it going? As always, we need to remember although when in wolf form, the creature is driven by primal instincts such as hunger and the thrill of the hunt, they also maintain their human intelligence and cunning. In essence they are doubly as dangerous especially as they work together in unison as a pack. There are no lone wolves out there…but what about inside the cottage?

Spoon is trying to wedge a dresser up against the door with the small window and a fist comes flying through and punches him. He falls to the floor as a cupboard door swings open and he is almost squatted like a fly as a huge cannister of Calor Gas pops out and just misses his head by seconds.

It is perhaps even more frightening when you discover that really was a heavy container! They had planned on using a much lighter prop, but it didn't seem to fall very fast necessitating the urgency for Spoon to get out of its way.

So, Darren being Darren suggested they use the heavier one and that he'd make sure he rolled away from it, which he did but just in the nick of time! He was pleased with the result, since it does look more realistic because he actually was in some danger!

Well, it might look good in the end but it's yet another of those heart in your mouth moments when you think we are not going to lose another one of our lads to a non-wolf death are we? No, but don't you dare rest on your laurels, dear reader, way more carnage is coming and very soon.

Joe has finally got his gun ready and just in time as the cheeky wolf has reappeared at the window and is ready to huff and puff and oh shit! Another one reaches through the window he is leaning against, and grabs hold of the collar of his shirt, making it impossible for him to aim correctly. He does manage to get some shots off, destroying more of the Uath's ornaments – actually pick-ups again by Keith's unit.

Spoon is back on his feet and grabs the magazine and gun whilst Joe realises he is actually in a spot of bother here and does exactly what I would have done in this situation - he yells, *"Cooper!"*

Coop rushes in to see Joe being pinned from behind and…

Quickly runs out again!

What can he possibly be doing?

Spoon drops his grenade out the window…

And then our knight in shining armour runs back into Joe, does an awesome roll over the sofa commando style (remember here, Kev hadn't done a film like this before, and he was still recovering from that broken rib. You'd never know from the way he was flinging himself about and looking the part) and what does he have, only the sword that could have someone's eye out! He calls out and swings it at the arm attached to Joe and we are treated to a grisly sound of torn flesh and bone and also a whine as it must have smarted a bit.

SCENE#   71   SHOT#   1 /3)

Joe then delivers a corker of a line as with the hand still attached to his shoulder he states, *"Cheers, mate."* And I'm sure the hand is another quick nod to Ash Williams AKA Bruce Campbell and *Evil Dead II*. Another homage to Sam Raimi's sequel also known as *Evil Dead II: Dead By Dawn* is the movie *Idle Hands* starring Devon Sawa. That is another very silly and funny movie which is my opinion there can never be too many of. There is a formula which works: horror + comedy + in camera practical effects = perfection and there's a rat-monkey from Skull Island to prove it.

There's commotion from upstairs and Cooper is quick to remember the re-stuffed with sausages, sleeping sarge is up there. Spoon has located a wee box of tools and there is another 'blink and you'll miss it but catch it and you'll piss yourself moment' as he is hammering nails into the door. Some hairy fingers suddenly poke through the letter box and he immediately starts hammering them too, because you would too, you know you would! Joe's got his cool back and his axe as he rushes the window again and Spoon throws Cooper's gun back at him as he passes by on his way up the stairs to Sleeping Beauty. He also has the sword as he runs up the stairs, doubly armed and dangerous.

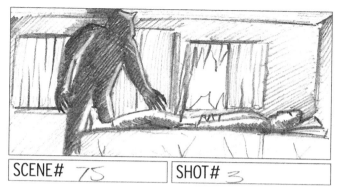

SCENE# 75   SHOT# 3

Next, we are finally treated to a superb shot of just how imposing and bloody terrifying this unknown enemy is. One has crawled in through the open bedroom window and is stood there, looming, imposing and like something straight out of a nightmare.

Pete supervising Ben-Wolf

'My original idea was to have something a bit more demonic, but Neil was insistent they should have 'real' wolf heads. I wasn't entirely convinced but he was the boss. Of course, he was absolutely right and the final result was both elegant AND monstrous. The costume had a sort of pulled in chest and ribcage, like a whippet rather than a big muscle suit. We kept the upper arms quite skinny and close to human, which then extended down to fatter forearms and giant almost comical hands. Same with the legs, skinny up top and then got fatter as they reached the stilted leg extensions. It was quite a stylized look."

Dave Bonneywell

Simon had also made the set dimensions slightly smaller than average, so the 7-foot wolves appeared even larger, dominating the space by having to stoop ever so slightly. The hair on their ears just brushes the ceiling. After many a disappointing creature before them, these really resemble something straight out of an old EC comic or 2000AD. You could imagine Slaine battling one of these guys!

Quick question. What would you do if you were Neil's flatmate and one day a wolf head was delivered to your house? Would you open up the box and then encourage your partner to try it on? And then when you realise the window cleaner is outside, would you suggest they sneak into the bedroom and pop up by the window giving said window cleaner a bit of a fright? Of course you would and this true story, again from Ian Flemming, made me chuckle as I know I would have done the same thing. I think we all would!

These spectacular costumes and practical effects most

definitely allow the film to stand the test of time against others which chose to use very expensive and easily dated CGI. And twenty years later, you still have the revered experts in the field like Greg Nicotero and Robert Kurtzman using those skills for things like *The Walking Dead, Creepshow* and *Black Friday* starring Bruce Campbell! The actual Bruce, not our Bruce because he's dead and, oh you know what I mean.

> *"A special effect is a tool, a means of telling a story. A special effect without a story is a pretty boring thing."*
>
> **George Lucas – *Star Wars***

The sarge of course is still fast asleep, knocked out on morphine, booze and a smashing (literally) smack on the nose from his best-mate. Cooper rushes in and fires at the wolf already in the room but wait, there are two windows! Another sneaky bugger is trying to get in and grabs Cooper's legs. He drops the sword, and the gun flies out of his hand and under the bed, where he tries to reach it whilst being held by the ankle. The wolf already in the room is ominously approaching Wells who isn't waking up yet despite the commotion.

Poor old Cooper is yelling like mad at him and lobbing books from the bookcase at the end of the bed, and Wells does start to sort of rouse a little. Cooper has found a camera and takes a photo now. What on earth is he doing, hoping to make a scrap book at the end of all this? Oh no, it wasn't for a memory box, thankfully the flash is on and for a second it disorientates the humongous creature. Sarge is now starting to stir, God only knows what must have been going through his mind, but I imagine he hoped he was still dreaming.

To build tension even more, we leave the bedroom for a minute and get a darting glimpse of Joe and Spoon back-to-back and firing bullets like there's no tomorrow.

3, 2, 1 we are back in the room (thanks, Paul McKenna) with Cooper and Wells and a huge fucking howling thing. Poor Coop is still trying to get Wells to realise exactly what is happening and to lend a hand but all that booze, drugs and being disembowelled is making him a tad groggy.

Ear-cutting sword

In the meantime, Cooper has retrieved the sword and is doing his best to bash the wolf that still has hold of him.

146

You can just about see here but he actually manages to cut off one of their ears.

| SCENE# 75 | SHOT# 11 |

Factoring in the money the costumes cost, it won't be too surprising to learn that not all of the heads were fully animatronic. There were various heads for different purposes and one they made just for extra scenes where they didn't need the movement, they called Vincent. It was Vincent used in this shot where the ear is cut off. Get it? Vincent, ear cut off...I'm telling you – too much fun.

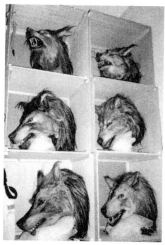

Many wolf heads

Just hearing Cooper shout, *"Fuck off!"* to the wolf as he finally manages to boot it in the face is pure class. He reaches under the bed for his gun just as Wells seems to finally grasp the urgency of the situation and then they both let rip at the wolf still in the room, Wells with two guns and the bastard goes sailing out the window.

Take that, mother fucker!!!

147

Ho. Lee. Crap

This was easier to shoot than in looks insofar as the interior sets were all one low level, so they just had to rig Ben the stunt-wolf-guy onto a wire which was then pulled backwards onto a soft-landing right outside the opening. It looks really smooth and is a great yet simple effect.

Wells sits up, still looking pretty shitty and holding his now nicely bandaged and glued up guts.

Will the guys get a breather now?

There are three quick shots of windows with nothing seemingly trying to climb through, indicating that at least for the moment, their attackers have retreated with their tails between their extremely long legs. It's very quiet, we can just hear Sam panting. We are still tense as we know quiet is often the catalyst for something major. Silence in horror usually has the complete polar opposite effect and is akin to ringing the klaxon or siren like in *The Purge*.

The black and white POV shows the wolves have indeed withdrawn back into the tree line, probably to lick their wounds. Perhaps it is over, at least for a moment...

Terry feeling brave.

Nah, of course not! Because Terry commits the cardinal sin of turning away from his post. All through the narrative thus far, he's been the baby-faced assassin, voice shaking and looking like he needs new trousers. But the adrenaline rush has kicked in, instilling a sense of bravado.

"Dogs," he says, his voice stronger although you can just about make out the tremor on his breath still. *"More like pussies."*

SCENE# 79   SHOT# 6(B) or 9

What happens next isn't much of a surprise, especially to those who are genre fans and can recognise certain tropes and plot devices but that doesn't make it any less effective or horrific.

The slatted blinds on the windows suddenly come down and then boom, two hairy arms reach in and pull Terry out through the window which is of course Neil doffing his cap to *Assault on Precinct 13*. We don't see anything here but my god, the noises. I have always hated hearing him being eaten since he was just a loveable dope of a character, but bizarrely the older I have got (isn't it annoying how you get older but the characters in the film don't? I have now reached the age where I am older than every actor when it was made) the more motherly I feel toward Terry. Terry, not the actor portraying him, Les. Remember he is over in Oz, tormenting me with visions of spiders big enough to put on the barbie…

Les went on to work with Neil again as one of the horrific crawlers in *The Descent* along with Craig Conway – David the camper from the start. He also portrayed Carpenter (wonder where that name came from?) in *Doomsday* again with Craig and Darren Morfitt.

Megan watches, resting against the window frame and cutting the palm of her hand.

Megan getting bloody

This was included as a moment of foreshadowing for the proposed sequel, a sign of her DNA being left. Even Neil has since jokingly agreed that the amount of werewolf blood flying around at the end would more than suffice and this tiny droplet left on a likely destroyed window ledge would be null and void, but it was originally intended to simply plant a seed and that was that. It has however led to some ambiguity in various reviews I have seen and read where people have speculated that this is the moment she is actually infected and becomes a wolf. No matter how clear a writer and director imagine they are being, there is always room for people to draw their own interpretations. I for one think that is the mark of a really great movie because it actually means people are reflecting on it and questioning things after the event rather than a one and done viewing and never consider the story or the characters again.

We cut back to a looking very sorry for himself sarge. He's resting again and says he's feeling peachy. However, by telling Cooper, *"Squad's yours, mate,"* and then looks lovingly at a little photo of his wife he carries with him, it would seem perhaps he's still not convinced he's going to make it through 'til sunrise.

Fun fact! That isn't the lovely Mrs. Pertwee Sean's gazing at but in fact Neil's sister, Sue! I asked her what it was like to have such an awesome cameo and if she still tells everyone she ever meets. If I was Sean's on-screen wife even in just a photo, I'd tell every person I spoke to. The postie, my hairdresser. The other mums in the playground. The lady on the till in Tesco…

> *"The "Annie" photo was taken just after I had had my daughter Molly, who incidentally played Jessie in The Descent. We held the premiere of Dog Soldiers at the Odeon in Newcastle it was such a special event, full of family and friends, Neil always tried really hard to promote Newcastle and the North-East within the film industry, we are very proud of our Geordie heritage. When the photo scene came up on screen (for literally seconds) all the cast and crew cheered me which was so special, they were such an amazing ensemble!"*
>
> Sue Kayll

Yet more evidence of the real sense of family that was born from this production.

Sean also added that it wasn't at all awkward meeting his 'wife' at the premier who just so happened to be the bosses' sister…

Cooper arrives in the kitchen to the sombre sight of Joe and Spoony looking downtrodden and dejected, staring mournfully out the window. Before he can ask what's happened, Ms State the Bleeding Obvious pipes up with, *"They took Terry"*.

Of course, Cooper's immediate response is to go and get him back, they're soldiers, right, they don't just let their men get taken. Ryan helpfully informs him there's no point as he is obviously dead and Cooper responds with the simple, *"Shit."* And then louder, *"shit!"* and that one word says it all.

Shit.

Joe and Spoon are still wondering why no one else has heard anything, there must be other people around, cars, lorries, combine harvesters, something passing by. Megan reiterates that the only other house within fifty miles is hers and do they have any idea how lucky they were running into her? Ryan cocks his head (whether this was intentional canine behaviour to imply the change was happening or just underlining his arrogance, it comes across as both pompous and annoying which was the vibe Neil intended) stating with that know-it-all candour, *"I thought you ran into us?"*

Spoon gets back to reloading the magazines which look massively depleted whilst Megan confirms the best thing to do is wait for sunrise, letting us know they still have around six hours to go. Joe goes back upstairs to check on Wells and to ensure no more stealth like wolves have climbed in the windows. They are sneaky buggers for sure. Anyone would think they know they layout of this cottage?

There's a quick howl – sending a message maybe – and shot of the clock which was purposefully broken so it would always be wrong and didn't mess with continuity.

More foreshadowing of Kev's future days on *Grey's Anatomy* as he plays Doctor again and tends to Megan's wound. This also subtly hints at that mutual attraction which constantly adds to her confliction. Even if seemingly innocent, cleaning a cut necessitates pseudo holding hands which is extremely intimate in the circumstances. Whilst likely enjoying the attention, she asks about their chances of surviving the night. Neil plants some more seeds in the dialogue here with the mention of things that lurk in the shadows and the fine line between myth and reality. As the majority of fans know, there wasn't just a sequel planned originally but a trilogy with Cooper as our lead protagonist not only fighting more werewolves but other supernatural entities like a rugged, handsome, Scottish Mulder. I am sure I speak for many, many people when I clutch my rabbit's foot and say PLEASE MAKE THIS HAPPEN!!! And I mean right now. The fans need it RIGHT NOW.

> *"I'm always pleasantly surprised when a fan asks me about* Dog Soldiers *– I usually like that kind of person."*
>
> My bestie - Kev McKidd

We are also privy to what some suggest is the most confusing and unsatisfactory story arc in the entire narrative. Megan confirms the fleeting glances between her and Ryan, were in fact not just odd choices of direction, but because they do know in fact already each other…

Dun, dun dunnn!

She says she was seconded to his team during his first visit. Yes, that's right, *first* visit. His team needed an expert, and she is a zoologist of course and had been there studying these creatures for quite some time. And…

Well, that is really all that is revealed. The reason why there is so much speculation around this, cements the fact that people enjoy a mystery and digging more into the plot to uncover the deep, dark secrets but alas in this case, there simply aren't any. You see, there was no connection between Ryan and Megan in Neil's original script. This convoluted backstory was added at the behest of David E. Allen, the American producer, and rather than take umbrage, Neil added what little he had to as to not impact too much on the story or characters. There were a couple of other lines added in here and there to the script, but they didn't make the edit. So, if you have been scratching your head for the last twenty years wondering about this prior relationship, there's your non-answer. Personally, I don't find it particularly confusing and instead of wondering about the mechanics, I draw three conclusions from this interaction/mini reveal.

1. Megan is capable of hiding stuff and may not be all she seems to be (understatement of the year once we get to you-know-what but bear with me).

2. Ryan is even more despicable than we first realised and did in fact know what they were going to encounter. He put the lives of our lads on the line and there is now no way I can ever feel anything but contempt for him.

3. Cooper likes to try to see the best in people and despite the knowledge that Megan hadn't initially admitted knowing Ryan, still entrusts her with the backdoor key and a gun. That or his gut feelings are masked because he fancies her and he's still chasing that first kiss…

Megan slots the gun in her jeans and wanders off to the window.

Nicely done for someone who shouldn't be au fait with a firearm.

I have often wondered about this; you'd have to have a good belt or tight waist on your trousers. Knowing my luck if I ever tried this, the gun would slip and either end up in my knickers or slide all the way down my leg and I'd accidentally shoot my own foot.

Although it isn't implicit and some of her actions are still questionable as to whose side she's really on, this was the moment for me which reinforced that she was in collusion with the wolves and at the very least she was able to communicate with them. And if that is the case, then everything else she does is an act because she knows the wolves won't touch her. What exactly is her end game?

It's all in the eyes.

Joe delivers the wonderful line, *"Fucking brilliant. We either stay and snuff it, or we all go – and snuff it,"* to which Captain Charming replies on beat, *"Decisions, decisions."* Which is just brilliant. Joe is now really wound up and ready to punch Ryan in the face which of course he deserves when Megan suddenly recalls there is a Land Rover in the barn.

Really, you couldn't have remembered this very important piece of information before our Terry got dragged off? Still, Joe claims he can hotwire it and then comes another fabulous little set-up.

"Alright," starts Coop, *"you're gonna need a decoy, something fast and loud."*

Joe, then Cooper, then Megan all turn and look at something which fits the bill.

The camera cuts to Ryan who also shifts his gaze to look at the fast and loud thing.

And of course, it's Spoon, sat chewing away completely oblivious. When he realises everyone is looking at him, he's non-plussed, merely asking, *"What? You what?"*

This little exchange is just 'absolutely fucking top fucking bollocks'.

Off we all trot up to the bedroom where Wells has drifted off again and yet to be awoken by his True Love's Kiss. Or he's still off his trolley and knocked out on mixing morphine with whiskey. Cooper puts Ryan in the corner and tells him to sit, stay, just like a dog which is a nice touch.

Spoon is ready to leap out one window, Joe the other.

Megan is tying up various sheets and ropes to allow Spoon to get back up the wall again. It is noticeable at this point apart from Spoon, the other soldiers are still in long sleeves, Joe has his jacket back on, but Megan has gradually stripped down from coat, fleece, shirt to now just a vest. I don't see this as something for the lads to gawk at but more to do with the fact that as she fights the change, she is starting to get hot flushes and sweat. There is a reason the werewolf cycle has been linked in mythos to the lunar *and* menstrual cycle in women. There are several parallels, fur aside.

Joe, bless him, is still sore about the football. He asks Megan, *"Don't suppose you know who won the match?"* to which she replies jovially, *"Didn't even know there was a game on."* Yikes.

Never use the G word with a hard-core footy fan especially when the match of his life is on and he's missing it for this party.

Keith Bell remembers this exact moment when they were watching the premier in Newcastle where a lot of the audience – mainly made up of cast, crew and their families plus local media etc. – were die hard Newcastle United Football Club fans and when Joe says, "*It's not a game,*" they all cheered! As the granddaughter of a Geordie who was also a NUFC fan, I whole-heartedly approve…

Anyway, Spoony jumps out the window. Well, I say Spoon but that must have been one of those specialist, circus performer type trained Hollywood style stunt guys, right? Or one of those tricks where it only looks like the actor is actually, stupidly jumping from out of the window, right. Right?

No. Darren really did jump from that height, which was of course the façade of the cottage. What was he thinking?

> "*Yeah, I shouldn't have jumped out of that higher window. Silly of me really as I could have fucked myself and the movie up. But I was young and over enthusiastic and wanted to give 110%. Bizarrely, I'd never imagined doing action type stuff - I wanted to do serious Ken Loach type drama, but after day one I was like 'This is fucking awesome - let's kick some fucking ass! I want to do this forever!'*"
>
> Darren Morfitt

See, I told you. Waaaaaaaaay too much fun…

> **"That's my advice with dealing with writer's block: follow the fun. If you aren't having fun, you are doing it wrong."**
>
> **Jordan Peele** – *Get Out*

Anyhoo, now comes one of the moments that gets cited over and over as a fan favourite. Spoon wanders over to the darkened treeline whilst we also get the quick black and white wolf POV. There are in the trees exactly where Spoony is heading. So far, so good.

There is real poetry in seeing a mouthy little squaddie from Hartlepool singing at the top of his voice, *"Come on you bastards. Come an' 'av a go if you think you're 'ard enuff!"*

It hasn't enticed them out of the trees yet. Maybe they were insulted. Maybe they're further away than he thought?

He's still looking around for signs of movement and lights a flare. Now we are starting to get glances of just how close those bastards are…

Zoinks!

Spoon holds his ground, adding, *"Well come on, you beauties!"* and we see him from the wolf POV which ramps up the tension to 110. He may be loud and fast but is he loud and fast enough? Shouting, *"COME ON!!!!!!!!!!"* like some sort of war cry makes me you think he can do this and luckily before any more heroics, he hears Megan shout, *"Spoon, run!"*

The most complicated character of the lot?

It's moments like this where the complexity of her character really comes into play. If she is truly just leading these men to their death, why does she help Spoon get back now rather than let him be ripped apart?

Or is she merely sadistic, enjoying playing with her 'food' and exerting her power over these traditionally and stereotypically very macho squaddies?

In the meantime, Joe is out his window and now the wolves are distracted with the loud and fast decoy, he legs it over to the barn to retrieve the vehicle.

Spoon isn't running quick enough for Megan and she shouts at him, *"Move your fucking arse, soldier!"* and we see him clambering up the wall, calling, *"I'm trying!"*

As he flies through the window and lands next to Megan, Spoon delivers another much-quoted line, *"I LOVE it when a posh bird talks dirty."* There's no time for her to give him a quick slap, as the damn wolf has grabbed hold of the rope, pulling the bed over to the window and trapping Cooper whilst it tries to get in. There's mayhem for a moment, Spoon is trying to cut the rope, Megan is taking photos using the flash to disorientate the wolf and Cooper is yelling, *"Fucking cut it, argh!"* and a few more choice expletives. Finally Spoon cuts through and the wolf falls from the window. Phew. There is one teeny moment of humour amongst the mayhem when the bed starts dragging across the floor and Wells immediately bolts up and demands, *"Fuck it what's happening, Cooper?"* like he wants a sit-rep in the midst of another attack.

Joe on the other hand has managed to get into the barn

and into the vehicle. He reaches down for the wires, and they ignite easily. Success! He turns the headlights on and oh shit, there in the haybales right in front of him is a wolf enjoying a midnight snack.

The problem is that is our Terry, who is somehow still alive despite being severely injured.

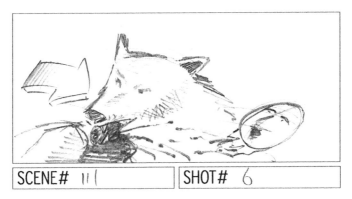

SCENE# 11 SHOT# 6

Terry reaches one pathetic arm out towards Joe and this part always gives me chills.

He is covered in so many wounds that there is zero chance he would have survived and of course we know the lore – if he *did* survive, he'd turn too, and they'd have yet another monster to deal with. It's still absolutely gutting to see his life end here though.

There's a moment in the DVD commentary where Sean comments on this scene. *"This is horrible,"* he says and quick as a flash in response we hear Neil say, *"This is great!"*

I'm torn between the two as I want blood and lots of it, but not Terry's. And just to make matters worse, what's a good horror film without a decapitated head being lobbed at you, right?

| SCENE# | 111 | SHOT# | 12 |

Those noises as the monster rips off Terry's head are absolutely horrific and leave you feeling a bit funny. Talk about reaching all the senses! Then of course the bastard throws the head at the Land Rover where it covers the windscreen in blood.

Little something on the windscreen

And comes to rest in the spare wheel on the bonnet. RIP Terry.

Oh, THAT'S where Terry went

Joe is visibly shaken by this but also is a professional soldier and it has no doubt stoked his fire. An arm shoots through the door but he manages to kick it out and he is ready to reverse out of there at top speed. And so was actor Chris Robson.

Kind of.

You see he had a small confession here, something he'd left out during his audition.

A minor detail really.

He couldn't drive.

It was too late to worry though and Neil got his own back by making him do the take anyway and to be honest, any panic on his face and juddery movements of the vehicle only went to reinforce what Joe was experiencing.

The Land Rover shoots through the back of the barn wall, reversing towards the cottage. Cooper sees this out of the bedroom window and gets everyone up together to head down the stairs and wait at the front door, so they can pile into the vehicle and drive the hell away.

Only it doesn't quite work out exactly as planned, does it?

Next is genuinely one of the creepiest moments of the entire movie. Joe is sat in the front of the Land Rover, no doubt still in shock from seeing his old pal Terry being used as a chew-toy. He's likely thinking they just might now have a fighting chance of getting out, getting Wells to hospital and all home for a nice six-pack.

However, it would appear he is not alone.

There is a distinctive sound reminiscent of Darth Vadar and we see the misty breath coming from behind him. Nice job with the dry ice here SFX guys. It's a scene suggestive of Ripley and the Xenomorph in *Alien 3*. What the hell will Joe do now?

Well, by this point he's had enough. Some reviews that have criticised his gung-ho response to this scenario, but we all know in high pressure situations the body goes back to the very basic principle of fight or flight. And Joe is pissed off. He's really angry and frightened and full of adrenaline so he chooses the only option that makes sense in the moment - fight. He must have known he would die; he's just seen what happened to poor Terry for Pete's sake. But he wanted to die fighting.

"You're behind me, aren't you," he says as the Sith Lord-esque noise continues. *"I'm gonna fucking have you!"* Joe's final battle cry is a valiant one and we see the vehicle rocking, hear him giving his all, doing his best for a few

165

short moments and then splat, buckets of blood all over the windscreen.

Buckets of it.

Shit...

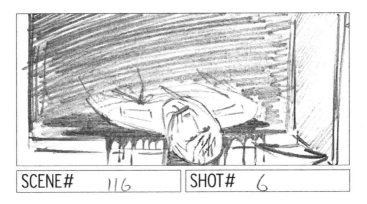

SCENE #   116   SHOT #   6

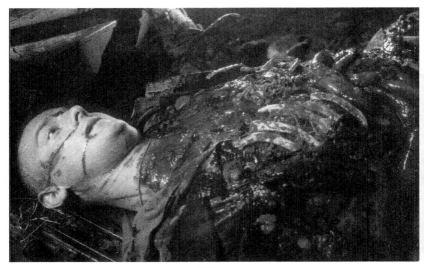

RIP Joe

The others open the door slowly; Coop and Spoon have their guns ready just in case.

Target!

Spoon releases the back door of the Land Rover and suddenly Joe's lolling head is visible and the blood. His body covered is literally covered in gore, some of which is oozing out of the vehicle along with his dog tags. And there, still feasting on Joe's sausages, is the wolf.

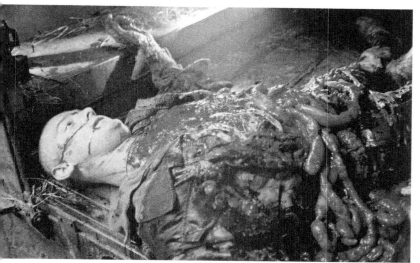

I hope they got a good deal on the sausages

Can I get the camera any closer?

168

It looks up and leaps out, knocking Spoon over and Megan fires at it, emptying her chamber before Wells slams the door, the wolf outside.

Megan looks visibly shaken here, a small amount of wolf blood on her cheek which she touches.

This was a moment where I considered she was perhaps fearful of the wolves rather than entirely complicit, and she knew her insubordination would be punished once they turned back to human form. I truly believe as well as her character being constantly conflicted during the film, so are people's opinions of her. No matter what else, Megan is certainly an interesting member of the cast. And as the band Space and Cooper's arachnid nemesis can attest, the female of the species *is* more deadly than the male.

There is a brief interlude from the violence and chaos for the characters, and for us. If the general viewer was even a quarter as invested as me at this point, they needed a reprieve, a short moment to catch their breath. Maybe change their underwear.

And for the guys, it is a minute to process their grief. They are a squad, a family. Brothers at arms and in the last few hours, they have lost three of their team. Half of their best friends are dead.

Great, memorable films, just like books, tend to be an emotional rollercoaster. The viewer/reader needs to be taken up and down and shaken all around. If the action is constant and you receive death after death after death, the violence is meaningless. Go play a video game if that's your bag. Just make sure it's *Call of Duty* as you will recognise the voice of Soap MacTavish…

As soon as a story plateaus, so do your emotions. Audiences are already massively desensitised to graphic scenes so what works best, when done well, is the pacing and placement of your shocks. It has way more of an impact that way. If you watch a typical 80's slasher, there is no real point bonding with any of the cast as you know only one virginal female is going to make it out alive as our Final Girl. The rest are merely cannon fodder. There is absolutely nothing wrong with that. I love 80s slasher movies, and sometimes mindless, ridiculous shallow characters being chopped up and drilled into is just what you need. But of the myriad of reasons why *Dog Soldiers* resonates so heavily with me, these men are at the heart of it.

So yes, the next few minutes are extremely melancholy. Megan plays the piano, injured hand on show. The tune is the haunting *Clair de Lune*, which means moonlight in English, by Claude Debussy to be precise. And the talented Emma really did learn to play the music. This is of course also an ode to *An American Werewolf in London* where all the songs had the word moon in the title.

Piano buddies

The lads sit at the table, in mourning for their fallen colleagues. No one would have blamed them at this point for just giving up.

As the camera pans around the sad faces, it really hits you. Every loss they feel, we feel and is a real kick in the teeth. You can hear the howling outside too as Megan plays. Is this song somehow actually for them, is she communicating with the pack? Could the song be a message?

Maybe.

Or perhaps they just prefer duelling banjos.

Next we see Cooper rushing back in through the front door and Wells and Megan hammering it shut again. I have seen some comments relating to confusion as to when Cooper left in the first place, in order to be able to come back in, but he does answer this non-mystery by telling the sarge about the dire state of the vehicle and that Joe's body has gone. I realise that I watch this film with rose-tinted glasses but much as you get very obvious scene breaks in a book, so do you on screen. You don't have to be shown every single action to fathom what just happened. However, sometimes where there is deliberate ambiguity, it lends itself to crazy fan theories which I am all here for. Ever fallen down a Reddit rabbit hole and you'll know what I mean.

Spoon announces they're pretty damn low on ammo. This is just yet another realistic moment in amongst the fantasy elements. All too often in films, especially action or superhero titles, the characters have endless supplies that never run out and they never need to reload. Now in those type of fun movies it doesn't really matter and is unlikely integral to the plot. But when you have a bunch of soldiers for whom weapons are as everyday as a pen is to me, you need some authenticity. And the lower the number of bullets, the higher the stakes (which are no good here, you need silver. Stakes are for vampires.)

Megan is back at the window, is she being helpful and standing guard or is she up to something? The latter seems to be the case. One of the theories I struggle with is that she was trying to get out of there the whole time, this was her ultimate escape plan. Because even if things had turned out differently, she's still a werewolf (spoiler but if you are reading this and haven't seen the movie, I'd be shocked – also, go watch it now, you fool!). If she had taken them to Fort William, then what? She could escape the pack, but she cannot run from the moon. Maybe her human instincts and pure desperation allowed her to find the squad and bring them back to 'safety'. I personally think any confliction ended fairly quickly, likely once her vehicle was attacked and she knew *they* didn't want her to leave.

This next scene was the longest piece of dialogue in the script running at eight pages, so two pages more than that first day bonding session. The guys were old pros now though, brothers.

Cooper is close to losing his shit and Ryan is about to rightfully take the brunt of his anger. The open hostility between them has been bubbling from the start and I think at this point Cooper just thinks, fuck it. He's done. He asks Ryan if he likes football, reminding him that Joe did, that he lived for it. Being unable to openly grieve right now, this is his way of honouring his friend. Cooper is getting more and more wound up whilst Ryan remains cool as a bloody cucumber, even managing to state, *"You just can't get past the dog, can you?"*

Cooper continues with the football analogies almost at fever pitch whilst Ryan kindly reminds him that if he'd passed selection, he would have been on his team and if Cooper had been on Ryan's team, he'd be dead **gulp**.

However now Cooper gets really mad, not about the topic but because Ryan keeps changing the fucking subject!

The Toffee-nose Twat concedes, and like just like when we were kids watching *Jackanory*, we settle down for a lovely heart-warming story although he does forewarn that we won't like what he has to tell us…

"We'll be the judge of that, Ryan," pipes up Wells and I don't want to say anything but the sarge is starting to

look a lot better than he did an hour or so ago and I don't think it's just the super-glue.

"Ever heard of Special Weapons Division?"

Wells isn't giving much away here, but we can presume as only a Field Sergeant, he may well have heard of SWD, but it would be massively unlikely he would ever know anything specific since all intel would be classified. Above his paygrade. And that really is a thing is the armed forces and emergency services. There were keypads on certain meeting rooms in the nick I worked at which you could only enter with specific clearance especially if they were being used by MIT (Murder Investigation Team). Not because they felt superior, but you have to make certain only so-many people know things to protect leaks. It is literally a need-to-know basis, and your everyday constable or squaddie does not need to know.

Just to make sure everyone is following; Ryan helpfully clarifies this.

"They're the men in white coats who teach dolphins to stick bombs on submarines and cute furry animals to tear your head off at the neck."

Oh, that Special Weapons Division.

He explains he was sought out to catch one of the creatures and bring it back. An actual fucking giant howling thing. At least it would be on our side, I guess. Only as Megan says, it turned out to be *them*. Remember, there was only supposed to be one…

Ryan is adamant that although it came from above – Head Sheds is a military term for Top Brass – it was *his* party. Well you loused it up, dickhead!

174

During this Wells is fingering the bug Bruce (RIP) found in their radio. That now seems like days ago, but it's only been a few hours. *"We lost good men,"* he says, *"yours and mine."* *Sniff*

"I want to know," he continues, whizzing the transmitter over to Ryan like a barkeep in an olde saloon, *"where we fit in?"*

The captain fills in any gaps from the bits and pieces we've seen and learnt – he needed bait and those in authority had given him approval to use Wells' team whom he'd recommended because of his prior engagement with Cooper. Because he never forgets, remember? He manages to relay all of this with a knife to his neck which no one would have blamed Cooper for slipping and accidentally slitting Ryan's throat (the knife was real, and Liam was mightily relieved when the take was over especially since Kev had previous convictions for inflicting Grievous Bodily Harm on Sean!)

Wells leaps up and punches Ryan in the face *raucous cheer*, knocking him to the floor and shouting in a fashion that tugs on my heart strings every damn time, *"They were my men!"* and I mourn Bruce, Terry and Joe all over again. *"Get up you shit!"* shouts Cooper and suddenly Ryan's eyes have taken on a rather yellow hue…

Well, that can't be good.

He goes flying across the table and Sean delivers one of my favourite lines here which is just so funny in the context – *"I didn't hit him that hard,"* as if somehow Wells punching him has shaken awake the beast that was just waiting to appear. Always makes me laugh, especially Sean's deadpan delivery.

There are several sounds in this movie that send shivers down my spine. I do that thing where you feel all wobbly and if you just move your body for a moment like one of those massive blow-up balloon people (not doll, get your mind out of the gutter) you see advertising car sales in the US, then the noise will dissipate, and your ears will no longer be assaulted. *This* is one of those times. When Liam drags his fingers across the tabletop, it's like nails on a chalkboard, metal cutlery across a plate, those things that set your teeth on edge.

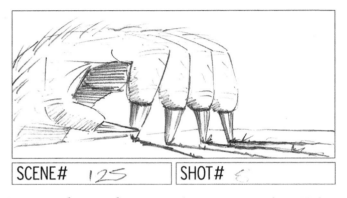

SCENE# 125   SHOT# 6

Of course, this is what we've been waiting for. We know the mythos - he's been mauled but survived ergo he is now a lycanthrope.

End of story, there is no Uno reverse card to play.

So, what tricks does Neil have up his sleeve to show us what's happening? Well, there is indeed a very clever transformation. We already know by now he is a huge *American Werewolf in London* fan and let's face it, it was the best werewolf transformation to date in 2001 and I would go as far as to argue it is still the best in 2022! He might be inspired and influenced by people like John Landis but that didn't mean he ever thought he could come up with something to rival that scene, especially not on his budget. I briefly mentioned earlier, another of Neil's favourite movies as a child, a film I used to watch over and over with my dad, whom my love of horror comes from. To this day he will sometimes text me if he's scrolling through the Sky menu and finds it playing on some obscure daytime channel. And that movie is...*Carry on Screaming* of, *"Frying tonight!"* fame. There is a monster transformation scene in that all-time classic, where main character Detective Sergeant Sidney Bung played by the late, great Harry H. Corbett is given a magic potion and falls behind a sofa. When he re-appears, he is a magnificent were-monster thing, resplendent with a funny wig, huge eyebrows, fangs and hairy hands and feet.

Fabulous.

It would also be remiss of me not to mention another legendary British actor who appears in *Carry on Screaming* as police scientist, Dr Fettle. He was played by the wonderful, late Jon Pertwee, proud papa of our very own Sean.

So in homage to this scene in particular but also all the old school movies that came before, we don't actually see Ryan change as he slithers down under the table, we just hear some suspect sounds and then voila, up he pops as a full-grown wolfman.

"It was so much fun, so silly. We all just laughed so fucking much."

Kev McKidd

I personally have never felt cheated by this although there are critics who say *Dog Soldiers* will never be the best werewolf movie due to the lack of a successful transformation scene. I think it was a brave choice of Neil not to even try and pull this off on his budget, since there was no way he would have been able to produce anything that didn't look cheap and silly. We all knew what was coming so it wasn't some surprise plotline of thinking the character had belly ache and oh shit, he's a werewolf.

Since there was no ta-da! moment, the decision to do it this way has always sat fine with me.

And that's why I am a horror fan and not a critic.

And as Wolf-Ryan rises up from behind the table and that music plays, it's like a love letter to Hammer and Amicus, and then of course the amazing sarge just drops the line, *"Bad dog,"* and we are back.

SCENE# 125   SHOT# 16

There's another wonderful Wells moment as he grabs a stick and yells, *"Fetch!"* This is one of Sean's famously

Fetch

ad-libbed lines. He was meant to grab the glowing log (according to Pete Hawkins, the batteries in the log still work today) and picked up the puny stick instead.

He called out fetch supposing Neil would edit it later but of course, this film was always meant to have humour and with the actors being fully on board and adding lines like this, there was no way it would be cut.

Megan is taking photos again, Spoony has his gun and Coop grabs the sword. Wells does select the correct prop this time and shoves the fiery weapon onto the wolf, causing a lovely hissing sound as it burns the fur and skin. I could almost smell this which is revolting as we all know what burnt hair smells like and it ain't nice.

Spoon is yelling at everyone to get out of the way as he has target, but first Cooper thrusts the sword through the Ryan-wolf's back, the hilt sticking through his chest. Then Spoon lets rip with the MP5 and Megan manages to just duck out of the way as the latest member of the pack flies out of the window, off to join his new family perhaps.

I love the final scene in this sequence as we look back into the kitchen from outside and witness the remaining four survivors just looking out as the wolves begin to howl…

Sam McCurdy certainly knows how to frame a really cool shot.

Wells fixes the boards back onto the window for about the hundredth time and Cooper begins to have something of an epiphany whilst looking at the Uath's photo again, about who exactly these wolves are and where the mysterious family could be. Because of course they are one and the same. It's no wonder the wolves want in, this is their house! And as Wells so eloquently sums it up, *"Well, that makes perfect sense, dunnit. I mean think about it, we bust into their house we eat all their porridge, we sleep in their fucking beds - no wonder they're pissed off."*

Too right and another *Goldilocks* analogy.

Shame Megan insists the family are actually good people (I'd be questioning her definition of good here based on the soup alone), because Cooper says they're going to have to kill them all. Wells then slams the hammer he was holding down onto the photo frame on the table, smashing the glass. This wasn't in the script but fits perfectly, to emphasise and reiterate these people are good as dead.

There's that look again on Megan's face, and we get the feeling something will be revealed and soon. She can't have many plays left – either she stands with the lads, or she will show her true colours and allegiance.

This next quick scene is a pick-up and those hands belong to producer Keith Bell. Neil said that whenever they needed an extra body for a shot it was literally all hands-on-deck and at one point even his shoulder is on camera. Whether it was a grip, or the lunch lady (okay maybe not the lunch lady as she was too busy making soup for Les to regurgitate all over Liam) or even Neil, people just mucked in and stood in as extra bodies when needed. I think that's pretty awesome and one day I'd love to be able to say, that's my big toe on the screen, doesn't it look—oh, I really need to check my cuticles…

I digress.

As Megan states, *"What self-respecting werewolf would have silver in the house anyway?"* and I love Cooper's response. Up until now he has been relatively calm – except with Ryan who deserved it – but you can tell now his patience is wearing thin, as it would. Since they are ordinary soldiers and not Buffy or Mulder, they are doing their best in exceptional, unprecedented circumstances, so he says, *"Fuck the folklore. Let's just burn them."* Woo hoo, grab your pitchforks and torches and let's go!

Only one issue, where are they?

Megan gives a zoologist spiel about alphas, packs and betas but basically insinuates they are in the barn which is warm and not too far from their food source – them.

But can they trust her?

Well whether they should or not, they do.

Spoon and Cooper began moving the Calor Gas cylinders we saw earlier that nearly squished Spoon and Cooper gets to deliver the line, *"That place is going up like Zabriski Point."*

Say what now, Coop?

For those of you who also don't have a Scooby, and I am going to go out on a whim and presume that is most people since this is not a horror movie reference, *Zabriski Point* is a 1970 American drama directed by Michelangelo Antonioni which has an amazing explosion at the end.

And Neil is a film ~~nerd~~ buff.

So now you know.

Spoon asks Cooper what we've all been wondering whilst simultaneously keeping our head in the sand as we don't actually want to know the answer.

"What about the sarge?"

Non-verbal cues are vital part of acting, of being able to tell a compelling story. Body language is massively important, and some actors just have a way of being able to convey a message perfectly with just one thing – their eyes. Kevin McKidd is one of these people and there are several moments during the feature where he doesn't need to say a word, his eyes do all the talking. This is one of those scenes. He knows what's going to happen. Spoon knows what's going to happen. We know they know (still following?) even if no one has verbalised it.

"The sarge is with us," he confirms, Spoon agreeing and saying he just didn't want him to go without getting his watch back. Go where? Leave the house with them or 'go' as in turn into the monster everyone knows is just waiting to bust out? I don't know but the loyalty

in this scene makes my heart full. My only problem with this exchange is now the music has started. And let me clarify what I mean, as the music is beautiful and enhances the mood and tone perfectly. You see that's the problem. This is already an emotional moment (it's about to get much worse) and Mark Thomas' score just does its job so well, it makes me want to cry. So it's not really a problem, it's just doing its job too well as I am now a wreck every time I hear it.

A lot of authors write to music, it helps them concentrate and get in the zone. I'm one of those people who get easily distracted – oooh look a squirrel! So, any background music has to be instrumental otherwise I'm singing along and typing the lyrics rather than whatever I'm meant to be writing. Horror movie soundtracks are of course perfect for this, since it evokes all sorts of emotion that's perfect to imbue into my work. And what else would I listen to other than the *Dog Soldiers* soundtrack, right?

Well, yes, until it comes to what's called Sarge's Theme.

Then I'm out.

It goes off.

Because I can't.

That's how powerful just the music is.

Moving on…

Cooper joins Wells back in the kitchen whilst Megan is shiftily playing with the backdoor key. She steps out of the room as Cooper asks the sarge how he is feeling. Of course, he's feeling fucking top fucking bollocks and that's a problem. That's an actual problem, not like me crying every time I hear his theme tune.

He shows Cooper his nicely healed stomach (great abs, Sean!) and basically tells Cooper he's done for. He also asks what if not all of the wolves are out there, implying of course they're not.

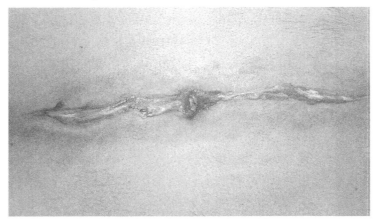

No more sausages

Cooper responds with, *"Then we get some of them. It's a shit load better than none of them and a marked improvement on all of us."*

Wells is insistent, he knows what's happening. He tells Cooper to get out, that he can hold the fort. But Cooper is incredibly faithful. He refused to leave Wells back in the forest when his guts were out and he sure as hell won't leave him now. We don't know much about Cooper, his background, upbringing and we don't need to. Wells is his best friend, a pseudo father/big-brother figure and his boss, his leader. He will not just leave him no matter what the evidence is. Sure, Ryan turned after having been attacked and miraculously healed just like Wells but, *"Shifty bastard could have been one of them from the start."* As he says, they've lost enough men and he won't lose Wells like this.

There is some hilarious dialogue at this moment and although it is not misplaced, because of the sombre nature of the underscore, the realisation that Wells will not make it out without either turning or dying and the fact I know what is going to happen means I can't enjoy it as much as I would like. It's classic potty humour and it actually is a really good analogy that anyone can relate to.

> **WELLS:** *"I dunno maybe it's like when you gotta take a piss or something I dunno. When you gotta go, you gotta go."*

> **COOPER:** *"Well maybe it's more like needing a shite. Just 'cause you need one doesn't mean you drop your kecks and pinch one off."*

In any other circumstances I'd be slapping my thigh. But each time I hear this exchange, in hushed tones and with that haunting underscore, I can't even consider a scoff let alone a chortle.

And then Wells manages to break the damn of my tears in one fell swoop with this beauty.

"You know, Coop, there's one more thing you gotta learn about command, mate." BEAT. *"Sometimes the people that you kill, are your own men."* Another BEAT. *"So I'm asking you, let me take care of myself. I can at least spare you the unfortunate business of trying to explain to Annie you had to incinerate me."*

Sean's voice catches a little as he says this too, bringing the emotion up to 101.

Fuck me.

That line coupled with Mark's amazing music is a kick

in the gut and a punch in the throat every damn time.

Something that I pondered before starting this book, was whether the characters would mean as much to me after I had spoken with the actors. Would it ruin the illusion, break the façade? Once you peak behind the curtain, you can't unsee. But of course, that hasn't happened at all. The cast may be older, greyer, wiser and a lot more famous in some cases. But they loved playing these characters and that shines through whenever they speak about them. I honestly believe they have enjoyed being able to talk about how much fun they had and sharing those memories as much as I have had listening to it all. So in actual fact, getting to know the people who played these men that mean the world to me, has only strengthened that bond. Now when I know Wells isn't going to make it, I not only mourn for *him* but for Sean, which is stupid as I messaged him the other day and he's fine. Obviously! Likewise, the rest of the cast but still, aside from reinforcing that at the end of the day I'm a soppy twat, what I'm trying to say is speaking with these guys was an absolute pleasure and in a weird way, part of me feels I was there too, on set.

I'll get my coat.

Wells reminds Cooper that despite telling him he's going to die, it's all fine and dandy and he is a Professional Soldier. But for now, what can he do to help? Luckily Cooper has the perfect plan - they're going to, *"Roast their bollocks off,"* which actually happens much later to Sean's character Talbot in *Doomsday*.

Back to the music now and whilst just seconds ago I

was reaching for my hankie, now the upbeat percussion accompanying Cooper as he drives the Land Rover with the gas cannister in the back (and leaking petrol tank that Spoon just cut) into the barn whilst Spoon attempts to light a match and set fire to the trail of petrol which will reach the barn and blow up the vehicle *and* those ~~pesky kids~~ lycanthropes.

SCENE# 135   SHOT# 4

The Land Rover reaches the barn and Coop jumps out spinning around shouting, *"Light it!"*

Quick story. Sam McCurdy recalls this moment only too well. They had rigged a camera onto the top of the Land Rover to capture the shots of Kev as he was driving. There was an extra in the car with him but crouched down out of sight and his job was to hit the brake just as Kev jumps out which would also stop it just before it got to the barn because it was now too high to fit through the opening with the camera on the roof. It was all going great, Kev jumps out and instead of hitting the brake, the dude hit the accelerator and crashed the vehicle with the camera straight into the barn door, smashing the camera and rig to pieces...

Oops.

This is a tense moment, and the atmosphere is increasing

by the second along with the score and that damn match refusing to strike. What will Spoon do? What will Cooper do? Are the wolves going to drag him into the barn with them? I can't even handle the thought of that right now! My chest is pounding and that fricking match still won't light. I can barely cope with the tension as Kev now gets to do his best action hero impression (so much better than Tom Cruise) and as he's legging it, Spoon calls out to our saviour, *"Sarge!"*

And out bowls Wells again looking more like a badarse than most of the Hollywood lovies put together, complete with Molotov cocktail which he lobs perfectly onto the fuel trail and up it goes! The path is lit, and Cooper still hasn't made it back, come on, son! There's a great moment where he leaps over the fiery trail and flies into the house and then we see the barn explode.

| SCENE# 37 | SHOT# 3 |

BOOOOOOOOOOOOOOOOOMMMMMMMMMM!!!!!

The look on Spoon's face - triumph, jubilation, fuck yeah that was awesome - sums up how we all felt after that close call. It was also the look on Neil's face when they filmed it and just for a moment, he forgot he was on set and the camera was running and burst out laughing. It was just pure giddy school-boy excitement. Luckily it didn't affect the shot since they didn't have the time or the money to build another barn to blow up!

And then –

Cooper is in the hallway; he turns around and is face-to-face with Megan.

They are both breathing hard.

She leans closer. This is obviously set up to make it seem like they are going to kiss. After all it's been teased that there is a mutual attraction and we've addressed that whilst it seems unlikely that you'd be thinking about a cheeky snog in this situation, adrenaline and near-death experiences affect the body in strange ways and all emotions heighten including sexual attraction. But of course, this isn't an Adrian Lyne or Paul Verhoeven movie and instead of leaning in for a kiss, Megan whispers, *"I'm sorry."*

Well, that can't be good.

To be fair, she does look a little torn here. I still believe Megan's motives and motivation are fluid and at times, perhaps even she is unsure where she stands especially regarding Cooper. That aside however, I won't forgive her.

Ever.

If you think Megan looks a little under the weather here, Emma actually was sick! Okay Megan was meant to be fighting a transformation and all that, but poor Emma had a real, stinking cold so that red nose is authentic. All of the male cast and crew had nothing but warm words of praise for how she held her own on set and in the bar! There may have been an abundance of testosterone, but

Emma never let that worry her.

Megan states she really did think finding them was her best bet of getting out of there, although as I mentioned before, that does raise the question of if they'd left right away, wouldn't she have changed anyway? When you gotta go, you gotta go, we've established this.

Anyway, Cooper works out there is no other house, there were no werewolves in the barn and of course, she's been busy snapping away with that camera – the same camera she used to take the photo of her 'fucked up family.'

Cooper appears to take this a bit more personally that perhaps he should, but we know he hasn't had much luck with women – there was more of this as we explored in deleted scenes – and Megan has done nothing to change his view.

"New woman. Same old shite."

Poor Coop.

Hopefully if he gets out of this alive, he won't be so completely messed up in the head that he never finds that certain someone to share a nice, happy future with removing all the cobwebs and putting out the spiders.

Megan bites, *"Being nice to women will get you nowhere. Being nice to me will get you killed. You may think they're all bitches but I'm the real thing."*

She then bends over in pain, and we witness the start of her change.

"They were always here. I just unlocked the door. It's the time of the month."

This is probably the one line in the entire film I don't care for. Not because I have any issues with linking lycanthropy to menstruation, I've written stories about it myself and turned it on its head to have a werewolf chasing a woman because she's on her period. And you have movies like *Ginger Snaps* that base the entire plot on it. It just didn't feel like something Megan would say.

It's behind you!

However, it doesn't detract in any way from the simply terrifying shot now of her closing her eyes and the wolves that have been there all along rising up right behind her. There is that Darth Vadar-esque/Xenomorph sound again that poor Joe (RIP) witnessed right before his fight to the death and the way they are framed behind her makes them appear about 12-foot tall.

Utterly horrific!

SCENE# 138	SHOT# 6

In the midst of all this, Wells has been loading the pistol back up with bullets and Spoon has been listening. We get one of the only pieces of CGI (some of the flashes from the guns were also added) as Megan's eyes turn from blue to yellow and she shows off some impressive fangs and then BANG, Wells appears and shoots her right in the face.

How'd you'd like them apples?

Now something that sometimes gets missed here is that she was in fact transitioning and therefore although it would have hurt, that bullet didn't kill her and she will reappear later resplendent with missing eye. A lot of people don't pick up on that, assuming the bullet from Wells killed her outright but that isn't the case.

Anyway, realising the wolves mean business, Coop and Wells head upstairs but Spoon gets separated from them and ends up in the kitchen.

Cooper and Wells run down the landing, Cooper letting off the last stun grenade. There is a really clever shot as it rolls down the floorboards but was apparently a bugger to film taking lots of attempts before Sam McCurdy got one to work and look right.

Spoon barricades himself best he can in the kitchen and is all too soon out of bullets. He starts to warm up for the fight of his life.

Darren actually is a boxer, and it is very clear from how comfortable he is here with the choreography. I wonder if he knew when he was training in the ring that one day those skills would come in handy – not in a *Rocky* remake but against werewolves!

Now we are back upstairs and through the smoke of the grenade we see the wolves approaching Cooper and Wells.

Dave Bonneywell recalls this scene fondly:

"One of my favourite moments in the movie is when the wolves are charging down the corridor towards the bedroom and as they move, they're slamming their hands into the corridor walls...it's a very powerful image and makes them look terrifying as they rip the place up. But it was simply Brian Claxton Payne the lead wolf performer helping to support himself and turning what might have been a disadvantage into part of his performance."

Dave Bonneywell

Some say he's still there...

Cooper runs into the first room he sees, locking the door behind him. It's a running joke that these things could likely launch themselves straight through the flimsy wooden doors if they wanted to and yet the characters still bother to put the latch on. It's standard operating procedure for a horror film though. He then turns and realises the bathroom is empty…

Where's the sarge?

Along with the urgency and crazy fast action, there is still room for some comedy here. It doesn't distract or lower the tension at all but is exactly what these characters would do and say in this bizarre situation.

It is fitting.

And we get a lovely dose of it right now.

Coop calls out, *"Sarge?"* and we pan to Wells, next door in a separate toilet. I love the little extra details, like the pile of books and air freshener. I think they'd need it after all that long-pig, it must stink in there. He's got a glow-stick in his mouth so he can hold his gun with both hands, and he sits on the toilet, feet up against the door.

He can hear Cooper calling to him and replies, glow-stick in mouth so kind of mumbling and also as to not alert the wolves immediately to his whereabouts, *"I'm in the khazi."*

"What?" comes the reply.

"I'm in the khazi!"

This was of course yet another of Sean's improvised lines and he thought it would be cut as there was no way anyone else would know what the hell a khazi was, especially the Americans.

195

But it was kept in thank God as I think most people will agree is it an epic and very quotable line with multiple uses.

| SCENE# 148 | SHOT# 1 |

See here for example -

MY KID: *Muummmmmmmmmmm!!! Where are you?*

ME: (no matter where I am in the house) *I'm in the khazi.!*

MY KID: **sighs* You are so lame…*

See, works like a charm.

And now ladies and gentlemen, fighting out of the red corner it's Private Spoooooney!

And fighting out of the blue corner it's a giant fucking howling thing!

Let's hope for a clean fight.

To get Darren geed up and in the mood, Neil bought him the *Gladiator* soundtrack to play in his trailer before the fight scenes. Darren says he still plays it sometimes at home, especially if he's writing.

Come on then!

The sight of Spoony sparring with the wolf never gets old. There are no Queensbury rules here! He gets in a few nice jabs and grabs a knife, managing to shiv it. The bugger pulls it out although the tip of the blade stays stuck in its skin. He then smacks it so hard we see a tooth fly across the room which is a very nice touch!

Back with Coop and he is being very creative, still leaning against that wooden door which the wolf is banging on and whilst putting his weight into it, also kicking the big old fashioned porcelain sink. We see it break and the pipes begin spraying as he now decides what to do next.

Meanwhile Wells is still sat on the bog, again wondering exactly what he can do to defend himself since despite pointing the gun at the door, is likely very low on ammo. I love this shot and it's such a cool POV looking up at Sean like that. They cut a hole in the flooring so the camera operator was lower down which was how they were able to get it right since these were sets and sound stages, not an actual two story house. Sam McCurdy said they didn't know any better back then, and if they needed a shot like that, it would just involve someone, possibly him, lying on the ground. They hadn't learnt all the tricks and gimmicks yet, but it doesn't make the cinematography any less excellent.

Wells is looking for something that isn't the toilet brush or a plunger, and he grasps the aerosol just as hairy arm comes crashing through and starts blindly grabbing at him.

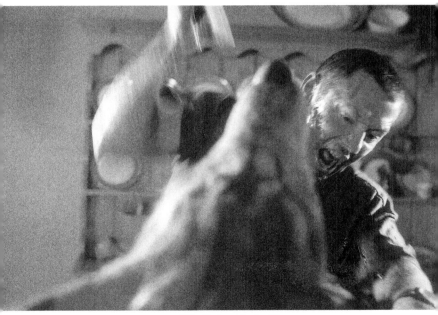

Take that you fucker!!!

Back with Spoon and things are about to get serious. He's managed to get the knife back and after a quick jab starts just stabbing it over and over and over and there is blood spurting everywhere, all over the table, the floor, the walls and Spoon. He looks like a mixture between Carrie at the prom and Jack Torrence. The damn wolf just sits back up as if it hasn't been almost gutted and knocks Spoon onto the ground...

Back to Coop and he's still smacking that sink whilst Wells has invented a makeshift blow torch and the sight of this is just magnificent, especially with him taunting the creature, *"Now get out of it, you bastard, how do you like them tomatoes, you fucking bastard!"*

I asked Sean about this and much like Kev's 'Top Bosie', it was just something that was said on set which made sense to them at the time and that came out at the moment and seemed fitting. The absurdity of it never fails to make me laugh and I kind of like the fact it doesn't mean anything – it was just something silly and fun.

Cooper has managed to get a tap free from the sink and is now using that to try and smash through the wall and get to Wells on the other side. As he's busy doing a super-speedy *Shawshank*, that darn wolf has finally realised it can easily break through the cheap PDF door. Coop realises this and starts banging at the wall faster, Wells 'helping' by yelling, *"Come on, Coop!"* He's being encouraging, bless him. However, Wells also lets him know that *"I'm running out, Coop, I'm running out,"* as the home-made flame thrower starts to sputter.

Spoon is back up off the floor and throwing everything except the sink (as Cooper has destroyed that haha) at his foe - plates, pans, literally anything he could get his hands on.

> *"No, I didn't go mad shooting the end fight, ha ha! I was just fucking buzzing. I love doing frantic scenes with loads of props where it's a real team effort between you and the crew. I think we actually did the stabbing of the werewolf and throwing pots and pans in one take. Sam (McCurdy) was wearing a crash helmet and riot shield and I had to make it look like I was hitting the camera without actually hitting the camera, or Sam! It was absolutely manic, but we all got a real buzz from it, including Sam!"*
> Darren Morfitt

Let the battle commence

And Sam agrees, again stating they didn't really know any better and just had a shitload of fun. Some of the props Darren was throwing were break-ways but many weren't. Hence the Perspex screen, mainly to protect the camera! Still, no actual Directors of Photography were harmed in the making of this movie and the end result is bloody amazing.

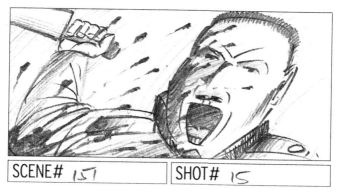

SCENE# 151   SHOT# 15

So Spoony is in the kitchen not going mad, and Cooper is trying to *Shawshank* his way into the khazi with a tap. That bloody wolf is through the door now and Coop always being inventive, grabs the other tap and stabs it into the top of its head.

If you look closely, you can actually see blood coming out of the tap too which is a wonderful little extra touch which Kev enjoyed immensely.

SCENE# 152   SHOT# 5

And then we get to one of the two big scenes that I struggle with more and more since being privileged enough to get to know the actors.

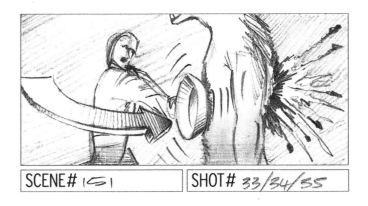

| SCENE# 161 | SHOT# 33/34/55 |

Spoon grabs the frying pan and starts whacking the wolf and we get that iconic shot where he is holding the pan above his head paying homage to Bruce Lee, covered in blood, eyes wide open like a crazy person and just when we think he is going to let the wolf have it...

It happens.

The wolf whips the pan away and pins Spoon against the wall.

Even in this dire moment where we know this is it, the final curtain, he manages to leave us with one of the most quoted lines.

"I hope I give you the shits, you fucking wimp," and then gobs his chewing gum into its mouth.

Both Liam and Kev stated this is their favourite line too, so it isn't just the fans.

Despite his wit, the pair of wolves close in...

gulp

Originally this death was a hell of a lot more graphic, with Spoon being literally ripped in half by the wolves.

Half a Spoon, please

They did actually film this gruesome departure which Darren said was really cool to get to do but ultimately Neil's decision to cut it was the right one. This was because he felt that the audience would have grown too fond of Spoon and despite being horror hounds who enjoy as much visceral violence and gore as possible, we would love this brave squaddie from Hartlepool even more. And of course, Neil was right. Spoon is often cited at as people's favourite character – from both men and women – and after feeling my heart break when we spot Terry (RIP) still alive in the barn, reaching out to Joe (also RIP), I know that I might not have been able to take seeing Spoon die.

The noises are bad enough.

And *that* is the mark of a bloody good writer as I love blood, I love guts, severed body parts and people being eviscerated but only if I don't love them like family.

SCENE# 156   SHOT# 3 (A)

<pre>
                    SPOON
        I hope I give you the shits.
</pre>

He spits in the WEREWOLF's face as two others rush in and tear into him below the waist! Still held firmly in the creature's grip, he loses consciousness as his bottom half is ripped away and his guts pour from his body! The two new wolves engage in a tug of war over one of SPOON's legs! SAM is barking wildly as the WEREWOLF, thirsty after the fight, laps up some water from the dog's bowl before, snapping at another thirsty WEREWOLF before going face to face with SAM! SAM shuts up as the WEREWOLF studies him, cocking its head to one side...

Thanks for the laughs, Spoon. You'll be missed...

Back to our two remaining lads, who have no idea of what has just transpired in the kitchen. Cooper is still trying to crawl under Wells and break through now into the next room whilst the Sarge continues to use the last of the blowtorch whilst simultaneously passing his knife to Coop. Wells also still has that stupid glowstick in his mouth and it is magical to hear him shouting, *"Go away!"* to the thing right outside the door that could gut him (again!) in seconds. I say excuse me Mr Giant Howling Thing, please go away would you, there's a good chap.

I remember feeling that we had lost so many men now that Neil wouldn't possibly put us through the ringer anymore. And then recalling there was very little hope for the sarge regardless. He must be on his way to beginning his transformation. I really hoped at this point that we wouldn't see a final standoff between Wells and Cooper, the sarge overcome with wolfy hunger or something. Witnessing one of them killing the other would have been too much.

We get the aftermath of The Spoon Incident and see the wolves digging into the blood and entrails covering the floor. He sure made a big mess. One of them moves slowly towards Sam (this is the second dog remember after the first had to be fired) and that poor pup looks really quite scared, baring its teeth and snarling. And I don't blame it. My dog would growl if you wore a hat and I guess you no longer looked like 'you'? I don't know, I thought Collies were meant to be clever, but anyway, the sight of a fucking massive version of itself that smelt human must have been confusing. This was actually just the wolf's head being used like a puppet, in case Sam decided to attack it. No one would have blamed him, poor boy.

Coop is giving the wall some serious jabs with the knife and kicks with his boot, and I like to think the same as with Wells, that him calling out, *"Come on you fucker,"* to the wall was helping in some way. We get to watch the hole getting bigger from the other side too which is nice, and it's another bedroom. They crawl through and huzzah!

But wait a minute, there's a hairy arm trying to follow, but it's okay 'cause Coop boots it again. Thank God for those steel toe capped regulation army footwear. They begin throwing stuff at the bed and piling things against the wall to close the hole including a chair which managed to land perfectly and looked pretty awesome. It's important to note than Wells *still* has that bloody glowstick in his mouth too. They stand back for a second and BANG, there's movement against one of the other walls.

This is a very cool shot the pair of them.

Wells has the glowstick in his hand now, holding it out in front of him and the other is held up in the air with the knife, ready to strike. Cooper is holding the MP5 which has the light on, and they do look pretty 'swag' as my 12-year-old would say. And we get a wonderful Wells/Sean line. *"Cooper, let's get in the wardrobe, son."* To which Cooper replies with the reasonable question,

"What?" So, as to clarify, Wells simply repeats, *"Let's get in the wardrobe,"* and clearly upon hearing it the second time, Cooper decides it makes perfect sense and he now just says, *"Yeah alright."*

A really simple exchange that contains no great revelations, isn't pivotal to learning about these characters or integral to the plot. Nevertheless, I love this conversation and the deadpan delivery. I was also privileged to hear Kev's impression of Sean when we chatted and I have to say, it is bloody brilliant.

So now they are inside the wardrobe with all sorts of fairy tale connotations. I mean of course the Brothers Grimm and Hans Christian Anderson, not the Disney versions.

More importantly right now though, what is that smell? Ah yes, of course!

It's the rotting remains of a shit load of skeletons they're now stood on, what else would any normal non-person-eating family keep in there? I guess the wolves are a tad slovenly and just bung their rubbish in the wardrobe but nonetheless it's a most unpleasant thing to be sharing a confined space with. It is also of course a very on-the-nose gag – skeletons in the closet for 10 points.

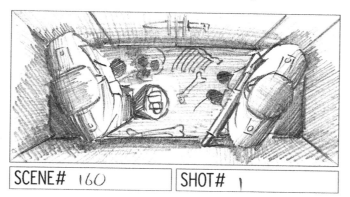

SCENE# 160   SHOT# 1

207

They can now hear their furry friends are in the room with them, Darth Vadar still needs a throat lozenge, and the wardrobe ominously starts to shake.

Segueing in some *Star Wars* trivia here, Kev is the voice of Fenn Rau in *Star Wars: Rebels* which fans of *The Mandolorian* have been championing to try and get his character to appear in. Also, Darren was a Transport Deck Officer in *The Last Jedi*.

"Give me your gun," orders Wells. *"Open your mouth, watch for your ears, mind your toes."*

Again. Cooper just obeys, no need to question, trusting Wells implicitly. I love the look on his face in this shot, reminds me of Edvard Munch's The Scream. Wells fires the MP5 into the floor and they fall through the ceiling onto the kitchen table below.

Nice.

Cooper rolls off the table and straight over to check on Sam. He then looks up, glancing around the kitchen. And asks, as my heart breaks again, *"Where's Spoon?!"*

Wells is stood by the bloody remnants of our beloved buddy and merely states, *"There is no Spoon,"* as he picks up his watch from the goo.

Despite this line obviously being an homage to *The Matrix* and Neo learning not to bend the spoon but himself because there is *no* spoon etc., Neil didn't, contrary to popular belief, name Darren's character specifically to fit this line. Along with Spoon's shits, it is one of the most quoted pieces of dialogue.

Again, the absolute raw emotion Kev portrays here is amazing. And that is in part down to him being a phenomenal actor who wholly deserves the myriad of success he has achieved since and Neil's spot-on direction, but also the almost unheard-of decision to shoot the movie chronologically. There was no saying goodbye to each other on screen and then continuing to party at the hotel bar every night. When an actor was killed off, they were gone, see you much, much later, Alligator. They were flown home making their absence very real and the guys actually mourned each loss and pined for one another.

Wells gets Cooper to quickly snap out of it and that damn beautifully haunting music begins again which I now have to switch off if it randomly starts when I have my iPlayer on shuffle. They start trying to barricade the door, flipping the table against it. Desperately looking for anything else to help, they spot the rug that was underneath the table. When they move it, a trapdoor is revealed which hopefully will lead down into a cellar. Cooper starts to climb down with Sam, and he calls to Wells. Instead of joining him, Wells hands over the gun, saying there is still one in the chamber, now get out of there.

Cooper of course doesn't want to leave his sergeant, his best friend and climbs back out. They have a bit of a scuffle – Cooper feels they should go together or not at all. He truly is loyal to the end, and he loves this man. He *knows* what is happening, that before long, this man who is like a brother, his commanding officer will go full-on Lon Chaney Jnr, but he will not just leave him. Wells however asks to him to obey his final order. He tells Cooper he *needs* to get out alive, not just for him but for all the lads. For Bruce, Terry, Joe and Spoon. Someone has to live to tell the tale.

We witness the urgency; the pain visibly increasing.

Wells winces as the cramps set in and no amount of morphine and whiskey will help this time. He slips his hand into his trouser pocket and pulls out the film cannister – remember those, back in the day when you had to send your piccies off in the post or take them to Boots to be developed. He gives it to Cooper before pushing him away, and at last Cooper admits to himself what is happening. It finally sinks in that there is absolutely nothing he can now do to help, other than getting out of there and telling the world what has taken place.

This emotionally driven scene was filmed with just Sean and Kev left, both already feeling the loss of the rest of the cast and the energy between them was so realistic and on point, that Neil and Sam just stood in the corner of the set and let them do what they needed. Sometimes that was the best way to get the takes, the actors knew what they were doing and the bond between Sean and Kev was obvious.

This sequence coupled with Mark's score is heart-breaking. I know I've said that a lot, but I really do mean it. Wells was always the character I most related to. I had many a kindly skipper in the police who I always looked up to. I also had a wonderful inspector, very much a father figure to the team. I'd still call him boss now if I saw him in the street despite having been out of the police for years and knowing he retired. Therefore, this beloved character coming to the end of his story, utterly ruins me each and every viewing.

As Wells puts out the flames in the gas furnace and cuts the mains pipe, we know what's coming. He's starting to look a bit rough again which is kudos to the makeup people since Sean is a very handsome man, but at this moment he looks truly ghastly. Almost like he's transitioning into a monster…

Then just to add salt to my already tender wounds, he takes out the picture of his wife Annie again (another cheer for Sue!) so he can be with his wife at the end. I swear if that doesn't give you all the feels then you must have a heart of stone. Usually by now I'm in tears and occasionally, I actually have to skip this scene as it's too painful to watch. And that hasn't changed. I still think of him as that fatherly figure despite now being older than his character and having been lucky enough to have spoken with Sean on several occasions. It hasn't lessened the impact, if anything it affects me more.

The wolves break through the door and now wander menacingly over to him, where he is resting against the cooker. Wells knows his time is up, but he doesn't look scared. He has a plan and is happy to be able to blow them to pieces – sacrificing himself before he becomes a monster. But more importantly, not only saving his best mate but allowing Cooper to escape and share what has happened with the world.

He holds out the lighter in a final 'Fuck You' stance but one of the wolves swipes it out of his hand. Now look very carefully at those wolves. Do you see one has an eye missing, the one at the front that hits Wells? That's Megan for all those who thought she died when Wells shot her. Still alive and doing her best to impersonate One Eyed Willy. The pirate you bunch of dirty savages.

Anyway, Wells ain't bothered.

He looks back up at them and Ho.

Lee.

Shite.

He's turned, he's now got the yellow eyes and…

SCENE# 167 | SHOT# 1

Before we continue, a quick story. I have been ridiculously nervous when I have spoken to almost every single person involved in this. Remember, despite having by-lines in various publications and being somewhat used to interviewing people, up until this project the majority of my prior communication with celebrities had been via email. I am in no way, shape or form a journalist and have no media training when it comes to speaking with famous people. Add into the equation, that to me these guys aren't just people off the telly, they are my idols, heroes, God like figures. So yeah, Zooming and FaceTiming the cast and crew has been an incredible honour and also cause for me to almost puke right before the call. Liam Cunningham was obviously such a person because he's Liam Fecking Cunningham, I don't need to explain. Anyway, we get on the Zoom, exchange a couple of quick polite Hello and How are you's and then he says, *"You tell fucking Pertwee that I want my eyes back!"*

Talk about a way to break the ice. Transpires the contacts Sean was wearing in this last scene were in fact the lenses that had been specially made for Liam and since they were only needed for this one, quick shot it was way cheaper to share them. Also bear in mind that Liam would have been back at home when this scene was filmed. Well, it may be twenty years later, but apparently naughty fucking Pertwee never gave them back and Liam is still a tad salty about it. I of course immediately text Sean after the call and I'm sorry to report, Liam that they are loooooooooong gone. So the moral of this story is never lend your eyes to Sean Pertwee as you won't *see* them again…

Anyway, Wells with his borrowed yellow eyes and bloody mouth makes a horrific noise now and slams his fist against the ignition button on the cooker and… BOOOOOOOOOOOOOOOOOOMMMMMMMMM!!!!!

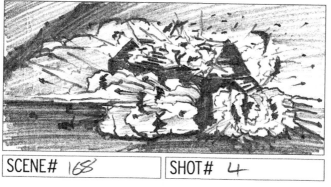

SCENE# 168   SHOT# 4

A couple of things happen very quickly when you are likely just focused on the house exploding and the fact that's it, sayonara - no more Wells (RIP) *sob*.

One: we see Cooper under the floorboards in the cellar, bearing witness to this audibly and that look of devastation on his face is just *gah*.

And two: in a blink-and-you'll-miss-it moment you can see an exploding werewolf head. This was filmed right at the very end when they'd finished all the major stuff and all the cast had left. The camera guys and crew still had a few hours and asked Neil if there was anything else he needed before they wrapped, and of course Neil said, let's pack a wolf head with fake blood and explosives and blow it up.

So they did!

I like to think that was Megan in a final moment of payback for luring these guys to their deaths.

It was also the cause of a funny war-wound type story from Sam McCurdy. According to Sam, he was proud of the fact that all through the entire shoot, he never got a single drop of the sticky, stainy, fake blood on him. That was until the very last day when the head exploded. He was behind some Perspex as usual to protect the camera and lo and behold just one rogue drop of blood flew through the air and landed directly on him. Right on his lovely new, cream Parka jacket.

And he wore that coat resplendent with blood stain for years after.

The house explosion is an amazing affect and was actually a model which Kev recalls fondly.

BOOM

"We were watching these expert model makers painstakingly recreate the cottage in miniature with real intricate detail, laying these tiny tiles on the roof etc. and none of us had ever seen anything like it, it was just up there on the sound stage as we were filming."

"The one day before a load of the lads went home about a week before the end of the shoot, it was time to blow it up. We were on a break, so we all sat round to watch it. There were about 15 cameras all on slo-mo covering all the different angles as they had one shot to do it. And then they blew it up and that was pretty cool watching this exact model of the house explode."

Kev McKidd

It's a giant!

To make things extra special, there was an honourable guest who got to press the detonator button – the Duke of Luxembourg's son who happened to be a big movie fan!

And then, there was one.

Well two if you count Sam.

The last man (and dog) standing.

Kev now gives what I always believed to be an Oscar Winning facial expression. Remember I said before that some actors can purvey an entire monologue with just their eyes? He sums up the entirety of the film, everything that has happened until this point with one long blink. The way he screws up his eyes, to me was always the physical representation of every single emotion, every death, every betrayal.

Give that man every award possible!!!

And then I listened to the DVD commentary.

Now don't get me wrong, I still love this scene and Kev and I had a good laugh about this, but in the commentary, he reveals that there was a shit ton of dust in the air and his eyes were killing him. This was confirmed by Liam when he was telling me how uncomfortable those lenses that Fucking Pertwee never returned were too because don't forget, although this was a working set, it was also in a steel factory where work was going on around them all the time! Anyway, Kev swears the dust just 'helped' and that it really was his amazing acting skills on display.

I'll believe him because he's awesome. But it does make me chuckle now, which is good as I am usually also ugly crying by this point, mourning Sean, I mean the sarge.

If you are reading this, then it is highly likely you are either a super fan like me or you enjoy the behind-the-scenes stories. Either way, if you haven't for whatever reason listened to the cast commentary on the UK DVD, treat yourself. I have watched a few over the years and although interesting, they are often pitched at an educational level, the director and maybe one or two of the lead cast talking about why they chose certain angles and what their motivation was.

Interesting - yes.

Educational – yes.

Entertaining? Not always.

However, *this* commentary is all of the above and more, all of the fun and camaraderie, the piss-taking and the sense of bromance is evident. The cast may have been helped by the fact it was about 11am and Pathe had provided them with several crates of beer. But if you have a good time watching this film and want to listen to the cast having a good time talking about that good time (are you still with me?) then definitely take time to enjoy all of the DVD extras.

Cooper is looking around the cellar but wait, what?

Cellar?

Simon only built two levels of set, what is this extra room now? Well, because Simon is a very clever chap, the cellar was actually the cottage living room redressed with loose floorboards replacing the solid ceiling. The walls were repainted, and the stone floor already laid for the living room remained in place. That's being cost effective for you! Poor Cooper is trying to find a way out when he realises, he has company – he appears to be in a pantry and there is plenty of food hanging from hooks.

Only problem is, the food is people, specifically the missing campers.

These bodies are actually the cadavers from *Event Horizon,* which both Sean and Bob Keen worked on. Perhaps Smitty is even in there somewhere because as we all know, if Sean is in a movie, then it is massively unlikely he will make it to the end credits. He will instead die in some horrific fashion.

Which is your favourite?

Event Horizon - explosion

Dog Soldiers – explosion

Wilderness – mauled and disembowelled by dogs

Doomsday – roasted and eaten

Howl – disembowelled by a werewolf

The Reckoning – burnt alive

Kind of a theme going on here.

Anyway, back to Kev…

Suddenly out of nowhere, he gets punched in the face. Who the hell can have survived and be down there? Of course, there was only one person it could have been, the shifty bastard Ryan still with the sword sticking out of his chest. Cooper says exactly what we would in this situation …

"You tried licking your own balls yet? I forgot you don't fucking have any."

Haha, take that, Ryan!

Wolf-Ryan doesn't like this witty retort however and gives Cooper a few nasty knocks causing some cuts and bruises.

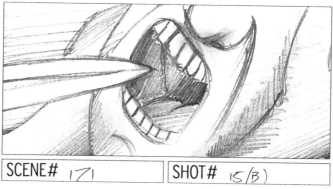

SCENE# 171   SHOT# 15/B)

Next comes the second of the moments that made me nauseous and have to cover my ears that I mentioned before. Along with Ryan's nails down the wooden table, the sound of the sword being forced into Cooper's mouth is absolutely horrendous and gives me the heebie jeebies each and every time. It also evokes my gag reflex so I'm covering my ears whilst making a gaggy face which isn't pretty for anyone. And more importantly of course I am wondering how the hell our Final Guy is going to get out of this conundrum and there is no way Ryan can be allowed to be victorious. Just in case you were wondering how far Kev would go for his art, that was a plastic sword and he had full control of how far it would go into his mouth whilst gripping it with his teeth. The utterly appalling squeaking was added in post.

Thankfully our hero Sam saves the day! I love this because it is the story coming full circle. Cooper loves dogs and refuses to shoot one for no reason. He befriends Sam without even considering the Collie might be anything other than just a dog and now Sam is repaying Cooper for looking after him and keeping him safe. He jumps onto Wolf-Ryan's back and starts attacking him, giving Cooper some leeway to roll across the floor and desperately try to find something to use against the wolf. The wolf who is of course the same Ryan who had no qualms shooting the dog at the beginning and was close to killing Sam if Terry (RIP) hadn't puked all over him.

And next we get another part of the story expertly wrapped up.

> *"I actually think one of my strengths is my storytelling."*
> **Quentin Tarantino – *Pulp Fiction***

Remember I said Neil isn't really a filler kind of writer/ director. There is a vast difference between extra scenes to build character or to keep continuity and filler pieces that have no real value. You won't find many of them in any of Neil's own creative endeavours. Red herrings of course are a different matter altogether. But most things will come back to bite you and one such object is that silver letter opener from the camping scene at the start. This technique is referred to as Chekhov's Gun. The essential premise being that if a gun is shown in the first act, it should be used by the third act, the basic principle of set-up and pay-off. Of course in this case it is a solid silver letter opener, but it doesn't have to be any kind of weapon. Just something that is established at the start of the film and brought back as an integral plot point at the end. It is also a very deliberate act whereas foreshadowing is usually more of a subtle hint at what is to come.

Here endeth screenwriting 101.

Cooper jumps up and pulls the sword out of Ryan's chest, shoves the silver knife in and it makes an awesome noise. He's obviously affected by the silver; it acts as a poison. But since Cooper knows Ryan's such a shifty bastard, he does a quick commando roll and grabs the gun that Wells gave him, with the one bullet left in the chamber.

Then in memory of Joe (RIP) he delivers the cheesy but perfect for this moment line, *"Think it's all over. It is now."*

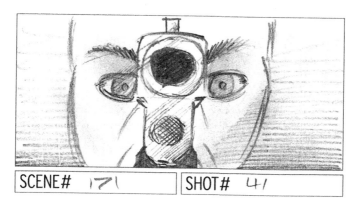

SCENE# 171   SHOT# 41

BANG.

Blood all over the camera.

Whooooo hoo!!!

We then get one final scene. Cooper steps out into the rubble, just him and Sam left. The weight of the world rests upon his shoulders but at least he has survived to tell his tale, to make sure although there is nothing left to take back to base (save the film cannister), he can make sure Spearhead Patrol are remembered as heroes.

That final shot with Kev stood holding his arm, is actually an homage to an homage. I'll let him explain it…

> *"One of the things that connected Neil and I very early on was I grew up with a father obsessed with westerns, and especially John Ford movies. Both I and Neil agreed the best John Ford/John Wayne collaboration was* The Searchers. *In the very last image of that film, John Wayne delivers the girl back to the house and the camera is inside the house looking through the doorway. You can just see him outside in the dust, being left behind. The camera pulls back and John Wayne holds onto his right arm and walks away as the door closes and the film ends. The reason they did that was because the horse master, Harry Carey who'd been with John Ford for decades would stand like that when he was watching the actors train on the horses, had passed away during the making of the movie. John Wayne stood like that as an homage to their friend. It is a final image of respect. So Neil and I thought it would be fitting for Cooper to re-enact that exact pose as he comes out of the rubble with Sam."*
>
> Kev McKidd

Beautiful.

There are just a few final treats if you sit through the end credits which as Pixar and Marvel fans, we are trained to do now anyway.

You see Cooper *does* make it back home thank God and he gets those photos developed and takes the story to the newspaper.

There's just one issue though, no one believes him.

And there we are.

End ex.

But this wasn't meant to be the end of Cooper's story…

More on that later.

CHAPTER
FIVE
POST PRODUCTION

What actually happens when a film wraps? Well, obviously every feature is different. On *Dog Soldiers*, the final takes had been secured by lunchtime and the remainder of the afternoon was spent filming any last-minute pick-ups and of course, exploding werewolf heads. After that all that was left was the wrap party which as all good parties should, involved a lot of beers and even some dancing from Mr. Marshall (sadly there is no photographic evidence of this, believe me, I have tried). Off they stumbled back to the hotel to grab a few zzz's before leaving in the morning...

Picture the scene.

You're fast asleep, your body desperately trying to get as much rest as possible to fight off the inevitable killer hangover that's going to hit you like a ton of bricks. You roll over and RING RING. RING RING. It's the hotel telephone. In your confused and groggy state, you manage to answer the call. "*Hello*?" you croak doing your best Zelda impersonation.

"Where are you, man? We're all on the bus for the airport waiting for you!"

Well that puts the kibosh on that plan.

Neil was so drunk, he'd overslept and since he hadn't packed the night before like a good boy scout, he now had not only the hangover from hell, but had to rush about in a blind panic trying to get all his gear together.

Silly boy.

Once he was indeed back home in Newcastle and the hangover had gone, Neil got to work on the editing.

> *"I love editing. It's one of my favorite parts about filmmaking."*
> **Steven Spielberg** – *Raiders of the Lost Ark*

Someone had done a rough assembly cut but there was an awful lot of for him to sort with the help of Susan and David Crosgrove at Imagine. Once the rough cut was ready, Mark could begin the composition of the music and the sound design people in London could begin adding in things like the gunfire and making it into the full surround sound. Neil admitted to not knowing every single date things happened since this was twenty years ago when most things were still recorded on bits paper and you can't reply on timestamped emails or texts. However he vividly remembers one date in particular when he was at Goldcrest in London checking out the work on the grading.

That memorable date was September the 11th 2001.

I also recall that day like it was yesterday. I'd only been back from the States for a couple of weeks. Admittedly I'd been in Florida not New York, but it still gave me extra chills. I was in the flat my then boyfriend now husband and I were renting during his final year of Law School. He was in a lecture, and I was just at home. I was flicking through the TV channels when I saw it on the news. I sat in the same position, tears running down my cheeks for hours.

Neil similarly recalls hearing it on the news and when he'd finished at Goldcrest, stepping out onto the street in Soho and it being completely deserted, like a ghost town. Bizarrely, right at that moment, Edgar Wright was just around the corner working on *Shaun of the Dead* and also recalls that surreal moment of Soho being utterly empty. Our thoughts are with all the families that were affected that day and as an ex-police officer, to every single first responder – thank you.

Life moved on and Neil was back to working on the post-production process. They had a cast and crew screening, and everyone was really pleased with how it turned out.

And then, they waited.

And waited.

Until a Fairy Godmother came along in the form of a horror loving Scouser by the name of Ian George. I'll let him explain what happened next but first, a little bit about why he was the perfect man to stumble across this film.

> *"Horror has always been my favourite genre. In my opinion, the best film ever made is* Deliverance *followed by* The Exorcist. *I started working in films back in 1994 and whilst I was at Warner Brothers, I was approached by Mark Kermode about a re-release of* The Exorcist, *and it was fantastic and made a lot of money. I then moved to Pathe and one of the first projects I worked on there was The*

Blair Witch Project *which the acquisitions team bought at the Sundance Festival and of course it went on to do incredibly well. So I have gained a sort of reputation if you like, people in the business knew I loved horror. I love the visceral feel of it, I like being terrified.*

Fast forward to the Berlin Film Festival 6-17 Feb 2001. I was walking around the stands and see these two guys, both holding pints of beer. It was Vic Bateman and Alistair Waddell of AV Pictures. I head over to say Hi and Vic says, "You like horror, don't you?" He then points at a poster on their stand and says, "Get on that."

I look at it says Dog Soldiers. *So I asked well what is it? And Vic says, "Werewolves. Soldiers. What's not to like?"*

I get on the phone to the acquisitions team, and they say they've already passed on it, everyone in the industry has passed on it. And I say this to Vic, but he insists, "YOU need to see it."

So once I was back in London, he sends over a copy, and I managed to drag a few people down to Mr Young's (now Soho Screening Rooms). The movie starts and we were all a bit like, okay, where's this going? And then there was the scene with the cow and the whole room jumped. I've never been in a screening like that before, never had that sort of experience.

I just sat there thinking OMG this is so fresh, this is so funny! You have this amazing calibre of actor with Kev McKidd, Liam Cunningham and Sean Pertwee and it could have all gone horribly wrong. It would have been easy for them not to get it, to dial in their performance but no one did that in this. I remember just thinking, this is fantastic, it's really funny.

This was the end of February, and I went straight back to the office and we did the deal with Vic.

We then had to worry about how to market it – we didn't want to lead with the comedy so needed to get the balance right for the horror side.

There's always this moment with smaller pictures made on a tight budget when you wonder if you've made the right decision. And then we started showing it to the press. And they loved it!

We got the most amazing quotes from FHM, Total Film, Loaded etc.

When then got to making the trailer which of course again we didn't want to give too much away with the look of the wolves, we wanted to keep that hidden as much as we could.

It worked well though as it was eye-catching and had just that bit of comedy in there to let people know what they were getting.

YOU'RE PART OF A SIX MAN UNIT

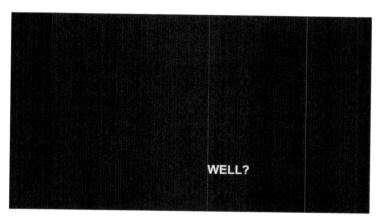

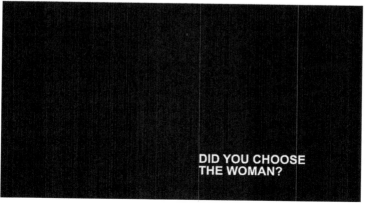

DON'T BE SO SEXIST

DOG SOLDIERS

A NEW BREED OF HORROR

Both Neil and Keith were intimately involved in the marketing which can be a recipe for disaster, but they seemed to know exactly what we wanted and completely got what we needed to do. I do recall Neil collecting up every single poster and item that was rejected and think he still has them all in his loft.

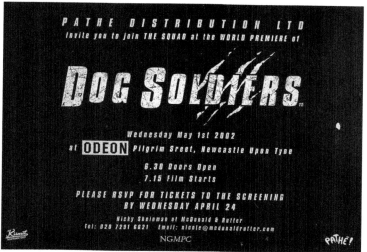

We had the world premiere at what was then the Odeon in Newcastle which was of course the cinema Neil had grown up visiting. When we got there, we thought it looked a little bare, so we dressed it in all this netting and camo stuff. The entire cast turned up for it and Neil and Keith both did an emotional and heartfelt speech. Then it was time for the multimedia press premier in London. It was one thing showing it in Newcastle where a lot of the audience were Neil's friends and family, but what would the jaded film reviewers of London make of it? Well, of course they loved it too.

Neil and producer Keith Bell

They scrub up n

A new talent had arrived on the UK film making scene. I must give a shout-out to Sam McCurdy too, he sure knows how to make simple things look terrifying. All in all, Dog Soldiers *was an absolute delight to work on and Neil to work with. You need passion and energy and to be able to bring that along with you. We saw something fresh and unique that was chocked full of talent and of course, everyone else was sick with envy that they'd passed on it.*

We were so happy to have been able to give it the big screen adrenaline rush fuelled fun it deserved.

Liam entertaining the troops at the premiere

Unfortunately, the opening weekend was marred due to it coinciding with the horrendous Potters Bar train derailment which of course took precedent everywhere in the media. Sadly, seven people died in the tragedy. Of course, a few years later, The

Descent *opened on 07/07/05 – the day of the July London bombings. Let's hope Neil's jinxes have ended. "*

Ian George

The rest as they say is history. The film did well in its opening weekend ranking third in the Box Office only behind *Panic Room* and *About A Boy*. It dipped to fifth the following week *Bend It Like Beckham* coming in at number four and of course, *Star Wars: Epiosde II - Attack of the Clones* leapt straight into first place.

By week three it was eighth and twelfth at week four. It played in 313 theatres across the UK and grossed $994,233.

By its fourth weekend it had grossed $2,860,893 and according to Box Office Mojo, ended up with $2,860,893 domestic and $3,530,620 worldwide.

The USA was a different kettle of fish altogether and our American friends were denied a theatrical release. Instead, it was bought by the Sci-Fi Channel. This never fails to make me chuckle. Without being mean, this channel hasn't always been synonymous with high-end, top-quality releases and there is of course a market for no budget features which are made for pure enjoyment.

I can only imagine what viewers thought after they saw this work of genius on a station that usually brought them Pound Shop *Sharknado* type offerings. Despite less of a fanfare, it became loved despite the very British humour, language and mentality.

I still see reviews today which state people turn the subtitles on as they were unable to understand the lads but in the main, no matter what language it is viewed in, it still has a universal appeal to anyone who enjoys seeing men running around with guns and fighting huge fucking howling things.

Pathe released it on VHS and DVD in the UK and Twentieth Century Fox Home Entertainment did the same in America.

There was a Shout Factory Blu-ray release in 2015 which despite Neil's best efforts to include as many extra bits as possible – despite not being paid a penny, just out of the love of the film and wanting to give the fans value for money – wasn't as well received as it could have been due to quality issues with the transfer. The original negative had gone walkabout and they were only able to use cinema prints.

Then in early 2019, German company Koch Media released a new media book DVD and Blu-ray having located the missing negatives.

Vertigo Releasing put out a 4K digital restoration late 2020 and at the time of writing, we are eagerly awaiting the limited edition 4K DVD transfer from Second Sight films. Having spoken with the guys and being privy to some of the extras on the DVD and the release comes with, I can assure you that it will be worth the long, loooooong wait.

As well as doing relatively well in the box office and of course going on to successful home media releases, there were a few awards picked up too.

"Neil and I attended the Brussels International Festival of Fantasy Film, where we watched it with a brilliant and bonkers audience. Full of horror nuts who cheered when the blood was spilled and howled when the werewolves appeared.

Keith and Neil at the festival

I went back a week later to pick up the awards from the Jury, headed by Christopher Lee, the Golden Raven, the festival's top award, as well as the audience prize, the Pegasus.

Keith accepting the award

Robert (Freddie Kruger) Englund was also there as a jury member. I remember him telling me that he loved the film."

Keith Bell

The movie continues to do well with reviews and ratings:

- **Rotten Tomatoes**
  79% Tomatometer
  79% Audience Score with 50,000+ ratings

- **IMDB**
  6.8/10 with 59,000+ votes

"The creatures themselves are beautifully designed, as stylish as they are terrifying, and the cast are exemplary in their delivery of both humour and terror, although Pertwee does deliver a film-stealing performance. Deservedly spoken of in the same breath as An American Werewolf in London *and* The Howling, Dog Soldiers *is pretty much the perfect horror film, now available in 4K clarity, with Marshall leaving a lycanthropic legacy that remains unmatched ever since."*

John Townsend for *Starburst Magazine - Oct 2020*

"Marshall treads the line between laughs and tension expertly and makes a virtue of his negligible FX budget by keeping his excellently designed (and thankfully non-CG) man-dogs where they belong: in the shadows. Pedigree stuff."

Adam Smith *for Empire Magazine*

"The result is one of the loudest, goriest, and unexpectedly funniest werewolf movies ever made."
Mike Cecchini – *Den of Geek* Oct 2020

"There's a critic's quote on the artwork for Dog Soldiers *comparing Marshall's debut with another iconic horror debut — The* Evil Dead *— and I truly believe that comparison is probably the closest thing you'll ever get to perfectly summarizing just why this film is so special. With his werewolf-centric story, Marshall demonstrates that you don't always need a huge budget to create a kick-ass movie (although budgets certainly helped his later works like* The Descent *and the criminally underrated* Doomsday*).* Dog Soldiers *also proved Marshall's ability to handle hugely ambitious material and found a way to bring werewolves back into the genre fold in a believably scary and ferocious way, something I appreciated as a fan of the subgenre."*
Heather Wixson for *Daily Dead* July 2015

"But besides Marshall's raw filmic savvy, the other breakout attribute here has just got to be McKidd, who steals the show. Previously seen as a young priest in Father Ted - making a portentous military-style escape from the lingerie section of a department store along with a veritable platoon of other clergymen under the command of Dermot Morgan's awesome Ted - he gives a performance of roaring strength and vigour. Not long after his barnstorming (quite literally barnstorming, as it turns out) in this, he would assume the bruising role of Lucius Vorenus in the great TV show Rome. *His introduction during the over-the-top brutality of his Special Ops Selection process is a terrific little*

action movie in its own right, McKidd perfectly coming across as a real, take-no-brown-stuff, hard-ass as well as revealing an immediately audience-winning affection for dogs. His adamantium-solid resilience and resourcefulness in the field may make him look like a cross between Rambo and Sgt. Rock, but everything we see him do is borne out of the situation and the character's absolute refusal to ever give in. His fierce Scottish brogue is also the perfect antidote to many a Yank stars' smug, committee-written one-liner and his terrifically implacable and stoic face is just the type to make any ravenous werewolf think twice about getting too close for a nibble. Undoubtedly the rock that this film is anchored to, McKidd should have an action figure released of his resolute Cooper. I mean they did bring the wolves out in plastic, after all."

Chris McEneany for *AVforums* – May 2009

CHAPTER
SIX
A SEQUEL

WEREWOLVES ATE MY PLATOON!"

Remember all those little nuggets Neil planted in the film, whispers of other creatures that lurk in the shadows? The mention of Special Weapons Division and werewolf DNA flying about all over the place? And not forgetting our Final Guy, the courageous Cooper who not only made it out alive but was extremely well loved and received by the majority of audiences. Well, for those of you who have followed Neil's career, you will likely know that at the time, he had not only intended for there to be a sequel, but there was to be a trilogy. Two more films would have meant a hell of a lot more Kev McKidd for one!

Despite Neil's wonderful career and a plethora of fantastic films and TV work, the questions he still gets asked more regularly than anything else is regarding that long, long awaited sequel.

But our hopes and dreams are for now at least still on standby. It's not confidential and Neil has been open and candid about why. Without getting into the nitty gritty legal details of Intellectual Property (IP), Neil didn't end up owning the rights to *Dog Soldiers*.

This isn't highly unusual in the movie business but does throw a spanner in the works for sequels if the person with the ideas and the person/s holding not only the purse strings but the permission slip, don't see eye to eye.

That is all I'm going to say on the matter since at the time of writing, things are still up in the air. Right at the beginning of this book I mentioned that if you were reading this hoping for juicy gossip or inflammatory slander then you'd come to the wrong place.

Both Neil and Kev have commented recently in interviews that they are still up for it and that the wheels are in motion. That things are looking far brighter than they ever have before.

But nothing is settled as yet and although the pendulum may be swinging in the right direction, nothing is set in stone.

As a fan I can only hope for now that Cooper's adventures are not over but I for one would only want to see more of this world if Neil is still the one creating it.

"I feel the horror audience is a great audience, and I would ideally make a movie that would give them as much energy as they're willing to give to the picture."

Sam Raimi – *The Evil Dead*

CHAPTER
SEVEN
INTERVEIWS

NEIL MARSHALL

JP: What are some of your own favourite horror movies past and present and have they influenced your own approach and style of film making?

NM: John Carpenter definitely influenced me, and I can say I am pretty much a fan of all of his work. *Assault on Precinct 13* was a massive influence on *Dog Soldiers*, also The Thing. From the way he chooses to shoot things to how he handles the music. Also, at the time *The Evil Dead* and *Evil Dead 2*, early Sam Rami stuff, early Pete Jackson stuff too, *Brain Dead* and *Bad Taste*. Showing what you could do with a budget and having a lot of fun with it. Also the tone, making it scary but also outrageous and funny. Also, because of the subject matter, *The Howling* and *An American Werewolf in London, Wolf Land* and pretty much any werewolf movie around at the time. So many of these films I saw in my early teens and that is the time where your future taste in movies is heavily affected by what you see at that age range. I watched horror movies from as long as I can remember, my dad would show me things like the old black and white *Bride of Frankenstein* and *Doctor Who* would have me hiding behind the sofa. As we got into the 80s, I started watched the then called Video nasties and the onslaught on VHS so that led me to *Zombie Flesh Eaters* and I *Spit on Your Grave*, grainy pirate videos. 1975 through the late 80s was my time period. *Alien, The Shining* all of those are my favourites. A more recent film that knocked me for six is *Lake Mungo*.

JP: When *Dog Soldiers* first came out, you stated it was meant to be a trilogy of movies. A sequel was rumoured for years, which you've been teasing again recently. Are we finally going to get part 2 and how can we ensure Sergeant Wells at least gets a cameo?

NM: Although I don't want to hex it, it is looking more hopeful now than it has pretty much forever. It's been a very, very long process but we might be getting there. It will be a different kind of sequel to what it would have been if I'd made it 15 years ago, but it will still have that similar kind of flavour – which is very difficult when you've killed off your entire cast. I have a story outline at the moment but not a script yet. There's been so many false starts over the years and attempts by others to go in the wrong direction, but we are closer than we've ever been. As for Wells, well never say never.

We need MORE Wells

JP: You chose to use practical affects and SFX makeup with Bob Keen rather than CGI and that is something which makes the movie stand out rather than looking dated. However, with technology being 20 years advanced and your reputation earning you a bigger budget, will you still employ the 'old school' techniques, or will we see computerised creatures?

NM: The technology was already there to a degree, *Jurassic Park* was around 8 years before, but I stand by my decision to use practical rather than CGI. The films from that time period that did use CGI look really dated now and yet movies 20 years older than *Dog Soldiers* like *The Howling* still look amazing because it's real. My film making principle remains the same – real is real and I use it whenever and as much as I can. CG is great for enhancing and you can do anything you want with it with the time and the money but even if I'd had more money, I'd have done it this way and IF there is a sequel, I will go practical again.

JP: In your honest opinion, why do you think *Dog Soldiers* remains so popular 20 years later when werewolf movies tend to be famed for being disappointing, especially regarding transformation scenes?

NM: Fundamentally it's the characters. So much work was put into making them loveable, likable and identifiable – I have always said, this is a soldier movie with werewolves not the other way around. Those soldiers needed to be as real and 3 dimensional and believable as possible. And funny, interesting and tragic. That's what resonates with everyone, they just love those characters. They love Wells, and Coop and Spoon, they got under their skin and into their hearts. You can now get the 4k version and it's still being found by new fans today. I tried to create the ultimate post-pub movie, you go out and come back and stick a movie on and it fills that Friday night need to watch something fast and funny and gory when you've had a few drinks.

I did a lot of research too and used my own experience from my father and grandfather being in the military, I grew up surrounded by that gallows humour and loved military history and just wanted to make my squaddies as realistic as possible and in a good light. It was a great reward to hear that troops over in Iraq were watching it and enjoying it.

JP: There remains some confusion revolving around Megan's relationship with Ryan and just why you showed her cutting her hand. Can you give some clarity on their previous meetings and was the cut solely about leaving DNA at the scene?

NM: I can't answer that because I didn't come up with it. David Allen financed the movie and insisted on there being this prior relationship between them which was never in my original script. I managed to whittle a lot of it down in the edit so what's left doesn't make a whole lot of sense.

Cutting the hand was to do with finding Megan's blood in a sequel and replicating it to make a clone of her, planting some tenuous seeds. It seemed like a good idea at the time but judging from the amount of blood splashing around I don't think it would have really made much difference.

JP: Both *Dog Soldiers* and *The Descent* focus heavily on character driven narrative. We almost don't need to ever see the creatures. The relationships and actions of the humans drive the story, fuel the atmosphere. How do you create such relatable people and do the actors rely heavily on your direction or bring something of themselves to the story also?

NM: Absolutely a collaboration, the trick of casting is to find people who will bring something to the table and every single person in this did just that. They all worked closely with me to create these rounded characters in both movies. I can only get them so far on the page, the actor beings the flesh and the blood and the bones to the role and a lot of their own life and personality comes with that, and their own ideas. There's a lot of talking back and forth and I love that part. And that's how these rich characters develop. That's why it was such fun doing an ensemble and using a lot of relatively unknown actors. They were young and hungry and put 200% into everything on set. It was an esprit des corps and by the time we finished filming, those guys would have fought and died for each other. They had been in the trenches and on some extreme piss-ups too! They really bonded as did the women on *The Descent* and they're all still friends all these years later. As a filmmaker, I like creating these groups of people who end up loving each other. We make a little family every time we shoot a movie. Everyone was just so nice and it was a real pleasure, we were basically going to work each day with our mates playing at being soldiers. What's better than that? I know let's add werewolves and now it's even better.

JP: You've kept a good working relationship with Sean Pertwee, will we be seeing him in future projects (the answer has to be yes!) and what is it about him and other actors and crew members that makes you want to keep working with them?

NM: I love the idea of just having this theatrical troop of actors and crew that you just work with again and again. First and foremost, they are brilliant at what they do and secondly, they're my mates. Getting to do what you love and working with your friends is a rare privilege. I will definitely work with Sean again. I don't know what it will be yet, but I have to. I want to work with them all again. If *Dog Soldiers 2* becomes a reality, I have to get Sam McCurdy back to shoot it, it's got to be done. They only issue is these guys are so talented, they get snapped up and are not always available for projects. I may even let Sean live although it has always been a pleasure to kill him off with a gruesome demise.

JP: Were there any lessons learnt on the set of *Dog Soldiers* on things to do and not to do when making a genre feature?

NM: One thing I learnt very early was if you have a very specific plan, bin it. It took me 6 years of writing, scripting, storyboarding and by Day 2 it was in the rubbish. Actors don't want to sit where you tell them to sit, they want to bring something to the role, and it was a very quick and good education about how to do it. Its good to have a Plan A, but you need to be really flexible and have a Plan B, C and D because nothing will go exactly according to plan, something will throw you a curve ball. Whether the weather, the timing, COVID, an injured actor, you have to be adaptable or you will drown. That was the biggest learning curve, working with an ensemble cast and addressing everyone's needs within a scene. It's a balancing and juggling act all the time. As a director, you need to be able to adapt and improvise. Everyone quickly clocked on to my passion for the project and they respected that. Sean and Liam were like mentors to the others, and everyone was so generous, giving away lines saying it sounded better from a different character and the like. We all just wanted to do what was best for the film, not for an individual. It was a shared passion and group effort. You have to lead by example and inspiration not by shouting at people, its stressful enough working to a budget and time, you don't need to be a dick about it.

JP: And on that, what can you tell us about *The Lair* and any other future projects you're working on?

NM: Another monster movie, a distant cousin of *Dog Soldiers* as it also deals with the military although more US and SAS as set in Afghanistan. All practical effects again. They encounter this 30-year-old science experiment that runs amok. It's an all-Brit cast (including partner Charlotte Kirk as Kate Sinclair and yes, she is a relative to Eden Sinclair of *Doomsday*), but some are playing Americans. It was filmed in Budapest, but you'd never know, and we spent most of last summer (2021) in quarries and covered in sand. It will be released in August. In the meantime, once final edits are done, we will begin work on *Duchess*, which is a gangster film. I can't say anything else about that right now, but we are already in talks about casting and hope to start filming in the spring.

Find Neil on Instagram - @neilmarshall_director

Extracts used in Scream Magazine April 2022

SEAN PERTWEE

JP: Sgt Harry Wells is an iconic, relatable and empathetic character for so many fans. How much did you bring to him and why do you think he remains so well loved?

SP: He is just everything to his squad, he's dad, uncle, leader everything they aspire to be. He's fallible, he is extremely loyal would lay down his life for his boys. He's a professional soldier and cares more for them then he does himself. He is totally selfless and that is a very attractive quality. He cares deeply and he really means it when he says he is a professional soldier.

I wish I could say I was as brave, or my pain threshold was as high! Neil just saw something in me, something that I didn't necessarily know that I had. With the right gauge of ammunition and the frisson between he, I and the other actors whatever he believed I could bring to the table came to fruition. He believed I could bring something special as the leader.

JP: Actors often improv and ad libs lines and actions. Was there much of that or was it mainly all Neil's script?

SP: We didn't realise what a film dweeb Neil really was and littered the script with references like *Zabriske Point*. It was only after we'd been there for a few days and had a few beers that we started asking what the hell those lines meant, this was 20 years ago before the days of checking stuff on your phone. Those lines went right over our heads, like with There is no Spoon. We respected him greatly, but he has the propensity to write these great chunky scenes and swathes of dialogue. Then after a while you reach your own vocal pentameter and your character heartbeat, then you can start to whittle it down and add your own sort of colour and nuance to the dialogue. Once I got there, I did add stuff as I have a propensity to swear a lot but always within the constraints of Neil's script.

The thing we are all most proud of is the acceptance and appreciation of the armed forces. The fact that members of Black Watch were watching it on a loop and sending us letters, saying how well we represented the foot soldier, the squaddie perfectly and that is down to Neil's experience and his writing skills. We absolutely trusted him with that.

The opening scene was 12 pages, we were straight on set first day, barely knew each other and suddenly we were in the trenches. We felt like we'd been there for about 3 months after doing that. We filmed and went for some beers and that was it, we were bound, a family. Still to this day it was the most fun I have ever had on a shoot, it was extraordinary. The palpable sense of friendship and loss on set. When people died, they were taken off set and flown home. Gone and we pined for people.

I remember Kev phoning me on his last day when he was all alone just saying this is so fucking weird, I'm all on my own! It was intense but so much fun. You never know at the time whether it would work you don't really ever know for sure, but we had so much fun doing it, we almost didn't care. But it had legs and it still does.

JP: I asked Neil about the line when you're in the khazi, "How do you like them tomatoes?" and he said that was down to you. Where did that come from?

SP: One of those things that just came from mucking about, and it stuck, and I thought it was funny! Even khazi was me, Neil wasn't sure whether to keep it, if the Americans would understand. We were just constantly flipping lines and seeing what worked, what we could come up with and Neil kept a lot of it.

It was similar with the "Fetch!" line later on, I was meant to pick up the burning log and picked up the stick by mistake so I just said fetch and didn't think Neil would keep it, but he loved it.

That's how things morphed into funny dialogue from all of us.

JP: I have heard tales about smelly rotten sausages and frozen trousers, what can you tell us about that?

SP: There was so much blood on the trousers, but you couldn't see it as it was always so wet, and the blood stains just blended in with the camo and dark. They used this sort of toffee apple mix that they needed to reactivate every day and I'd end up taking them off and they would stand up of their own volition as they were so rock hard from the cold. It snowed whilst we were there and it was bloody freezing at times, so we'd often congregate in my trailer to try and keep warm.

The trousers and my guts were a disgusting and very uncomfortable experience.

The props guys had used some sort of organic matter to begin with and they were on the turn. We kept the kit on for lunch as it was a very low budget affair, we didn't go off anywhere for lunch, half the time we were just sat in the woods, and no one could work out what the stench was. The props guys built this horrible sort of cocoon nest thing out of gaffer tape for my guts to rest in, but they had to be replaced as they'd started to rot. They replaced them with some sort of plastic things in the end because the whole thing was so unpleasant. And that was for weeks by the way.

JP: I have to ask what you remember about the scene where Cooper punches you. Just how much brandy really was consumed and how did Kev react when he realized he'd clocked you?

SP: Filming was going really well, I took Neil aside and said look, Wells has been through the mill he is turning into a lycanthrope. He's had enough morphine to kill an elephant and now a bottle of scotch. He's in the process of transitioning - no one can do that; he'd be off his maracas. I can do drunk acting but how do you feel about experimenting with some Martell brandy. And he went, okaaaaay, but you should tell Kev. So I told Kev, I'm going to be consuming some alcohol and I think we let Chris Figg know too. We were meant to keep it under tabs legally but the amount I consumed it was hard to keep anything quiet by the time we cane to shoot it. I still to this day don't know if it was a missed blow by Kev or slightly on purpose. I think I annoyed him so much, all that you pussy was impro. I just recall a blinding white light, seeing blood all over the SFX guys and just giggling to myself. They were all asking are you alright mate and I just thought it was fake blood, but no, Kev had clocked me right on the nose.

The set was so clever but small and there was nowhere to go with the cameras, so Kev and Emma were literally on top of me in that scene.

The first time I actually saw it properly was at the premier and when I saw the punch, I just thought oh…I would love to know it was an accident or if it was just a nudge from Kev saying, wind your neck in, Sean.

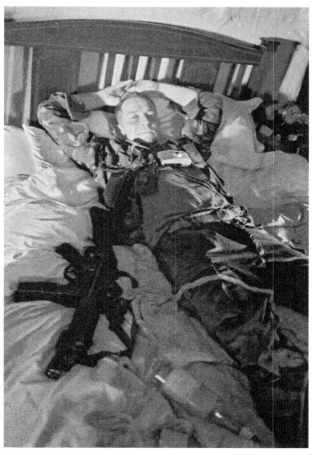

JP: You might be actors, but I think 2 important things were very apparent in the movie. 1 – you were all very close and 2 – you were having way too much fun. Is this true?

SP: We shot the movie chronologically which was a very old school way of doing it, like my dad did for Hammer Horror, where you'd shoot a movie in five days – the beginning, middle and end it order and it works. There was such a high calibre of skill in the cast too and we all built up such respect for each other. There is an old adage that the art of acting is reacting and it's true so you can turn of the hilarity of a scene when a huge dead cow comes flying at you and that's called NAR – no acting required which happened throughout the whole movie as these things terrified us and we just reacted immediately. I love the scene with Liam when he's in the kitchen changing into the werewolf and we just see the hand claw back and we did that because we didn't have the money for an AWIL transition scene, so we said let's do the old fall behind the sofa gag and it worked better! All of that tension, all that laughter, we were on edge and nervous like we would have been if we were there with our mates and freaking out. With everything that happened, there was very little need to put our scared head on, it all happened for real in our experience. It's also flattering to be seen as relevant and that new directors – as Neil was at the time – wanted to work with me.

JP: Did you have any British forces or firearms experience before this?

SP: I was a Marksman in the Combined Cadet Force at school, but I learnt so much when I trained with SAS for *Bodyguards*. We spent a lot of time in Herefordshire learning about looking after our principle, tracking, positioning etc. so I was already comfortable with that sort of thing and handling the weapons, small arms and things like Kalashnikov's. We also had some very basic firearms and procedures training from a chap from the Foreign Legion and that especially helped the younger actors who weren't as used to weapons and protocol. Most of all it looked like we knew what we were doing which was important and we all helped out.

Sean looking the part

JP: Neil seems to come up with the worst death possible for you – is it in your contract – must die a horrible death? Which of the 3 so far – Wells, Talbolt or Moorcroft - has been your favourite demise?

SP: Oh, Talbot for sure, it was horrible. They left me up there while they broke for tea! All these South African crew and extras, just smoking and flicking their ash at the giant BBQ I was strapped to! People didn't believe me when I told them, but it was true. And I'd love to work with Neil again, anytime I can. I couldn't do *The*

Lair but hopefully we will find something.

Find Sean on Twitter - @seanpertwee

*Extracts used in Scream Magazine April 2022

JP: How did you get involved in *Dog Soldiers* in the first place?

KM: I had done a few things before obviously been in *Trainspotting* and was considered an up-and-coming actor but was a slower process for me than people like Ewan McGregor right up until around mid-30s actually. My agent at the time, Sally who was a pretty big deal said to me, "Oh darling, this horror script has come in, it's a bit silly and I don't think you should do it." So I was like okay, but I read it anyway and I just starting laughing and the way he described the action was funny. I got it, I understood the tone immediately, that it was a real British comedy set in the horror genre. One of the things Neil did when he described the house blowing up, was he'd written like half a page with the word BBBBBOOOOOOOOOOOOOOOOOOOOMMMMMM!

And I think that was one of the things Sally didn't like and I hadn't seen anything like that before in a script, but I liked it and I wanted to talk to him. We hit it off straight away, we got talking about hiking in Scotland and the fact it was set in Scotland was a big deal for me. I ended up saying to Sally, I respect your opinion but I'm doing this movie. We flew out to Luxembourg to do some pretraining doing special ops in the woods, we were doing this tactual thing on first day and I was really into it fell on this utility belt I was wearing on this metal canteen and cracked my rib. I was so worried I was going to get sent home, so I didn't tell anyone for a week wincing through the pain and then I told them and of course it was all fine. It was the first time I played an action type lead, and this was what I wanted to move towards. Meeting Liam and Sean, the 3 of us became close, Liam was the father figure of the whole set. People didn't know what this film was going to be like, like the start of filming for *Star Wars* where Harrison Ford and Carrie Fisher were like okay George, don't know if this is going to work but let's give it a try! We had that much more experience and just knew something was working here, but that we needed to play it serious. We geed everyone up and said there feels like there's something here. Neil was so busy with everything being a first-time director that we sort of took the others under our wing in a non-official capacity to help him out a bit. He had a ton on his plate and at that point, not much experience of working with an ensemble cast and getting everyone on board tonally, all singing from the same hymn sheet, but we were able to help with that. We just trusted his vision and felt very much a part of that.

Kev having fun at the premiere

JP: So you helped out the lesser experienced cast, was it easy to bond too?

KM: Everyone bonded so quickly but by the very nature of the film, people died, and you could feel that sense of loss, it was real. By the end of the shoot when it was just me, I was like where are all my pals? That was very clever of Neil. I phoned Sean on the last day, and I was like I miss you mate. It was a real lovefest, a true bromance. We worked hard and we partied hard like actual squaddies would have and that shows on screen.

JP: This question comes courtesy of The Vomiting Cavalier - what does Top Bosie mean?

KM: I make up words all the time, I have this language with my kids where I just have all these words. For some reason and don't ask me why on day one we were all just running around and pretending to be soldiers and the words Top Bosie just came out of my mouth 'cause I was having a great time. And for some reason it just caught on and everyone was saying Top Bosie Top Bosie and it became this weird on-set catchphrase. I've had other words I've used on other films, but Top Bosie was only ever used on *Dogs*. It doesn't mean anything, it's complete gibberish, *Monty Python* speak. But it meant I was happy.

JP: Like McGuffin then in *Brave*?

KM: Exactly, it has literally become my thing I'm known for.

JP: There's a clip on the DVD extra, but what can you tell me about the Kryptonite tea-towel?

KM: There's this point where we have to tie up Liam with a tea-towel and they were meant to have rigged it so it rips easily. So I was like okay, and we started shooting and I must have picked up the wrong tea-towel and it was very embarrassing, and I was trying to look all badass and was like shit so that wasn't a good look for me!

JP: I have to ask as the other person has spoken about this many times…in the bedroom scene, did you mean to hit Sean on the nose?

KM: Haha he was all like I'm gonna drink, Kev and then he was definitely annoying me that day as he just wouldn't shut up. We were trying to concentrate and get the scene right and he kept going come on then hit me hit me, being all method.

I caught his nose, but I did not intend to break it, my aim was just too good. He definitely deserved it though and he was egging me on to hit him, he was literally asking for it and I obliged. I love you Sean! I hope he doesn't hate me now…

JP: Did you have a favourite scene or one that meant a lot to you?

KM: The scene where I'm running back from the Land Rover after blowing it up, that was fun, felt like a real action hero like Tom Cruise running along.

The scene in the bathroom where I grab the tap and stuck it in the werewolf head and then turn it on and the blood comes out, that was the scene I read in the script and just knew I had to be a part of this as it was so funny.

The scene getting in the wardrobe with Sean all like, "Get in the wardrobe" and I'm just like, "Alright", that was just so much fun and just silly again like Monty Python. We would just do the take and then laugh and laugh.

YOU'RE TRAPPED

Darren was just so funny, so any scene was great with him in it and he had my favourite line of the whole movie, the I hope I give you the shits right before he's literally eviscerated. I love that line.

The scene where I slide across the floor over to the door, again felt like an action hero

But my favourite scene to watch being filmed was actually when the cottage blows up. We'd all been watching the model makers making each individual bit, laying these tiny tiles. Then about a week before the end when everyone was due to leave, it was time to blow it up and we all just sat around watching and that was really cool to see. There were about 15 cameras all set to slo-mo and it was fascinating and awesome to see all that hard work gone in seconds.

JP: We know the script is littered with film references and Easter Eggs. Did you get them all like your line with *Zabriski Point*?

KM: No, that's all Neil stuff. We all got the Spoon reference from *The Matrix* but there's a ton and some he explained and some he just left alone. We didn't need to know.

JP: Were any of the scenes difficult for you, either emotionally or physically?

KM: Some of the exterior scenes were hard physically it was a 12-hour day and horrible weather, so we were all pretty beat up but was also strangely satisfying. Once we got inside on the sets in the house it was so much fun and shooting guns was just such a laugh. Nothing seemed arduous because we were just enjoying ourselves so much but was definitely tiring. We'd shoot all day, before we'd limp back into the hotel all wet and bedraggled and get showered then head to the bar and reminisce about how great we were, lol.

JP: Did any of your own favourite movies influence your performance as Cooper?

KM: One of my favourite horror films is *The Thing* and all of us watched over and over to get inspiration, since it has a lot of parallels being all boys stuck together. We all took a lot from it, mainly how the whole cast played it straight.

JP: Have you met any big *Dog Soldiers* fans whilst in LA?

KM: When I first arrived, Frank Darabont invited me for coffee at his home to talk about possibly casting me for *The Mist*. I thought he was going to say it was because he'd seen me in *Trainspotting*, but no, turned out he loved *Dog Soldiers*.

Find Kev on Twitter - @TheRealKMcKidd

DARREN MORFITT

JP: How did you get involved with this project in the first place?

DM: It was just a normal audition. There was no script beforehand, so I turned up an hour and a half early just on the off chance there was something to read. I bumped into Neil and the casting director, who said they weren't giving out scripts yet, but I begged Neil to let me have a read and he let me take it away for an hour or so. I don't know but maybe my enthusiasm to read the script helped me out.

JP: You made a very realistic soldier, had you any prior experience with the forces or handling weapons?

DM: I had worked on Peter Kosminsky's *Warriors* about the war in Bosnia, so I had spent 3 months with the Royal Green Jackets, so I did know a little bit about guns and driving tanks etc.

JP: Spoon has some amazing lines. Was that all scripted or were there some ad libs in there too?

DM: I have a feeling all my lines were in the original script. I don't remember add libbing too much but I could be wrong.

JP: You all looked like you were having the most amazing time and way too much fun on set, but Spoon especially seemed to be 'bloody loving this'. Was it as much of a blast as it looked or are you all just absolutely amazing actors? (That as well of course!)

DM: I was 'bloody loving this'! I'd been in things before where they had wanted you to look cool, but they always gave shitty costumes and dialogue and make up. I remember thinking 'finally make up that makes you look better instead of worse'. It was a total buzz shooting the movie, we all got one really well and would shoot all day and party all night. It was awesome for us that were less experienced to learn from Liam and Kevin and Sean.

JP: I've heard you really did jump out that window a bit further than your agent/the insurance people probably would have liked? Did you enjoy the physical side of filming?

DM: Yeah, I shouldn't have jumped out of that higher window. Silly of me really as I could have fucked myself and the movie up. But I was young and over enthusiastic and wanted to give 110%.

Bizarrely, I'd never imagined doing action type stuff - I wanted to do serious Ken Loach type drama, but after day one I was like 'This is fucking awesome - let's kick some fucking ass! I want to do this forever!'

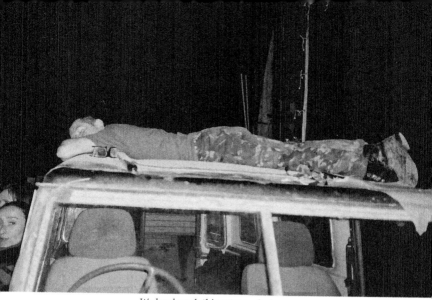
It's hard work this actor malarky

JP: Your original death was way more violent on-screen, there is a rare set photo floating about of you being split in half. I know Neil made the decision to cut it because he rightfully guessed fans would love you, but do you think it was a shame to miss out on such a cool SFX scene?

DM: I enjoyed filming everything so shooting my death was cool, but I think Neil made the right decision to not show that.

JP: Did you really go a little bit mad during your final fight scene? Between the boxing, the frantic stabbing, lobbing any and all objects and the frying pan, it really does come across like you'd lost it and that's brilliant! What was that scene like to film?

DM: No, I didn't go mad shooting the end fight, ha ha! I was just fucking buzzing. I love doing frantic scenes with loads of props where it's a real team effort between you and the crew. I think we actually did the stabbing of

273

the werewolf and throwing pots and pans in one take.

JP: You worked again with Neil on *Doomsday* and got to make it to the end (spoiler!) – would you work with him again if the opportunity arose and why?

DM: *Doomsday* was like a glorious reunion in one of the most beautiful countries in the world, South Africa, with a lot of Neil's old actors and crew from *Dogs* and *Descent* getting back together. It was an exhilarating shoot, and I am still blown away at the fact I had such an amazing opportunity to be involved in all those cool scenes working with South Africa's finest stunts and crew. But you won't see me in anything else I'm afraid. I decided to leave the acting game in about 2019. After having the excitement of shooting Neil's movies, the day in day out reality of shooting other stuff just felt a bit boring to me. Obviously, I'd make a comeback if Neil needed a little fucker with a big fire so never say never!

JP: Why do you think *Dog Soldiers* is still so popular 20 years later, what makes it such an enduring fan favourite?

DM: 20 years later... It's funny, now I'm at parents evening at my kids' high school and their science teacher is like "Erm...are you Spoon?" Yes I am!

JP: How did you get involved in *Dog Soldiers* in the first place?

LC: It was important for me to do a werewolf movie. I'd grown up watching Lon Chaney Jnr as the Wolfman. I remember my uncle got married and he couldn't afford a big party, but he invited all the family around to his house and put up this big sheet showing *Frankenstein V The Wolfman* and I remember being in the same room as this noisy projector and seeing Boris Karloff and Lon Chaney Jnr beating the shit out of one another so when the opportunity to do a werewolf movie came up, I wanted to do it. But I wasn't that impressed with the first script, and I said no. Then about 9 months or so later they sent a new version, and my agent was like do you want to read it and I was a bit meh because of the first one but I gave it a try and right away I was pissing myself laughing. Neil had formulated it into *Goldilocks and the Three Bears*. Neil had created these wonderful characters and is the hardest job in the world to write an ensemble with all great characters and he'd done that. It was wonderful, a different movie, I said to agent this is gold, sign me up. I'd done a mummy movie and a vampire, so I needed this to complete it.

JP: What did you think about the stellar reaction to the movie?

LC: It was such a coup, such a compliment to us that actual soldiers wanted to watch this thing over and over. We'd portrayed the army as ordinary lads and they loved it over in Afghanistan. We had that real camaraderie on set and just all the time, you weren't afraid to throw an idea out as no one laughed or took the piss, it started a conversation build a momentum of a scene. Just a wonderful laugh and the ridiculousness of the whole thing. There's something about having fun where you don't notice the long days and you go the extra mile when you enjoy working with people. Everyone would fire ideas around and all the cast took a very serious responsibility to the characters. You could tell something magic happened, it could have gone wrong, listen we were doing *Goldilocks* but with werewolves. It was a disaster on paper, but we managed to pull it off and the whole thing is exactly what an ordinary person would do in these extraordinary circumstances. It's exactly what the people in the audience would do, they can relate. The banter and humour is exactly how these people get through very dark times.

Seeing that first kill with Bruce and the tree it was like oh shit this will be gory and it is also ludicrous how he gets killed, not even by a wolf, if makes the audience sit up and think oh!

Fun at the premiere

JP: Ryan is very much the antagonist. Some actors when they take these parts purposefully keep themselves

276

away from the other actors to enhance that feeling of being on separate teams. Did you do that at all?

LC: I've no time for that, we were altogether doing scenes, you can't be like that. If you come across as aloof it can be 'actor aloof' and you can't have that when the lads are punching you off a chair and you're working out the moves. The audience have got to want me to get another one and it has to look real, they all want me to get punched. The guys got a real kick out of me being Irish but playing this toffee-nosed bastard and I'm sure a lot of your ordinary Joe soldiers feel like that they despise these guys because it's chain of command. I tried to make him extra plummy and annoying. He doesn't give a fuck about these guys and that kind of character is fun to play, we did have a laugh. The scene when Terry throws up all over my head, you had to have that comedy in there. People enjoyed that, and I just say, "Bathroom?" to try to bring some decorum back. It's just incredibly layered and clever. I still recommend it all the time to people, and I still see it every Halloween, people are suggesting watching it all over Twitter. It's great, still very fresh,

JP: Did you have a favourite scene?

LC: It has to be the transformation scene, I felt like I was under a lot of pressure – they were all looking forward to what I was going to do, how I was going to play it. I had the eyes and the teeth, but we didn't have the money for a big makeup budget or anything digital to we went back to basic old school principals, we went back to Lon Chaney Jnr paying homage to those old movies. We choreographed the scene, and the guys knew what about to happen, the audience knows what's about to happen after they throw me over the table and you just see the nails, but everyone was just smiling, and Neil is so good with editing – I said we need to hide the face as long as possible and we'll get that chalk board sound in, we'll build the tension. The audience had enjoyed the film so much by now that they allow us to get away with it. When I just pop my head up, we were all just laughing so much. The audience were expecting it, waiting to see which way it would go but there's something warm about it and it still brings a smile to my face now and I know that I got to be a werewolf.

Surprise

I also love Darren's line – it's exactly what he would say and when he's stabbing the wolf, I hope I'd be that heroic and it's wonderful and a lovely demonstration of blue-collar English dudes. There was just a magic that came from a generosity of spirit. It was a joyous shoot that we took very seriously when we were working but could also really enjoy and have a laugh when the camera wasn't rolling.

And we definitely left a lot of money behind the hotel bar.

JP: And did you have a scene you found difficult?

LC: The transformation scene again because of the eyes. I'd never worn any type of contacts, and these cover your whole eye and were a bugger to wear. They're meant to only be used in a clean environment which we didn't have in this dusty hanger, and I was kind of in constant pain. I'd just sit on the corner and wipe my tears away. If it had been an annoying Hollywood set, you would complain and ask to see a doctor or something, but I just sucked it up. It seems silly but the idea of their mission was they were putting up with a ton of shit and somehow maybe the awful weather and things like my contacts helped with that and I just don't remember anyone complaining. We were all so happy and you can tell from the commentary, we were taking the piss out of each other, but we looked out for each other and there's not as many productions that do that as people are protecting their corner.

JP: Keith Bell told me to ask you about the running scenes?

LC: Oh yeah, where I'm being carried because I'm injured, and we are running through the woods. They needed the 180 shots, the staccato like Spielberg used in *Saving Private Ryan* those 90-degree mirror on the camera. We did a lot of running – we ran for decades I think was the saying in this movie. Neil loves a good running shot; he was the same on *Centurian*. It was tiring but we did it then we'd drive back to the hotel. Shower, eat, bar, sleep and back next day to do it all again. It was just great fun.

JP: You've worked with Neil a few times now, what is it about his style of directing that you like?
LC: There's no airs and graces with Neil, he's very approachable and laid back with a deranged imagination. You can see his eyes open up when you throw an idea at him that he likes, give him a 'what if?' and he gets very excited. I just know what he wants now to the extent that we can communicate nonverbally as I understand his intentions. When we worked together on *GOT*, he was just communicating via hand gestures, and it was great, the rest if the crew didn't have a clue what we were doing and how we could understand each other. He's just that kind of director.

Find Liam on Twitter - @liamcunningham1

LESLIE SIMPSON

JP: How did you get involved in *Dog Soldiers* in the first place?

LS: Holy moly, we are going back in the mists of time. Craig Conway and I were involved so long ago, Neil was considering Boris Karloff for the lead. Long-time fans of *Dog Soldiers* may remember when it was first released on DVD sometime in the early nineteenth century, there was a bonus short film called *Combat*, also written and directed by Mr. Marshall.

Eagle-eyed viewers should recognise Craig and me from that film. *Combat* was effectively my audition.

And

Well, that's the short answer.

My actual audition was an afternoon in a Carlisle pub talking movies.

Neil and I got royally bladdered. Neil is insanely knowledgeable about film, and I like films a lot too. So our informal introduction became a marathon 'Scene It' movie drinking game. At the end of the afternoon, Neil staggered away, careening off the bar, muttering something about being cast in *Combat*, and nabbing a role in his squaddies-versus-werewolves flick.

For the next year or more, I was in, out, in, out, and shaken all about because the producer man fella, who went to Eton College where they're programmed to think everyone from the lower classes is an oik who can't do maths, didn't know who I was. I hadn't heard of him either.

Thankfully Neil was unceasingly loyal and kept at it. With a couple of weeks to go before shooting was due to begin, Craig Conway was cast as Winston Smith in a UK Theatre tour of *Nineteen Eighty-Four* (I think that was the play?) and his agent advised him to take it. But that meant he wouldn't be available to play Terry Milburn. Personally, I think Craig would've been fantastic as the Vomiting Cavalier. Anyway, I was dragged to London to meet some bloke in an office who took the credit for Neil casting me, and that was that.

I think that happens a lot.

JP: Did you have any prior military experience, as an actor or maybe as a cadet etc.?

LS: Yes. Of course. Pfft! Wasn't it obvious? Look at my gun action thingy in the film. It's immaculate.

Wait. What was the question again?

Er, no. No I haven't.

I've had short hair before, if that counts?

And I went to Cub Scouts once but didn't go back because the sandwiches were rubbish.

I'm only in this game for the free haircuts.

Unfortunately, during *Dog Soldiers* I became a junkie for the taste of fake blood - I was turning into a fake vampire. I recently found out fake blood is a laxative, which explains my nickname on set. Fortunately, there's a support group for fake blood addicts, called Sweet FA. I'm half decent at pretending to do lots of things, but completely useless at doing anything for real. I can't even change a lightbulb unless someone's watching me, so I'd be no good to anyone in the army.

JP: What were your favourite parts to film?

LS: I'm a method actor, so when I work, I'm always in character. I made sure everyone called me Terry all the time and had slaves to wheel me round Luxemburg in a shopping trolley on my days off.

Terry's favourite scenes were in the bar after we'd finished shooting.

They seemed to go on all night, but that's when you have to dig deep - commit to the role. You have to appreciate that people pay hard cash to come and watch you, so you go that extra mile and that extra drink.

The Hotel Intercontinental where we stayed had one of the best stocked whiskey bars in Europe. To be fair, that wasn't entirely conducive to usual military exercise conditions, so it did take me out of the work a little, but one just has to grin and bear it. It was hard going, sure, and Terry took a few weeks to shake off, but hopefully the results speak for themselves.

The lads hard at work

JP: What was hard to film, whether physically or mentally?

LS: Getting up at 5 AM for Make-Up after 20 minutes sleep. That takes commitment.

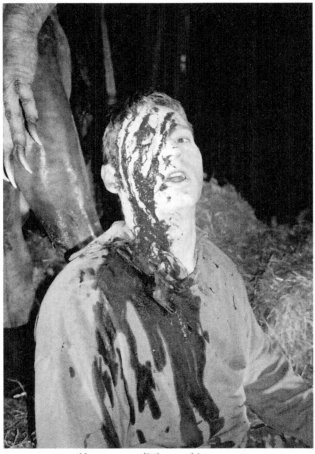

Um, you got a little something on you

We shot all the exterior scenes in the first couple of weeks. The Location Manager was either a practical joker or a sociopath, because most of the locations were on hilltops, when there was no logical need to be.

And on the days we were outside, it rained most of the time. So we had three layers of clothing - the first layer was a thermal tee and long johns, then a pair of plastic pants to stop us getting soggy feet or Trench Foot (it didn't work), and finally our kit. And when I say our kit, that included a full-size Bergen Kitbag which we had to carry ourselves when we marched up, and back down the hill.

To be honest, even that wasn't hard. We were having a blast. Everything's a breeze when you're having fun.

JP: Terry is lovely but a bit of a plonker. Did you bring any of yourself to the role?

LS: Yes.

JP: I want more stories about the other guys, but funny stuff like 'Top Bosie'. What can you tell me!

LS: Yikes. I can't really remember much about specific individuals. Well, nothing that can be made public. But below are a few things that happened, generally.

The obvious choice is Kevin McKidd and the tea towel, but someone must have mentioned it already. It wasn't pretty, but it was bloody hilarious. There's a short extract of the scene on the DVD/Blu Ray gag reel, but that was after they'd cut the towel almost in two, but Kev still couldn't rip it apart. That's why he shouts, "Is this fucking made of kryptonite, or something?" in the clip. By that point he was exhausted, and his biceps were as weak as the underdog in the final of an arm-wrestling competition. You can see the tea towel is in a bit of a state, because it had been going on for ages - about 25 minutes. Kev was really embarrassed but we were all wetting ourselves, laughing. The props department kept prepping the towel, distressing it to make it easier to pull apart, but whatever they did, Kev just couldn't manage it.

The financier, David Allen's day job was the owner of a US food company. We didn't see much of him, but he was always pleasant enough. He kept trying to place cans of Popeye Spinach on the set, in a sly attempt at product placement. So there was a little dance going on between Neil and David. Who eats spinach in Scotland?? So, between takes Neil would go hunting for Popeye Spinach cans and turn them round to hide the label. And every time David sauntered through, he'd look round furtively to see if anyone was looking and turn them back.

We were all excited to see the helicopter turn up - yeah, everyone, all cast and all crew - and we all wanted to have a ride. That was when I learned a hard lesson about film insurance. None of the cast were allowed to have a go, and we could only get in the helicopter when it was on the ground. We were told we were too important by the assistant director, Sam Harris, and we weren't allowed to do anything without approval. Just then Neil bounded over, excited as the rest of us about the chopper. He wanted a ride also, and Sam said, 'sure, hop in'. Neil was beaming from ear to ear, punching the air because he got to have a go before his cast.

As we watched him fly off, Sam said, 'yeah, he's not as important as you lot. If the helicopter crashes, we just replace him. If anything happened to any of you, we have to start all over again'.

When Neil came back, celebrating like a loon, we told him why he went first. He instantly turned into a five-year-old boy, his bottom lip sticking out by a good half mile.

During the shoot, we created a maelstrom of good vibes and camaraderie, and it seemed everyone we met wanted to be involved - below are a couple of examples.

There was another film shooting while we were there, a horror called *Feardotcom* (heard of that? No? Well, well). It had a much bigger budget, and starred Stephen Dorff, Natasha McElhone and Stephen Rea, alongside genre icons Jeffrey Combs and Udo Kier. The actors and their crew were often in the hotel bar too, and apart from some mutual friends (and some not so friendly), we generally kept apart, and we were considered poor half breeds. After about a week, word filtered through what was happening over at our little film and the buzz we were generating, and suddenly our corner of the bar started to get a little cramped. Then we started seeing people on the set we'd never seen before. Apparently, some of their crew jumped ship, and were asking if there was any work on our movie.

Speaking of Jeffrey Combs, I was in the hotel lobby one day and needed a car to go into town, so I strolled over to the Concierge. Jeffrey Combs was one of my horror heroes, and there he was, standing right next me. All I could say was, 'Oh my word, Jeffrey Combs!!' He turned to me, his eyes lit up, and shouted, 'Oh my God, Colin Powell', I replied, 'Jeffrey Combs!' he retorted 'Colin Powell!'. It was surreal, and as my real first name is Colin, part of me was trying to process whether he'd actually heard of me (not likely), so was deciding whether to tell him it was Simpson not Powell, but could only repeat, 'Jeffrey Combs -?' His jaw was on the floor, and he garbled, 'Colin Powell', again. It turns out that the then US Secretary of State, Colin Powell, the guy who led the invasion of Iraq was standing right behind me, and I had no idea. So that's how I didn't get to meet

Jeffrey Combs

* Appendix - I did actually sit down and have breakfast with Mr. Combs on another occasion, when I discovered he was staying in the hotel. On our first night shoot, which was about ten days in, we made light work of the scene and wrapped early. I got back to the hotel first, and as I walked in, the bar staff raced over to me, with genuinely worried looks on their faces. They asked, what was wrong? Was everything was alright? I'm not kidding. I just stood there, confused. We were so popular, and always in the bar, that the first night we weren't, the hotel staff started acting like the sky had fallen in.

Sean mentioned too many beers by the lift shaft…

Well, that's where we split to go to our rooms. And our rooms were the only place we were apart for the duration of the shoot.

Sean was a great bloke. He was our Sarge. And it was clear he was having the time of his life as well. I remember when we were on a night out, and he and Liam told us to enjoy every minute, because the spirit in this group was rare, and it wasn't likely we'd ever experience a shoot like this again.

Chris, Darren, Tom, Sean, and I were all on the same flight from Gatwick to Luxembourg (Kev, Liam and Emma came later), where it was the usual subdued, uncomfortable introductions. Sean was polite, but barely engaged with anyone, and sported an outsized handlebar moustache, which he thought screamed 'Army Sergeant', but looked more like an eighties Freddie Mercury throwback. You could almost read his thoughts. It was just another payday with an untested director, and a B-Movie genre script - and until the proper actors turned up, he was down among the Z-men. By the time we got to the hotel in Luxembourg City, he was yarning like one of the lads. We'd been rehearsing for about a week, but our first full day was the helicopter drop and exercise orders from the Sarge. On the way to the location Sean was complaining we couldn't do seven pages of dialogue in one day. It was impossible, and a nightmare start. For the less experienced on the shoot, (i.e., the rest of us, except Kev and Tom, who kept their mouths shut) it was worrying. On the way back, when we wrapped early and everyone was completely on point, Sean was bouncing off the walls of the car, and whooping.

A day later, he came dancing into the bar after shooting his first encounter with a werewolf, declaring Neil the new Sam Raimi. Being a friend of Neil's for some time, and having confidence in the mission he was on, I said, 'nope, he's the first Neil Marshall'. The template was set.

Sean went home for a week for a pre-arranged break during the shoot, and I've never seen such glee on an actor's face than the day he came back. Apparently, he couldn't wait to get back, and told everyone who'd listen about how good the film was going to be. He was having the time of his life.

JP: What was it like having your head chewed off?

LS: Not as bad as having my feet tickled. I have a Burmese cat called Sirius who likes licking my underarm hair, and that's bleedin' horrible. But you know, he's a cat. I can't tell him his show of affection is well rank, so I let him get on with it. Getting my head chewed off is better than that.

The werewolf was a vegan and wasn't told he'd be eating anyone when he was hired, so it got a bit hairy at one point. The werewolf called in his handler, Neil called in the producer, but try as they might, they couldn't persuade the beast to touch me, not even with a barge pole. They locked themselves in a room, and eventually Mat and Pete on the practical effects team agreed to mould a full-sized model of Terry Milburn out of a giant turnip (the one from the kids' book), and the wolf agreed to eat that. I was impressed. Mat and Pete really know their stuff, and thanks to their attention to detail, the turnip was actually a better actor than me.

On me 'ed!

CRAIG CONWAY

JP: How did you become involved with *Dog Soldiers*?

CC: I'd worked with Neil on *Combat* along with Keith Bell, Sam McCurdy and Les Simpson and at that time Neil had shared the script of *Dogs* with us. I thought it was brilliant and took it to my agent. Unfortunately, they didn't agree and promptly signed me up on a two-year theatre contract instead. I was gutted, Neil had actually wanted me to play Terry which of course ended up going to Les. But I was still desperate to be involved in some way. Then I get this phone call from Neil, asking if I want to come over and open the movie. The catch was I had to be there the next day. So I phoned in sick and flew out to have my Drew Barrymore at the start of *Scream* moment. It was sort of bittersweet as I'd really wanted to play one of the soldiers but at the same time, I was over the moon to see how well Neil had done and was incredibly pleased for and proud of everyone involved.

JP: Although poor Sarah gets ripped to shreds albeit off camera, we don't see David die. Was there ever any discussion about you coming back for a sequel?

CC: Yes, and I've waited for years for something to materialise, living in hope. If anything ever does happen, it would be like coming full circle. I will have done a cycle with a character. And I'd love for David to now be a werewolf and have an epic battle scene with Kev McKidd.

JP: Have you got any behind the scenes stories you can share?

CC: Well it was a bit weird flying in and meeting Tina, who was playing my on-screen girlfriend for the first time. We needed to film in the morning, and it was already evening, so we just had time for a quick rehearsal before dinner. And that rehearsal was running a few lines and a little snog, in Neil's hotel room, so you know, haha. Then we all went down for dinner and that was even stranger. We're sat at the table and the chef wheels out this thing that I think was venison but looked like one of Paul Hyett's creatures! It still had a load of skin and fur, and the chef was just stood there grinning with this great carving knife and I wondered if the film had started!

JP: You've worked with Neil a few times now, on *Combat*, *Dog Soldiers*, *The Descent* and *Doomsday*. What is he like to work with?

CC: Neil is just so calm on set. He gives you a sense of confidence in your performance, you trust him. Sometimes you'll be in the middle of a take, and he'll call cut because he already knows he's got what he needs from you. That's the editor in him, he can already when you're done and he has the moment. He's constantly editing in his head and that's brilliant. I'm also very comfortable with Neil. You know you can do something and fail, and it won't be a big deal. He'll now say, that was a bit shit, let's try again! And that's what you want, to make it the best for everyone. None of this, that was interesting when we all know interesting just means shit anyway. Neil lets us all play and you feel like you're actually doing something you love which is why we all got into this in the first place.

Also working with Sam McCurdy is always a joy. He is just so talented, but also he lets you know what he's doing, he tells you the angle or lens he's using so you know to get it right and a lot of DoPs don't do that. You might be giving it your all but it's a wide lens and you have to do it all again whereas with Sam it feels much more like you're working together. People don't always realise how intense and how much hard work goes into shooting a genre feature. It's so much fun but it's also really demanding, especially making it look authentic and sometimes hours in uncomfortable prosthetics and make-up. But it's worth it and I can't wait to work with Neil again hopefully.

JP: You were only on set for a short time, what was it like getting to see the final feature at the premier?

CC: Attending the premier in my hometown surrounded by friends and all these amazing people who'd been talking about films for years was just amazing. I was blown away and everyone attended, Liam, Kev and Sean who I've gone on to work with on loads of stuff. I even lived with him for a while, his wife couldn't get rid of me! I remember walking onto the set of *Doomsday* and just hearing, oy, come and put some cream on my back and it was Pertwee on the sun-lounger haha.

But I remember looking around at all these people and thinking, shit – we've done it and just feeling so brilliant. It's beautiful to see all your friend's names on the credits. It was just a real boost of confidence for everyone involved.

Find Craig on Instagram - @conwaysinsta

CHRISTOPHER FIGG – PRODUCER

JP: How did you get involved in *Dog Soldiers* in the first place?

CF: Neil sent me the script, as simple as that. I like a good horror movie so long as it is fantasy horror, something that can't happen in real life and isn't degrading to women. My sort of horror is made up, as much splatter and gore as you want, but I don't like torture-porn.

JP: What was it about Neil that you liked?

CF: I enjoyed *Combat* and I think people that come out of editing make good directors, assuming they can tell a story and are good with people. Neil had written the script so he could tell a story and he seemed to be someone who was good with people and was entirely confident with what was going on. He's very collaborative.

JP: There are several producers listed on IMDB which is often the case with feature films. Do you all have different roles

CF: Well, Keith was there as Neil's partner as acted as second unit. David Allen was there as he'd brought in the money and Tom Reeve was there as to make a film in Luxembourg you had to have a Luxembourg producer, even though Tom is actually British. It was a fun time on set but rather stressful having to scrape all the money together

JP: I'd just like to say THANK YOU for recommending Kev for the part of Cooper.

CF: Kev was on holiday when they did the publicity poster for *Trainspotting*, so he missed it. People sometimes forget he was even in it, and I always felt a little bad for him and wanted to get him another chance.

He's a great actor, very talented and I thought he'd be perfect for the role.

JP: You were incredibly busy, but do you have any fun / interesting anecdotes from the set?

CF: The crew were from all over Europe, French, Dutch, German and Italian, you name it. They all got on and there was a lovely atmosphere, but they really teased each other relentlessly too. It was all in jest and much like the banter the chaps were having on set. It was the first time I had been on a set that was still a partial working steel plant. There was a rather morbid health and safety sign which told you how many deaths there'd been on site. When we arrived, it said the number was 2 and every day I had to go and check it just to make sure it hadn't become 3. Thankfully, it didn't!

JP: There was a pretty amazing set of people working behind the scenes.

CF: It's wonderful to see how successful Simon Bowles, Sam McCurdy and Mark Thomas have gone on to be, since it was pretty much the first major work each of them did.

Mark in particular is very good at 1+1 =3, he's great at creating subtext that you fill in with music. The story has to work first without the music and then you bring it in to embellish, to enhance. The score should be secondary to the picture but with Mark his work just compliments it beautifully.

KEITH BELL - PRODUCER

JP: How did you first become involved in *Dog Soldiers*?

KB: Neil was the year ahead of me at film school and we had worked a bit of each other's projects and had many discussions about similar taste in films. I remember for his third-year end of year project he made a zombie movie when no one else was doing anything like that. After graduating, I'd moved down to London for work. During that time Neil had co-written a gangster script with our friends Fleur Costello and Casper Berry called *Killing Time* and they asked me to come up and help. It was a good learning experience. I then moved up to Glasgow to work for the BBC and it was in 1996 that Neil first told me about his pitch for *Dog Soldiers*. I loved it but at that time, no one in the UK especially wanted horror, they all wanted the next Guy Richie movie. A bit later, Neil came up again with our mate Colin Lang. We were in this pub, and had rather a lot of beers and I got this napkin, and I wrote on it that I promised to produce Neil's first feature and that it should be *Dog Soldiers*. We had so many false starts and by time we finally got to Luxembourg Neil was so ready.

JP: Tell me about the shoot

KB: We had 36 days in total, 6 x 6-day shoots, Monday to Friday. I'd obviously been on board from the beginning, there are different types of producers, but I was there from start to finish. I basically acted as a second unit. We'd get to the end of the shoot, and we might need another shot of someone's hands or an alternate shot of the dog, so I went around doing the pick-ups. We saw the actors grow each day, I remember Sean finishing a scene and coming over and saying, "I'm having so much fun."

Every single person mucked in and the SFX team were the unsung heroes for sure, they always are especially in low budget productions and our guys went the extra mile. When we were meant to film the Land Rover seen when Emma finds the lads, it had snowed overnight. So we put the vehicle in the barn Simon had built and rigged up a load of lights. The grips were banging tree branches against the roof and windows and rocking it and Pete was on the roof with the wolf arm. The actors saw what the crew were prepared to do and really gave it their all. Everyone spurred each other on.

Keith with Les and Mat

JP: Tell me a bit about the actual production of the movie?

KB: Back in 2001, we shot everything on Super 16 film, which was later blown up to 35. There was no one in Lux to cut the negs so we had to fly the rushes back to London everyday who worked on them and converted them to VHS, then flew them back to us to watch and make sure we'd got the shot we needed. It could be days before we knew if a scene even worked but that was the nature of the game. Take the model of the cottage blowing up for instance. That was amazing, these experts painstakingly creating this exact miniature replica of the house just so we could blow it up. Because they were constructing it right behind the sound stage, we all followed its progress. So when it came to the explosion everyone came to see it. We had the cameras set to extremely high-speed so the shot would work but because of having to send the film away, we didn't get to see if was captured properly until we were back in London.

JP: Have you got any fun behind the scenes stories?

KB: On one of our days off, we went to the local cinema to watch *Enemy At The Gate* as Jude Law was in it who is very good friends with Sean. The place was almost empty apart from a couple of locals and us. I was sat in front of Liam, Sean and Kev. My god, they were live-critiquing and moaning about it the whole time! Never go to the cinema with actors, I was crying with laughter. Kev was quite diplomatic, but Liam and Sean were brutal! Actors talk all the way through a film, they even did it at the premier.

I also remember vividly after Darren had gone home, Sean and Kev turning to look at one another and saying, "We're the last ones left." They really did feel that sense of loss that everyone mentions, as did the lads back home! I remember Les saying he just wished he was back as he missed everyone. You know if people had a good time on a project by what they do after it's completed. When we held the premier every single actor turned up for it, they all did publicity and were happy and proud to talk about it. That shows they enjoyed themselves.

At the premiere

SAM McCURDY – CINEMATOGRAPHER

JP: How did you become involved in *Dog Soldiers*?

SM: I'd known Neil for quite some time, and we'd already made a short *Combat* together and worked on some other things too. One of the reasons why we tended to get on so well was because we shared the idea that movies should be fun and entertaining. We'd both grown up watching *Indiana Jones*, *Star Wars*, *The Goonies* and that was the feel we wanted to bring to our work. We also loved horror, but we wanted our movies to be enjoyable. Whenever I've worked with Neil, I've always been lucky to get the scripts early. With *Dogs* it was years in the making, so we had a lot of time to prep. From all that time planning and talking, I knew this wasn't just a horror movie. It was a soldier movie, that was the aesthetic. It wasn't a slow build-up of tension, it would kick off right from the word go like all good action / war features. Having the script that early meant we'd shot it before we ever actually shot it.

JP: Neil shared his vision with you, making your role far easier. Are all directors like that?

SM: Directors like Neil will shot list and story board an entire movie, especially if there is a lot of prep time. I've been lucky enough to work with James Gunn on *Peacemaker* and he did that, he also shot listed all of *Guardians*. Working with someone like Neil, he knows exactly what he wants from you. We knew it was a long lens soldier movie rather than a wide lens, steady cam horror kind of feel. It's a luxury to have that long to prep something but we wondered for a hell of a long time whether it would ever get made, at one point we were just going to head up to Scotland and do it with no money. But thankfully Neil's determination and enthusiasm paid off.

JP: Tell me what a Cinematographer/Director of Photography does?

SM: It's my job to give the audience the photographic experience of being there, in the film. Being part of it. However the director sees it, I try to deliver those feelings photographically, to create what the director wants the audience to feel. I make sure everyone involved knows what we are doing, what look we are creating, what we want people to feel. I have an army of crew to do the technical stuff but it's that vital insight from the director that triggers the emotion, so I know the aesthetic. I get inside their head, use my creativity to translate onto film what they're seeing. For example, saying *Dog Soldiers* isn't a werewolf movie, it's a soldier movie, told me all I needed. We used lots of off-set frames.

We were also very new to the game, there was stuff we

just did because we didn't know any better. A lot of the time we were dictated by mood and what felt right. For one of the tunnel scenes in *The Descent*, we stripped down a camera and nail gunned it to some woods and shoved it into the hole. I'd never do that now, but it worked, it was right for that movie and we just didn't know any better. That's one of the many reasons I have such fondness for both those movies and still talk about them so much today.

JP: Tell me about some specific shots / camera work from the film?

SM: Well we shot on 16mil and blew it up to 35, of course using actual cameras and film. There are a lot of running and action shots in the movie and we used 45 or 90 degree shutter angles. This helps create the short, staccato effect edit as the angle reduces the mirrored light in the camera to almost a stop frame. This look was famously used in *Gladiator* and *Saving Private Ryan*. It changes the look of the film, making it gritty and dirty but more realistic. It also takes away the blur usually caused by movement which can make the viewer feel disorientated if a scene goes on like that for too long. It can be distracting in an extended scene as your eyes aren't used to seeing things in perfect clarity at speed. We used a lot of action movie gimmickry as well as horror stuff.

We didn't pull walls down or do anything clever – if the camera needed to go somewhere, we put it there! We'd strip it to get into tight spaces. I was often on the floor. But you look at *Dogs* and *Shaun of the Dead* and they're fucking good movies. People suddenly realised Brits could make stuff that wasn't costume drama. People like Neil and Edgar brought back the idea of having fun.

JP: Any final thoughts?

SM: I remember sneaking into a cinema in Piccadilly Cirus on a random Thursday evening and sliding into the backrow. The place was packed, and the audience were loving it. Screaming at the right places, laughing, jumping – just having a great time and it felt amazing watching their reactions. We had so much fun making it and people were having fun watching it.

Follow Sam on Instagram - @boardboy535

SIMON BOWLES - PRODUCTION DESIGNER

JP: How did you become involved with *Dog Sodliers*?

SB: I had been working over in Luxembourg for a few years on various films (starting with *On Dangerous Ground* with Rob Lowe) and had become part of their industry as Art Director. I was approached by Christopher Figg and asked if I wanted to come over to London to discuss a project with a new director and of course it was Neil. We got on straight away, laughing and joking. I'd worked on the first *Tomb Raider* as a concept artist and Neil was very interested, so we poured over the pages and just clicked. I'm sure some of it was because I was already over in Luxembourg, and I could see the relief on Neil's face that they'd got something sorted. Neil came over and we went on some location reccies and looked at all of these amazing stone structures sticking out of the ground that the location scout had found. The thing with Neil is he's like a mountain goat and goes running off so one moment you're talking to him and the next he's gone and he's up the top of the hill somewhere. We ended up making a pact where we would distract everyone and then run off together.

That's how we found the bit where the Special Forces camp is ruined. It was beautiful but really hard to get to and film in.

JP: Tell me about your work on the film

SB: The location scout hadn't been able to find any authentic looking cottages, so we had to build the exterior. We found a great clearing which already had a hardcore layer for us to build on and had an access road. We needed to build the bare minimum due to time and budget restraints, so we just constructed the front and side and part of the roof with the chimneys. We also built the barn too, although people often think it was a model. I recall the SFX guys walking in with these binbags full of petrol to blow that up! That was fun.

I dressed the windows with curtains in so couldn't see through to other side, the chimneys had holes in them so we could run a smoke machine and looked like real fire at night. A lot of inspiration came from real Scottish cottages and my parent's house in Somerset which had those huge stone walls.

We also had to see how small we could get spaces on the set inside the studio. Part of reason for shooting on 16mm camera not only money but the camera is far smaller than a 35mm which enabled Sam (McCurdy) to be able to whip around without having to float walls there was no time to dismantle set.

The interior was two sets for the two levels. We also dressed about 4 foot each side of windows of the interior set for when camera was peeking in, and outside of door, the porch, bushes etc so guys could run up to door and into the hallway.

We had a brilliant construction manager Bruno who came from a car-welding background but was so good at this job, he just managed to work his way up. Sonia Klaus was set decorator who I'd worked with previously on *Tomb Raider*. We were incredibly lucky to get her, and she was able to pull in loads of great favours from prop houses.

Every single item used and on display tells a backstory to the characters, I have to create the narrative in my mind to help design and dress the set as a lot of the time I don't have any of the cast there with me. I have to put myself in the shoes of the character. There are layers of lives in that house, I take a lot of time just being there, making sure even the saucepan handles are facing the right way as it has to look believable. As soon as the audience doesn't believe you can never get them back as they query the whole thing.

I got the carpenters to sand the stairs so there was tread on the left and right as if decades of footsteps had trodden there. And we did the same on the flag stones on the floor in the entrance way, made it look worn and lived in. Again, it has to look authentic, or you lose the audience.

We also used a solid ceiling on the set, partly to make the wolves more imposing. I asked Bob Keen the exact measurements of the werewolf costume, I wanted the ceiling to be the exact height where the hair on the top of the wolf ears were just brushing against it. Also, again it helps with the authenticity and look of the set when it isn't all open like a soap opera. With a real ceiling, you have to light the set properly with things like the fire etc. and it helps the audience believe in this world you've created.

It was also my job to source things like the Land Rovers and get them over from the UK, so they were right-hand drive and things like the armoury and weapons.

JP: What are some of your memories from working on the set?

SB: Before we even got over to Luxembourg, I remember being in Shepperton with Neil, Christopher Figg and Claudio the draughtsman, drawing up these intricately details plans. Then when we got over there, I unravelled this piece of paper and the construction people looked at his detailed sketches it was wonderful to witness their relish, knowing that they were going to be creating this world.

I vividly remember working on the house and seeing the cast running past during the bootcamp with the foreign legion guy who was busy whipping them into shape.

The house became a celebrity too, and locals would drive up to see it including one very special local, the Duke himself along with his son.

The cottage exploding at the end was of course a model. It was made by a team of local art students and it took them ages to create. They started with mini stones and built up the walls with mortar, made all miniature scale furniture, even pictures on the walls. The roof had all individual tiles so when it exploded, they would all shower up onto the camera. The first take was too much like actually looking at a model, they had the camera looking down. So for the second take, the had the camera facing up from the platform the model was resting on so all the pieces that flew up into the air showered down and that's the money shot that everyone loves.

There wouldn't have been time to insert the explosion

packs into the wall during the shoot, so it all had to be done during initial construction of the walls. Neil and I had to decide where the bullets were going to go so the windows and walls could explode before the scenes were shot. The detonators were already there built in since no time to replaster paint etc. once we got rolling.

We didn't need to take the set apart at the end, we just swept it up! Every single thing was destroyed, all that vintage crockery! But it had done its job, the story of that set has been captured for ever though, that's a part of me that might be transferred onto hologram one day for my great-great grandchildren to see one day and I'm super proud of that.

Overall, not only was it a lot of fun, but I am still really great friends with both Neil and Sam and try to work with them whenever possible. From a great film came lasting friendship.

Follow Simon on Instagram - @simonbowlesdesign

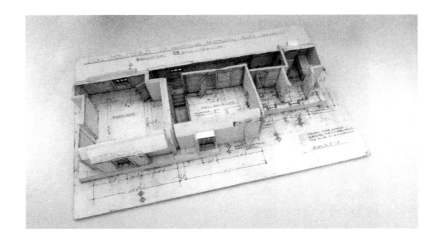

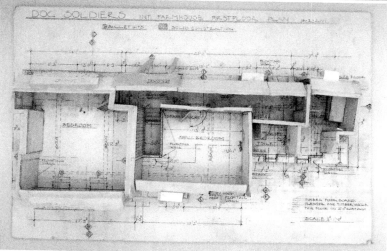

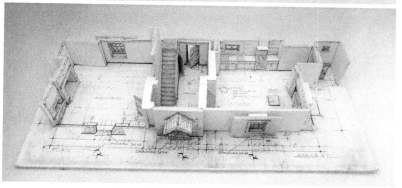

311

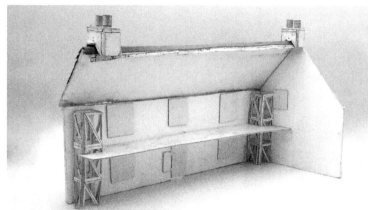

313

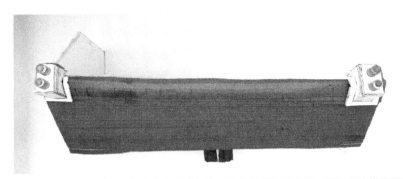

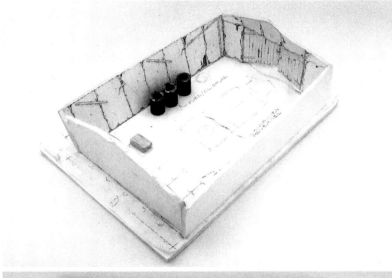

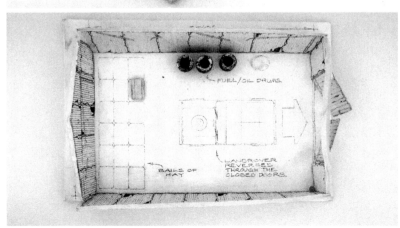

FUEL/OIL DRUMS.

BAILS OF HAY

LANDROVER REVERSES THROUGH THE CLOSED DOORS.

314

MAT OTOOLE – SFX MAKEUP ARTIST

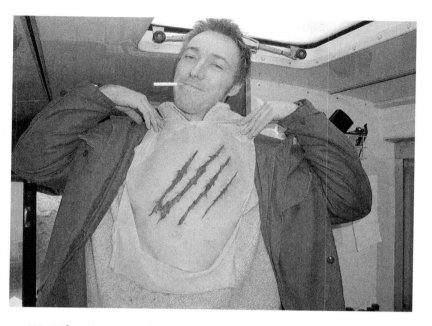

JP: Why did you choose to work in SFX?

MOT: SFX wasn't really my thing growing up I was more of a comic book guy, constantly drawing, and eventually sculpting. I was working as a sculptor/designer for a computer game company, Bob Keen was bought in as a creative consultant he and I got to chatting and he asked to come down to London for work

The game company eventually folded so I took him up on his offer and worked for him on the movie, *Event Horizon*, of course I was super pumped working on a big film, I was hooked.

JP: How did you get involved with *Dog Soldiers*?

MOT: Working at Bob's it was one of the projects that came in, Dave (Bonneywell) came in and said, 'We've got a werewolf film.' I remember we were all cautiously optimistic about it.

JP: What were some of the things you worked on/ helped to create?

MOT: At the start of the job, we was going through all the things that needed to be made, starting with the main sculpt of the wolf. Dave, I thought, was the natural fit as he was the supervisor and good at everything, but I remember him pulling me aside and saying I'm gonna give you sculpting job, I'll be too busy running the shop. I was super flattered and pleased, we life cast the performer Brian (Claxton Payne) who was tall, thin but muscular perfect for what we needed.

Got a fibre glass cast of him, then Pete (Hawkins) welded up a box frame armature/stand that we attached it to, ready for sculpting. Justin (Pitkethly) helped me out with the sculpting duties, it was a lot of fun we used regular water-based clay for speed, but also for getting those big shapes there's nothing like regular clay. I remember enjoying sculpting the body more than the head weirdly

I think I did the 'flesh vest' sculpt as well, that was a flesh-coloured tight tank top made by the late Lisa Crawley (lovely lass who did a lot of the fabrication work and died way to soon, RIP) that we cast the silicon slash wound on to and could be worn like a regular t-shirt by Liam after being found with his wound by the squad.

There were many responsibilities that we all did, moulding, casting, seeming, painting hair work, gag work, mixing blood, all sorts.

JP: What was the most fun to work on?

MOT: Hmmm that's a hard one, the whole job was a blast. I would say maybe the gore on set, because to me it felt like everything worked out so well, even when we had problems, I had a real sense of confidence because of the guys I was working with. It was like there was nothing we couldn't handle, that and the fact it was gore and gore is always fun hahaha,

JP: What was the most challenging aspect?

MOT: I would say the time constraints, we had to get, I think three suits done in very little time, along with everything else. Dave could tell you the exact time we had.

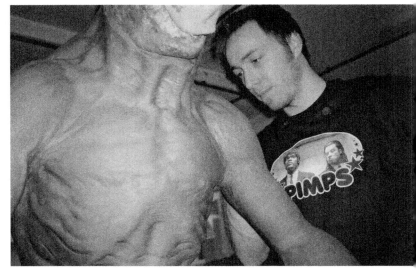
Pimps!

JP: Are there any scenes or moments that stick out for you?

MOT: Watching the film there are a few. Sean's monologue about the devil tattoo on the soldier's arse, the big reveal of the wolf standing up in the bedroom, Liam's transformation.

From a behind the scenes perspective, moments that stand out are probably the comradeship of going out with the guys, drinking, partying, having a blast, same on set minus the drinking/partying haha!

JP: Any BTS stories you can share?

MOT: I have vague memories of getting a massive chunk of dry ice (we used the dry ice for wolf breath in the animatronic heads) and dropping it into the catering guy's massive container of hot soup. It was wrap so the ice wouldn't last for the next day and the soup was done with, but I remember filling the woods with low level fog.

I also remember dressing the SAS camp with blood and gore from the off-screen attack, it was on a slope so the whole crew was slipping and sliding as it was raining all day. I went skidding down on my arse a couple of times.

Another great memory is I remember Neil getting me to be the eldest brother in the photo on the mantle that Sean hammers, I love that in some small way I'm kinda canon in that universe.

JP: What are some of your own favourite creature features and effects in films?

MOT: Hmmm that could be a very long list. I think a standout for me is the *Predator*, the original suit has never been topped for realism and performance, also C3PO is an amazing suit that's overlooked for how well it's done, as is the simple effectiveness of Chewbacca's snarl. Gory stuff very rarely makes me wince but the arm chop in *28 Days Later* always gets me. There's also a fantastic head shot in *Extraction* (Chris Hemsworth movie), there are a whole bunch of makeups that work really well these days with the advances in silicone, age, likeness, character and weight make ups that are beautiful. But I still think the helmet off look for *Robocop* is one of my favourites.

JP: Any final thoughts?

MOT: I guess my final thoughts are that maybe I remember it through rose coloured glasses but when asked what's my favourite film I've worked on in my over twenty-year career doing this silly job, it's always *Dog Soldiers*.

Everyone felt fresh, but not in a green way, in an enthusiastic way. It was fun and hard work at the same time, there was an appreciation for work well done and an understanding of limitations. The above the line hung out with the below the line and we all made a bloody fun movie.

JUSTIN PITKETHLY - SFX MAKEUP ARTIST

JP: Why did you choose to work in SFX?

Justin P: I chose to work in Creature Effects because I grew up in the 70's and 80's and loved horror and fantasy films. It was something that was developing and getting better with each film, there were lots of behind-the-scenes footage and "making of" documentaries. These and the magazines at the time - *Fangoria, Cinemagic, Cinefantastique, Cinefx* fuelled the fire, and I had my heart set on getting into the industry.

JP: How did you get involved with *Dog Soldiers*?

Justin P: I was working at Image Animation at the time, I'm guessing it was actually known as Image FX by then. Although we were all freelance, we did tend to stay and do a run of different projects there with Bob Keen whose company it was and with Dave Bonneywell as workshop supervisor.

JP: What were some of the things you worked on/ helped to create?

Justin P: I did some sculpting on the creature suit alongside Mat, but we all knew Mat, who was always drawing amazing *Conan the Barbarian* like characters, was master of muscles and anatomy so he did the majority of it.

I remember working on Spoon's death. I made a severed torso that we tested out by having Pete Hawkins (I think) poking his head, shoulders and arms through a piece of fake wall we made. We attached the torso to Pete's shoulders and hid the join with clothing. So it basically looked as though Pete had been chopped in half and his top half was stuck against the wall. We also had a hole in the wall just above the line of where the torso ended so that we could drop the famous sausage skin guts out of.

I understood the shot was going to be Spoon being pinned against the wall by a werewolf while coughing up blood and as the camera pans down we see he is missing his lower half and werewolves were devouring what was left. But this sequence didn't end up that way in the film sadly.

JP: What was the most fun to work on?

Justin P: I have to say looking back at working on *Dog Soldiers*, the fun part of the job was always the people that I worked with back then. We did work hard often staying late, but we genuinely had lots of fun, we used to all go out clubbing together at the weekends and had a good time! Strangely the most fun thing I worked on was a glowing log! It was enjoyable because I got longer to make it than I usually would. The shooting crew Dave, Matt, Pete and Lisa had gone off to Luxembourg to start the shoot, and a few of us were finishing off a few things in the workshop. I moulded a real log and made a hollow fibre glass version that slid apart and had a torch and a little circuit with flickering lights in it. I remember sending it out to the guys with a little set of instructions, I really enjoyed making that! Sean Pertwee uses it to burn Ryan once he has fully transformed into a werewolf.

Ant Parker with the log

JP: What was the most challenging aspect?

323

Justin P: I'm sure like all these films the most challenging aspect was to make all that we had been asked to make in the time that we had been given. Full foam latex creature suits don't always come out of the oven perfectly every time! Everything we make is usually a custom one off and a lot of time and effort goes into each thing. It's a great job but it's also really challenging. Once it's been made and is being shot, trying to get every effect to work is the challenge, and we are always under pressure to get it right first time. When filming has finished for the day the shooting crew would have been continuously repairing damaged suits and making them look good for the next day - it is hard work.

JP: Are there any scenes or moments that stick out for you?

Justin P: There is a scene that sticks out for me, and it is a shot of a werewolf that comes through the window of the bedroom and shows the creature slightly silhouetted, the camera is low, and I thought it was the nicest shot of a werewolf from the film.

JP: Any BTS stories you can share?

Justin P: As I didn't go on set, I don't have any behind the scenes stories, But the shooting crew came back with lots, so I'm sure they will fill you in!

JP: What are some of your own favourite creature features and effects in films?

Justin P: Favourite Creature Features that spring to mind are the real obvious ones - *Alien, Aliens, The Thing,* and *An American Werewolf in London.*

E.T I think was done incredibly by Carlo Rambaldi as it was such a believable character. Yoda by Stuart Freeborn also amazed and inspired me. Rick Bakers Harry from

Harry and the Hendersons was incredible, and of course *Gremlins*! Walt Conti's animatronic dolphins are the most convincing animatronics I've ever seen, I think!

I have always loved horror films too, and am a big fan of *The Evil Dead*, *The Fly*, *The Blob* (1988) *Pumpkinhead*, *Chucky*, *Return of the Living Dead*, to name a few. I also love a creature feature that dares to push the boat out no matter how bizarre, so have a special place in my heart for Frank Henenlotter's *Brain Damage* and *Basket Case*.

ANTHONY PARKER - WORKSHOP CREW

JP: Why did you choose to work in SFX?

AP: When I was a child, I was interested in animation and would spend hours in my bedroom drawing and making plasticine models that I would animate with a super 8mm camera I had been given by my uncle. I loved horror movies and had posters of Freddy Krueger and things that would have given most kids (and some adults) nightmares on my bedroom walls. I decided to make that a career and moved to London when I was 18 with the intention of finding my way into a career making monsters and gore for movies.

JP: How did you get involved with *Dog Soldiers*?

AP: I had been in the industry for about 5 years when I heard that Image FX were crewing for this werewolf movie called *Dog Soldiers*. At the time, I had not worked for Image before but knew people who worked for them. I heard that the werewolves were going to look really different, with mostly hairless bodies and very realistic furry wolf heads. At the time I had done quite a lot of fur fabrication and painting of fake fur to make it look realistic, so I was really interested in doing that on a werewolf movie. I had an interview with Dave Bonneywell and started soon after.

JP: What were some of the things you worked on/ helped to create?

AP: I was part of the Image FX workshop crew and my job was the fur on the wolf heads. There were hero animatronic heads for each wolf and stunt heads too. Foam latex skins were cast out of the mould of the sculpt and these had to be painted and then covered in fur and painted realistically to give each wolf their individual look.

There was also a lot of hair work. As part of a team along with Tacy Kneale, Bobbi Roberts and Shirley Sweeney, I designed how the fake fur was going to be pieced together on the heads and also how they were going to be painted. The heads were furred using a technique called fur replacement. Fake fur comes on a roll with a material backing. In fur replacement, the material backing is shaved away from the fur and replaced with a glue. It is then transferred to the foam skin. The fur was painted using inks that are used in taxidermy. They were airbrushed using these colours.

328

Everyone mucking in with the wolves

JP: What was the most fun/challenging aspect?

AP: Definitely, for me, the most fun and challenging aspect was helping to come up with the different colour markings for each wolf. I remember I had a book of wolves that I had marked and labelled the photos of wolves I thought had interesting colours and markings, to use as reference for the different wolves in the film. They all had their own distinct look.

JP: Are there any scenes or moments that stick out for you?

AP: One of my favourite scenes is the 'what scares the Sarge' scene, where they are sat round the campfire on the first night and Sarge tells the story of Eddie Oswald and his laughing devil tattoo being all that was left of him after he triggers an anti-tank mine. Then an eviscerated highland cow lands out of nowhere in the middle of the camp!

JP: What are some of your own fave creature features and effects in films?

AP: *Killer Klowns from Outer Space* by the Chiodo Brothers was always one of my favourite movies when I was a kid. I've always loved werewolf movies though, another reason I was eager to work on *Dog Soldiers*. Particularly *The Howling* series and *An American Werewolf in London*. The transformations in the original *Howling* movie and *American Werewolf* are still a couple of my favourite effects.

JP: Anything else you want to add?

AP: *Dog Soldiers* has very special memories for me. Aside from being an extremely rewarding project to work on in terms of the job I was doing, it was also the first time I worked with and became friends with the woman I would eventually marry! Lisa Crawley was a creature suit fabricator for Image FX and on *Dog Soldiers* took care of the internal fabrication of the wolf suits, making sure they fit together and fit the performers correctly, that the heads fit to the suits and could be removed and reattached seamlessly, and that the heavy animatronic hero heads could be supported as comfortably and safely as possible while the performers were wearing them. She was also on set for the movie to dress the werewolf performers and help look after them. We became good friends during and after *Dog Soldiers* and in 2007, we finally became a couple while we were working on *Hellboy 2* in Budapest. Our son Zack was born just over a year later and we got married on Malibu beach in 2011, while our son played in the sand. Tragically, Lisa passed away in 2017 after being diagnosed with Motor Neurone Disease (ALS) in 2015. *Dog Soldiers* will always be very special to me and hold a special place in my heart because it is how we first met. Making werewolves.

CHAPTER
EIGHT
FAMOUS FANS

Something that became evident in the early planning stages of this book, is just how popular *Dog Soldiers* remains today. People love this movie. Not only film-fans, but people in the industry. I spoke with some of the people who inspired Neil himself to make movies, some who were in turn influenced by Neil to make their own stuff and also people who have made their name and earn their living due to loving horror.

> *"After the 1980s, it was hard to imagine anyone breathing new life into the werewolf subgenre. After Joe Dante and John Landis had completely overturned lycanthropic cinema with* The Howling *and* An American Werewolf In London, *where could anyone possibly take it? Well, Neil Marshall had an answer. His* Dog Soldiers *was a smart and canny—and ferocious—werewolf movie with more than just teeth. The juxtaposition of warfare and werewolves was brilliant: fast-moving action with full-on scares, beautifully choreographed and*

presented, with a game cast and a promising new filmmaker showing promise for a remarkable movie career. Dog Soldiers *is one of a kind, and the world is better for it!"*

Mick Garris – producer *Hocus Pocus* and
Masters of Horror

"I have a lot of love and appreciation for Dog Soldiers. *Firstly, as a fan of all things lycanthropy related, I love that Neil tackled this subject and put his own creative spin on it. It was really exciting to see such a unique take applied to a familiar sub-genre by blending action with the horror. It was a well told story done smartly despite its low budget.*

I remember very well — ordering my DVD from the States and watching the featurette and the commentary to learn everything I can about the making of this movie.

Secondly, this low budget movie was very inspirational to me. It came out during the period where Leigh Whannell and I had spent a few years writing and trying to get our little indie film off the ground in Australia, so it was tremendously inspiring to see a movie like Dog Soldiers *— telling a classic genre story with all the thrills of Hollywood filmmaking but outside of the Hollywood system — come along and get people's attention. It made us think that we could do the same with* Saw. *I'm really glad to see* Dog Soldiers *having a long shelf life after its initial release, and new generation of horror fans discovering this gem of a movie."*

James Wan – director *Saw* and *Malignant*

"Getting offered the role of Spoon in 2001 was a

huge deal for me. I had only really done television up until that point and although I was very proud of Spaced *and* Big Train, *I had my heart set on breaking into movies. Neil offered me the role straight out, which was amazing to me. It was the chance to not only play a lead role in a movie but also be part of a great ensemble, hanging out in the wilds of Scotland, on a project which occupied a genre space that I absolutely loved.*

At this point Edgar Wright and I were deep into developing Shaun of the Dead *and when I told Edgar about* Dog Soldiers, *he didn't seem too enthused. When I asked him what was wrong, he confessed that he wanted* Shaun of the Dead *to be our first horror movie. Shaun was incredibly personal to both of us and as much as it pained me, I could totally understand where Edgar was coming from. Edgar and I were putting everything we had into our movie and part of that was our novelty value as unknowns in the field. We wanted our film to have the biggest splash it could possibly have and in Edgar's mind, my involvement in* Dog Soldiers *threatened to diminish our duel debut.*

I realised, I felt the same way and in the end, I bit the silver bullet and decided to pass. I never expected to make a decision like that so early in my career. I didn't actually watch the Dog Soldiers *for almost 20 years because of the lingering sense of FOMO that turning it down had left me with.*

When I finally watched it with my daughter recently, it was bittersweet but I loved it. Darren Morfitt is so great as Spoon. He's funny and relatable but also brings an authentic toughness to the character that I think I would have struggled to convey. It was great to see everything turned out as it should. Dog Soldiers *will forever be my 'one that got away'."*

Simon Pegg – co-writer and star of *Shaun of the Dead* and *Hot Fuzz*

"Just when we thought The Wolf Man, I Was a Teenage Werewolf, *and* The Curse of the Werewolf *had pinned this monster's story to the wall, along came 1981 with* An American Werewolf in London, The Howling, Wolfen. *Surely this was all there could be, though, right? What other stories can there be left to tell? How can the werewolf be taken any farther? Like this:* Bad Moon *and* Ginger Snaps *at the end of the century, and, crashing through walls into room after room, a little movie called* Dog Soldiers, *giving us probably the best werewolf silhouette since Eddie Quist's. Those ears, yes? That muzzle? Those claw-tipped fingers? No: the adrenaline.* Dog Soldiers *traps you in an old house in the middle of nowhere with a bunch of soldiers who didn't ask for this — nobody told them to stay off the moors. This is just military exercises, for them. Until it's so, so much more.* Dog Soldiers *reminds us that the werewolf story is always red in tooth and claw. And getting redder every minute."*

Stephen Graham Jones – author of *Mongrels* and *My Heart is a Chainsaw*

"I remember seeing Dog Soldiers *at the cinema and thinking, wow this is great! I never thought for a moment I'd end up working with Neil. He's such a lovely guy and a pleasure to work with. There's a real difference between doing stuff with someone who's so supportive and makes you want to give*

110%. You get some directors who you know aren't like that but you'll get paid the big bucks so you put up with it, but you wouldn't want to be barked at on a low budget horror shoot. He's not like that at all, you always want to do your best, work late, match his enthusiasm. I took those sensibilities with me to my own directing jobs. He's not only a real geek and super nice guy, but he also truly knows his stuff. He has such vision and can always answers questions installing a real confidence. He is always prepared and led by example. He actually gave me lots of feedback on my first movie, I was expecting a few words and he gave me pages. He shares, he's a genius but he's so open with those ideas. There is also never any fear to make suggestions. You can listen to what he has to say and then add, that's great but what if? He's so collaborative and never precious about who comes up with ideas. He cares about how it looks in the editing room, not who thought of what. And the audience are never going to be asking, oh I wonder who decided to do it that way anyway! He feeds off his crew's talents, and that makes him a dream director.

I always look forward to working with him having done The Descent, Doomsday and Centurian now. The funny thing is a lot of people just presume I also worked on Dog Soldiers. I go to conventions and people will bring over a load of DVDs to sign, and often Dog Soldiers is one of them. I'll say, this is a great movie, but I didn't work on it and sometimes they argue back that I did! So, I end up just signing it anyway. I've also worked with Sean on a lot of films, as a director too. He's just the loveliest guy, full of on-screen charisma and up for anything which is good as I have killed him off in so many ways. The cast and crew were just wonderful, and I've worked with a lot of them since. Neil ends up finding the best people to work with and it shows."

Paul Hyett - SFX wizard and director *Howl* and *The Seasoning House*

"I think that deep down inside all of us who have dedicated our lives to genre cinema secretly want to make a werewolf movie. I've longed to make my own werewolf film ever since first flipping through the hauntingly beautiful pages of Stephen King's Cycle of the Werewolf *at my local bookstore as a 9-year-old boy. Bernie Wrightson's illustrated werewolves are still the most realistic and fear inducing depictions of the fantastical creatures that I have ever seen. Who can ever forget the first time they feasted their eyes upon the terrifying drawing of the werewolf reaching through the car window and ripping the driver's face off? The sheer fact that I still find Wrightson's drawings to be infinitely more frightening than anything offered on screen says a hell of a lot about how difficult it actually is to create a worthy cinematic werewolf. It goes without saying that Rick Baker's iconic creation in* An American Werewolf In London *changed the game and remains a feat of timeless cinematic glory, but even Baker's incredible depiction was still much more wolf than man once fully transformed. Even four decades later with the tools of modern CGI at our disposal, a great werewolf movie is nearly impossible to find. Sadly, the horror genre is largely condemned to the low budget world of filmmaking and the challenge that comes with*

creating a convincing werewolf on a modest budget is precisely what keeps so many of us on the side lines and afraid to create our own.

But then there's Dog Soldiers.

For all that Neil's film has going for it, it was the brilliant choice to design the creatures with actual wolf heads that makes it one of the truly great werewolf films. The creatures in Dog Soldiers *brought me right back to the feeling I had as a kid standing in the bookstore and gazing upon Bernie Wrightson's* Cycle of the Werewolf *illustrations for the first time. The werewolves in Neil's film looked so damn cool that I enthusiastically suspended my disbelief and went along for every second of the violent, gory, and action-packed ride. Budget hurdles be damned, the werewolves in* Dog Soldiers *represented everything I had imagined when first learning about lycanthropy and they were the closest thing to the Wrightson illustrations I had fallen so madly in love with as a child. Even more importantly, the film signaled the arrival of a new voice on the scene that demanded the attention of not just genre fans but of other aspiring filmmakers as well. Somewhere out there a fellow traveler had tackled a sub-genre that most indie filmmakers wouldn't dare touch and he had done it with total grace and style. In the end, Neil pulled it off by committing to very specific and stylized choices that mattered far more than any of the budgetary limitations he was up against. As someone who first saw* Dog Soldiers *in the early stages of putting my own first real film together, there was a fearlessness behind Neil and his film that I couldn't help but feel infected by as I set off to make* Hatchet.

Someday I'll find the courage to make my own werewolf film and it will be all Neil's fault."
Adam Green – writer / director *Hatchet* series

"Dog Soldiers stands out against the other low-budget genre offerings of the early 2000s by going the Evil Dead *route and serving up cleverly staged set-pieces punctuated with juicy gore gags, fully delivering on the* "Night of the Living Dead *but with werewolves" premise. The siege-movie structure affords it a generous momentum fuelled by tense action, with engaging characters and banter that keeps you entertained even when there's no mayhem onscreen. It's a movie that feels like a video game in the best way possible, an exciting slice of survival-horror that still holds up decades later."*
Steven Kostanski – writer / director *Psycho Goreman*

"I had just completed my Degree at Wimbledon School of Art where I studied Theatre Design and specialised in sculpting, model-making, prosthetics and animatronics and was in the middle of making my own film debut, a 30-minute stop-motion model animation called Butterfly, when Dog Soldiers *arrived.*

As a lover of horror and specifically monster movies and creature FX, I always had my eyes open to new horror movies. Werewolf movies are unique and good ones are quite rare. They are a hard monster to pull off right. Zombies and Vampires are essentially quite easy to render visually but if you are going to make a Werewolf movie, you have to commit to the monster... I loved The Howling, American Werewolf, Company of Wolves *and* Wolf *and the last good one back then had been* Ginger Snaps, *a Canadian movie that cleverly subverted the genre and had some cool makeup FX.*

When I saw the Dog Soldiers *poster, I remember staring at it and thinking it looked cool and enticing and the high concept 'Soldiers VS Werewolves' idea that it proposed immediately had me curious. And then I noticed that it was coming from the UK!*

The cross-genre blend of action and horror Neil managed to juggle in his debut is no mean feat. It felt similar to something like Aliens *or* Predator *and* Dog Soldiers *didn't hold back with the gore either with wonderful practical FX and iconic creature design.*

Yeah, if you are going to make a Werewolf movie, you have to create great Werewolves and Neil pulled off some of the best-looking monster silhouettes in a long while. And he wasn't afraid to place them right in amid the action. It instantly earned its place as one of the best in its hairy-clawed sub-genre!

Dog Soldiers *also helped inspire me when putting together my own practical-FX heavy debut feature,* The Hallow, *a decade or so later, after which Neil had already followed up with the equally impressive and terrifying, monster-filled* Descent *movie.*

I am looking forward to revisiting Dog Soldiers *again later this year when it gets its new glorious release."*

Corin Hardy – director *The Nun* and *Gangs of London*

"I think something that's really appealing about Dog Soldiers, *and Neil Marshall's filmography in general, is that it harkens back to the kind of low-to-mid-budget genre movies pioneered in the 70's & 80's by guys like John Carpenter, Sam Raimi & Joe Dante. You get the infectious feeling of seeing a kid that grew up reading 'Famous Monsters of Filmland' & watching late-night horror flicks finally making good & directing exactly the kind of movie that they wanted to see, but for some reason nobody had made yet. I mean, it's basically* Assault on Precinct 13 *with werewolves & a British twist. What's not to like?"*

Brandon Tenold – Brandon's Cult Movie
Reviews

"This is a film that holds such a fond and nostalgic place in my heart, something you wouldn't expect for a film of such calibre. Dog Soldiers *isn't just a werewolf film for me, it's a piece of my history that strengthened the bond between my dad and I. The first time I watched this film I was a teen trying to establish independence and that meant pushing my parents away. My dad sat me down and got me to watch it with him; safe to say we both adored it! From the impressive British idiosyncrasies to the barbaric guts and gore to the dogfight sequences, it was definitely our cup of tea.*

I think that's why the relationship between Sergeant Wells and Private Cooper feels so tender and special to me, because it reminds me of my dad and how we'd sacrifice ourselves to bloodthirsty werewolves for one another. Re-watching Dog Soldiers *transports me to a sentimental place that means so much to me, and comforts me like an embrace.*

It's also an absolute gem of a classic British horror film! Is there really another werewolf film you can have just so much fun with? I think not. It stands the test of time, it is bloody hilarious and for me, has to be one of the greatest werewolf films ever made!"

Zoe Rose Smith – Editor in Chief Ghouls Magazine

"Things get hairy in this siege thriller that brims with bloody action and spectacle, yet still finds the time to make you care about its characters, just as they're about to disappear into a meat grinder. Dog Soldiers *wears its love of genre history comfortably on its sleeve, whether we're talking about the nightmarish imagery of its emaciated bipedal doggos slinking through fog-strewn forests, or the splatterly wolf attacks that provide us with all the red meat we can eat. This one sits on its haunches at the crossroads of yesterday and today. A little bit Larry Talbott. A little bit Eddie Quist. Neil Marshall brings a welcome burst of energy to a subgenre that can always use more of it, clawing out a place in history as one of the best werewolf movies ever made."*

Matt Serafini - author of *Feral* and *Rites of Extinction*

"Dog Soldiers *is one of the few modern films that I'd call an all-timer, that I didn't see first in a theater. And part of me regrets that, but another part of me, as an American teenager, a middle schooler, when the DVD first came out here late in 2002, it makes me nostalgic for that very particular time in not* *only horror cinema, but movie distribution. When the internet (we had just gotten it in our house, at that point) didn't pick apart every little bit of a film before you actually got to see it, but at the same time the popularity of DVD (and the shops that rent/sold the format) meant that you were seeing international movies in high quality, with a very short lag time from when they were released in their home country. Oddly, because of those factors, I would argue horror fans at the time were a lot more adventurous and outgoing, a lot more cinematically omni voracious, than they are now, now that there's "infinite streaming options" but the algorithm has us locked into tweeting about the same one or two movies each week. There weren't "limitless" options for seeing films like there are now, but there was this perfect storm of availability, variety, and a newly widened whisper network that made it, so you didn't have to work *too hard* to seek out what was new and great."*

Adam Cesare – author of *Clown in a Cornfield*

"I can clearly remember the first time I saw Dog Soldiers. *I'd spent a day with some friends in Bristol, and we decided to finish up with a trip to the cinema to watch a new, low budget werewolf movie before heading back down the pub.*

I didn't need much convincing – werewolves have been my favourite cinematic monster ever since I'd seen Oliver Reed in Curse of the Werewolf *as a child. My love had been cemented by* American Werewolf *and* The Howling. *However, ever since then, I'd been disappointed by the genuinely terrible movies that had followed on. It seemed that no one could create a good werewolf movie anymore. So, while I was enthusiastic about a night at the cinema watching a horror movie with old mates, my expectations were suitably lowered.*

I needn't have worried.

Dog Soldiers *was an absolute revelation to me. I was hooked from the moment the troops landed in that remote Scottish forest. I'd spent a few years in the military, and the banter between the lads in that unit rang absolutely true to my ears. And the inclusion of not one but two characters from the North East (where I grew up) made me feel that the movie was speaking to me personally, capturing the essence of the region in a way I'd rarely seen on film before.*

And then the film cranked it up a gear, and I was a lifetime fan. Even more than twenty years later, the werewolves remain some of the best designed to date. They actually looked and moved like wolves, rather than some unconvincing bloke in a gorilla suit with a paper mache dog head stuck on top of the costume. The gore effects were brilliant, convincing, and made me physically wince more than once (Sausages anyone?)

However, what really made the film for me was the masterful use of humour amongst the carnage. The ability to get a laugh from the audience right before dropping them off an emotional cliff opened my eyes to how best to make a comedy horror. It was hilarious by the nature of the characters, who were so well written. The plot itself wasn't funny, despite the peppering of cultural references. What made the film a classic was how the characters played off each other.

That stayed with me for another six or seven years until I started writing my own werewolf novels. And right from the start, I knew that thematically, I was aiming for a cross between Dog Soldiers *and* Stand by Me, *set in the North-East of England in the 1980s. A coming of age monster story that used the same levels of horror and humour to get an emotional response from the audience.*

Dog Soldiers *is, for me, still the best werewolf movie ever made. I have watched it every Halloween without fail for almost twenty years, despite knowing the lines and scenes off by heart. And if I'd never had a low budget horror movie speak to me the way this one did, I doubt that my own writing career would have ever even happened."*

Graeme Reynolds - Author of the High Moor Trilogy

CHAPTER

NINE

COMMENTS FROM SQUADDIES

I'm lucky enough to know a few people who have actually served in the forces – thank you – so I asked them what they thought of the movie and the portrayal of the soldiers.

> *"I like the film - basically the blokes sound, move and act like British Squaddies (don't get me wrong to make it 100% it'd be peppered with the C word). The best bit being the one where Spoon says (as a werewolf kills him) 'I hope I give you the shits'. I think the cast got pissed a lot off set too. So in essence the cast of* Dog Soldiers *depict the average British Infantryman faced with bloody great big werewolves in the arse end of nowhere The other thing I love about* Dog Soldiers *is the special effects are real not CGI which makes it better."*
>
> Conrad Ball – serving police officer and ex-Armed Forces

"*Dog Soldiers is one of my favourite movies and I appreciate it as a filmmaker myself and as an ex-serviceman. One of the many realistic aspects are the nicknames – Spoon, Coop, even Left-Hand Charlie – as almost everyone had one or at least a truncated version of their name. And you were given that name, you couldn't turn up to the barracks and say, 'Oh yeah people call me such-and-such,' that name was awarded to you.*

The entire movie is played as if Neil knew how squaddies minds worked. Their reactions were authentic. Some of them chose fight, others flight. Some forgot all their training, others it instinctively kicked in. Just like it would in a real-life situation.

Something that can be annoying in films is when characters are placed in these scenarios and don't arm themselves to the teeth. Again, when the lads come across the SS camp that has been destroyed, they grab all they can. And they would, it's what they've been trained to do – get the weapons, fill your pockets with ammo!

The whole thing is played out with authenticity without losing any of the fun or atmosphere and squaddies watch it over and over."

David Creed – director and ex-Armed Forces

"*I love this film, so when asked to write my thoughts on why this was a favourite with military and ex-military alike, it gave me an excuse to watch it again. And I'm glad I did.*

From the moment the Squad de-bussed from the helicopter the attention to detail becomes apparent. From the wet and weathered worn in look of the uniform and kit and broken in boots, to the constant banter and piss taking one would expect from Squaddies. Sentences made up of bad language and the word 'fuck'. It's like a language I can easily understand. Camaraderie at its best.

The fighting withdrawal through the woods showed tactics similar and the fact they had even been thought about raised my eyebrows. Even when the Squad realised what they were up against they took this in good military fashion. It is what it is, expect the unexpected and deal with it. Commands given with the same level of thought and discipline.

What can I say, the military emphasises attention to detail and this is no different to the Squaddies portrayed in this film. Piss taking, camaraderie and the willingness to get involved in a good scrap. Makes you want to do it all over again."

Eddie Sundarajoo – ex RAF and police officer

DOG
SOLDIERS

A NORTHMEN PRODUCTIONS FILM PROPOSAL

Imagine you're leading a six-man squad on a routine army exercise....and it all goes horribly wrong. You're behind enemy lines. Your men are inexperienced. Your radio doesn't work. You're cut off and on foot in a vast, hostile wilderness. You've got a critically wounded man to look after. You've been set up by your own superiors. You're the bait in a trap laid by heavily armed Government forces. You're not carrying any live ammunition. You can hear something howling in the distance and the sun is going down. It's a full moon night, your men are scared shitless, you're missing the most important football match of the decade, and there's every chance that you're about to be eaten alive by a pack of vicious, snarling, blood-hungry seven foot tall Werewolves!   ...What do you?

RUN FOR YOUR LIFE

DOG SOLDIERS

SYNOPSIS

A lone soldier, Corporal Lawrence COOPER, shattered and torn, flees in desperation from an unseen menace. Seemingly animal in nature, the pursuer soon runs COOPER into the ground and at the last moment the beast, a DOG, is yanked back by its handler. It's just a test, but in being caught COOPER has failed Special Forces selection.

Some weeks later, a Chinook helicopter swoops low across the highland wilderness of Scotland pausing briefly to drop its cargo of six soldiers in the middle of nowhere before thundering off into the morning haze. The six-man unit is being led by Sergeant WELLS, and consists of Corporal COOPER, JOE, TERRY, BRUCE and SPOON, a motley bunch of tough-nuts from across the U.K. They are on exercise, being supposedly a 100km behind enemy lines it is their mission to get back across their own lines, evading hostiles and avoiding capture, within the next 48 hours.

Aside from a few false alarms the first day passes without incident and is spent yomping through spectacular landscapes bantering about girlfriends, card games and the weather while regularly exchanging ruthless quips. We soon come to know them both as individuals and as a unit. As the sun sets that evening, the men bed down for the night in the only available shelter, a cave beneath a rocky promontory. Later the men eat, drink and joke together until COOPER decides to regale them with a scary local legend; concerning hikers mysteriously vanishing in these mountains. Sensing tension within the group, WELLS seeks to displace it with his own 'true' story, a ghostly tale with a joke ending. The men laugh away the fear, dissipating the tension completely, and only then does the first shock come, slamming home with maximum impact as a mutilated COW quite literally drops in from the cliff above and lands slap-bang on top of their campfire! Recovering from this sudden and violent intrusion, the men quickly conclude that something is awry and decide to investigate the next morning.

Following a trail of blood, tracing the COW's path back to the place it was attacked, the men hike across miles of rugged terrain until they stumble upon the site of another attack - a second group of SOLDIERS, heavily armed and yet decimated in the night. Blood covers their camp, all that remains are shreds of clothing, smashed equipment, and one badly wounded survivor - Captain Richard RYAN. WELLS orders an immediate evacuation, but the radio has been sabotaged. They're cut-off, a hundred miles from the nearest town or village, the sun is beginning to set, and just as things can't any worse, the howling starts. At first far off, but quickly moving this way, the sound alone is enough to send a shiver down anybody's spine. As the unseen horror approaches, the decision is made to withdraw, rapidly!

The chase is on. The winner lives. The loser....is lunch. BRUCE hangs back to cover the retreat but is quickly cut down by this savage, unseen enemy. WELLS goes back to help him, but he too runs afoul of one of the creatures. He's slashed across the belly and must literally pull himself together. As the others run, COOPER returns for his friend, blasting one of the beasts out of the way before dragging the injured WELLS clear. Finally, we get a glimpse of the creatures - huge, seven foot tall WEREWOLVES, running around on two legs, lashing out with deadly clawed hands! Running hell-for-leather through the night, made darker by the canopy of the forest, the remains of the squad, carrying RYAN and caught up by COOPER and WELLS, run into the path of a young woman driving along a remote mountain road. Her name is MEGAN, and she has little choice but to agree to take this frantic bunch of armed men to sanctuary - a farm owned by friends of hers.

Arriving at the FARM they get no response and break in. There's nobody home except the family dog - SAM. They find the telephone line is cut off and the decision is made to evacuate and drive to the nearest village. But there's one problem, her car has vanished, from right outside the door. The hunt has now become a siege, with the soldiers trapped inside and the WOLVES at the door!

In this initial period of reprieve, as the WEREWOLVES watch and wait, WELLS is sewn up by MEGAN and COOPER, who begin to grow on each other, while the rest of the men turn the house into a fortress, bolting the doors and barricading the windows. Then the first attack comes, ferocious and intense, claiming TERRY as the second victim. But by the skin of their teeth, they manage to hold out. During this time, RYAN does little to help, and COOPER (having assumed command of the squad now) grows suspicious of his rapidly improving health.

Their ammunition, salvaged from the remains of RYAN's camp, is running low and so is their time. Desperate situations requiring desperate measures, JOE volunteers to make run for the BARN, where MEGAN informs them an old Land Rover is kept. With SPOON creating a diversion, JOE makes it to the car and, despite being attacked from all sides, manages to reverse up to the FARMHOUSE door but is slain at the last moment by an unwanted passenger.

The vehicles fuel tank is rupture and leaking badly their options have run out. Realising the futility of his actions considering the situation they're all in, RYAN finally succumbs to reason and confesses all. His team of Special Forces operatives are part of a covert Government-backed agency who have known about this area for years - the local legend, the missing people, and the firm belief that there was something on the loose out here, something very dangerous, something worth investigating. It was RYAN's mission to catch he beast, and it was COOPER, WELLS and the other's misfortune to be the live bait. Only 'it' turned out to be 'them', and now they're all going to die.

Enraged by this, WELLS takes a swing at the now fit and healthy RYAN who, having been wounded by a WEREWOLF, promptly turns into one and escapes mto the night! WELLS knows that sooner or later he's going to follow RYAN's example and tum, but COOPER's not going down without a fight. Loading the Land Rover with canisters of propane gas, COOPER turns it into a moving bomb and drives it headlong toward the BARN! Just before it smashes home, he jumps clear and SPOON lights the trail of fuel left in its wake. The fire ignites the fuel tank, bursts the propane canister, and blows the BARN sky high!

Swept up by this brief moment of rapture, COOPER moves to embrace MEGAN, but she backs off, finally revealing her true self. She has betrayed them all, she's been lying from the first moment they met, she is one of them, and this is their house! Beginning her own transformation, COOPER shoots her right between the eyes. He knows it won't kill her, but it's the thought that counts!

All hell breaks loose as the family of WEREWOLVES surge into the house! WELLS and COOPER flee upstairs while SPOON engages one of the beasts in hand-to-hand combat in the kitchen! He puts up a good fight but is finally torn to pieces. Upstairs, hiding in the bathroom as the creatures pound the door to splinters, WELLS and COOPER tear throu h a wall into the neighbouring room and take shelter inside a wardrobe. W1th the WEREWOLVES rocking them back and forth trying to get inside, WELLS cuts a hole through the floor, and they drop down into the now deserted kitchen. Using the table to block the door and buy them some time, WELLS urges COOPER (and SAM the dog) to take shelter in the basement while he remains behind and makes the ultimate sacrifice. Turning on the oven but not igniting it, WELLS fills the room with gas and bids his friend farewell. As the WERE OLVES force their way in and comer him, WELLS flicks his lighter, sparking off the gas and blowing himself, the WEREWOLVES, and the whole house to ashes!

Recovering from the blast COOPER finds himself surrounded by the spoils these creatures have collected from their victims over the years. But just when he thinks it's all over, he's attacked by one last werewolf - RYAN! But valour intervenes in the fearless form of SAM the dog, taking on the beast ten times his size and giving COOPER enough time to dig out a SILVER steak knife from the surrounding booty! At the last moment COOPER slays his nemesis, before staggering from the smouldering wreckage of the house with his newfound saviour and companion close at heel.

...But there is something strange about SAM as he sits, looking directly at us. His eyes begin to change, slowly, almost imperceptibly, becoming less canine... and more human!

THE END

CHARACTERS

COOPER

Having served for six years and missed out on any major conflicts, Cooper secretly yearns for some action. After failing official selection for Special Forces duty, Cooper ultimately succeeds through natural selection. When the storm comes, Cooper remains a calm harbour of reason and morale until the bitter end. He's loyal, selfless, determined, courageous and a good mate to have around in a crisis.

CAST SUGGESTIONS - Sean Bean, David Thewlis, Gary Oldman

WELLS

A professional soldier to the hilt, Wells has worked his way up through the ranks and picked up a lot of experience along the way. He's seen some action and paid his dues, and watches over his men with a firm but fair hand. He sees in COOPER his former self, and is always prepared to give him the benefit of his wisdom to avoid him making the same mistakes.

CAST SUGGESTIONS - Bob Peck, Pete Postlethwaite, Maurice Roeves

RYAN

Morally corrupt and vehemently ruthless, Ryan cares for no-one and nothing beyond his own personal gains. Swathed in cloak and dagger secrecy he is as much a creature of the night as those he is dispatched to capture.

CAST SUGGESTIONS - Colin Firth, Iain Glenn, Nigel Havers, Angus MacFadyan

MEGAN

All flowing hair and radiant features, Megan is the kind of woman who'll break your heart and then eat it, literally. A Zoologist by trade she's gone to the dogs. Dark and seductive, you want to trust her... you really want to trust her.

CAST SUGGESTIONS - Catherine McCormack, Emily Watson, Emily Woof (or possibly a newcomer)

SPOON

Short of stature but big of balls, Spoon is a quick-witted, cockney wide-boy with a hair-trigger finger and a put-down for every occasion. He's a silver tongued Devil with a machine gun, and he won't go down without a fight.

CAST SUGGESTIONS - Rick Warden

JOE

A full blooded Geordie to the last, he lives and breathes for only one thing -
football. The beautiful game is his life and death. This army lark is just something to do between matches.

CAST SUGGESTIONS - Stephen D. Thirkeld

TERRY

Joe's brother in arms and partner in crime, Terry is a gambling man who doesn't favour the odds he's found himself up against.

CAST SUGGESTIONS - Mike McNally, Bob Mortimer

BRUCE

The smart, silent type, Bruce is a by-t e-book soldier, in for life, tight in every sense of the word but a dab hand with a headset and wireless

CAST SUGGESTIONS - Ewan Bremner, Colin McCredie, David O'Hara

WEREWOLVES

The aim is singular. We intend our LYCANTHROPIC characters to be the most frightening and convincing ever committed to film

Closer in nature to the looming bipedal creatures of the 'The Howling' 1980 than the squat, dog-like monster of 'An American Werewolf in London' 1981 and it's less than convincing sequel, 'An American Werewolf in Paris' 1997, our Werewolves will be humanoid in form yet wolf in feature, giant, savage, drooling, snarling and absolutely real - in other words, not CGI.

Due to extreme over exposure, contemporary audiences have very quickly become complacent, unconvinced and in many cases just plain bored with the so-called fluid motion and ethereal nature of CGI creatures. With the possible exception of only one film - JURASSIC PARK - CGI effects are rapidly and noticeably becoming less effective. They don't look solid, like you could reach out and touch them, and because of this they don't achieve any sense of reality. Since our werewolves are half-man half-wolf hybrids that have arms, legs, clawed hands and run around on two feet, we want to do it the old-fashioned way and put a man in a suit - but not just any man and not just any suit. We want to use basketball players, because of the their size, agility and physique, and the suit should be a like a second skin, detailed and textured, crowned with a fully functioning and highly expressive animatronic wolf's head.

It is our opinion that the man to wolf transformation

sequence in 'An American Werewolf in London' is about as good as it gets and would be a hard act to follow, let alone compare with. This is just as well because DOG SOLDIERS was never intended as a 'transformation movie'. There are transformation sequences contained within the film, but instead of being dwelt upon they will either be handled in a very matter-of-fact way, or, using modem techniques such as motion control, do the old 'disappearing behind the furniture' trick, (paying homage to the classic Wolfman/ Dr. Jekyll movies of old) but doing so within a tracking shot, which is something that has never been done in this context before.

Another important element, from a purely visual standpoint, is the Werewolves point-of-view. In contrast to the frenzied, hand-held action of the soldiers, the Werewolves sight will be smooth, gliding at great speed through dense forest or over rocky glen. Since dogs cannot see in colour, have a wider field of vision, and can see much better at night than humans, the POV will be monochrome, anamorphic and over-exposed. Not only is this more accurate, but it will also be visually arresting in the extreme.

VISUAL STYLE

To be shot in widescreen 35mm 'DOG SOLDIERS', as we envisage it, has that rare characteristic of being both epic and intimate, panoramic and claustrophobic, and can be divided into two visual segments:

The first half, set almost entirely outdoors, should encapsulate and exploit the vast splendour and underlying mystery of the Scottish Highlands. Our introduction to the characters and the world they inhabit should be predominantly natural in its colour and gritty in its feel - browns, greens, heather purple and granite grey. Even in bright sunlight, the landscape should be magnificent yet verging on menacing, gentle yet deadly, as Scotland really is.

The second half will be an assault on the senses using glaring and contrasting colours - the orange glow of fire, deep blue moonlight, red phosphorous flares and blinding white powder flash. As the action intensifies, so do the images.

SOUND

The intention is that the WEREWOLVES various cries, howls, snarls and guttural bellows will cut deep into our very souls searching for that same instinctive reaction that instilled primal fear into the hearts of the first humans ever to know the howl of a wolf, the growl of a bear or the roar of a lion. Employing the latest in post-production technology we will manufacture sound effects of such volume and intensity the audience will be able to physically feel them hitting their bodies like shock-waves, the echo resonating long afterwards, and be left exhilarated and enhanced by the experience.

EDITING

The intention of the edit is simple - to compact two hours worth of script into a 100 minute package, without spilling a drop. It's an action movie, not just in terms of content, but in style, and it should move accordingly. We're going to start fast and keep the pace at break-neck speed until the last shot is fired, the last line is delivered, and the last frame passes through the gate.

LOGISTICS

In the production of DOG SOLDIERS we will follow the lessons learned from 'Killing Time', i.e. the three p's - Preparation, Preparation, Preparation. The work contained in this document is only the tip of the iceberg as regards insight, planning and resolution of what Neil and I propose to be contained in the finished Film.

As the script currently stands we intend to shoot on Location in the highlands of Scotland for four weeks in September this year (budget and actors commitments permitting). On completion of this we will move into the studio, (London based) where our sets will already be constructed and waiting, to shoot all FX and interiors for a further four weeks.

Locations have to be finalised but the front runner at the moment would be to have our Production HQ in Cannich approximately 25 miles west of Inverness with all the location filming taking place around Loch Affric. The cast and crew would be billeted in Inverness.

We are looking into assistance from the Ministry of Defence for logistical support (Helicopters, Weaponry, Uniforms) as well as having technical advice from either retired or serving armed forces personnel.

The crew will be a mixture of professionals who we have worked with over the years as well as recruiting local Scottish people to assist us on location. We believe it is vitally---important in choosing the right crew and will be looking for extremely competent and experienced personnel in the SPX department and as this is Neil's first feature, a well-seasoned First with some experience on Action films.

In respect to Post Production we will have daily transfer of negatives to the lab with transfer to Beta (VHS for director and producers viewing on location). All Beta tapes will be sent straight to our edit suite in Newcastle to be digitised with the edit beginning one week after completion of principal photography. Utilising the latest Avid Film Composer technology, the edit will run over 7 weeks in Newcastle at Imagine - Non-Linear Post Production, with Sound mixing, dubbing and final effects to be completed in London.

On our current schedule all Post Production, music composition and final cut of the film ready for prints to be made would be completed by March 1999.

NEIL MARSHALL - DIRECTOR

Keith and I first met in 1991 when we both attended Film School in Newcastle. Although in different year-groups, it was clear that we shared the same dreams and aspirations as far as movies were concerned and so a very strong friendship was formed and has remained so ever since. I graduated in 1992 with the satisfaction that I'd succeeded in subverting the course rules by directing a twenty-minute action Zombie movie which gained a rapturous ovation when it was screened at our degree show.

Attending that screening were Producer Richard Johns and Director Bharat Nalluri (who made 'DOWNTIME' for Film Four last year). We met and they became interested in one of my scripts, promptly forming PILGRIM FILMS with the view to producing it. During this time I worked side by side with Bharat on the Tyne Tees drama 'DRIVEN' as editor, storyboard artist and directors assistant, followed by 'PRESS-GANGED', again as storyboard artist and directors assistant. In 1994 PILGRIM asked me to write and direct a 10min short for Tyne Tees Television. I came up with 'DOG EAT DOG', a fast and furious 'video diary from Hell'.

Away from PILGRIM, I edited the 30min drama 'REFUGE' for Tyne Tees Television, and was commissioned by Paul Brooks of Metrodome films to write two feature scripts based on treatments I'd sent him. The first, entitled 'THE SPIRAL DOWN' is completed and in search of funding. The second, 'HEIGHTS OF ABRAHAM' is still in development.

In February 1995, PILGRIM FILMS commissioned me to come up with a script for an action/thriller to be made with very limited resources. The result was 'KILLING TIME'. Shot on 35mm and filmed on location in and around Newcastle in October of that year, I worked not only as a writer, but again as storyboard artist, directors assistant, action co-ordinator, and finally as editor. Observing the pre-production, being on location and directly involved at a hands-on level through every moment of the shoot, and finally cutting the work into a coherent whole was both a totally exhilarating and highly educational experience. 'KILLING TIME' was acquired by Columbia/Tri Star at the Milan Film Market in November '95 on the basis of a two minute trailer that I'd cut only days after the film wrapped. It was released in the U.S. on January 29th, 1998.

Throughout 1997, while surviving as a freelance AVID editor, I have devoted every spare moment to writing 'DOG SOLDIERS', consulting with Keith along the way and hammering out draft after draft until, in December, we agreed that it was ready to go.

KEITH BELL - PRODUCER

I left school at sixteen, worked in numerous jobs, including a year as a Cinema Manager for ABC, before travelling around the world for a number of years courtesy of The Royal Navy. It was here that I finally decided what I wanted to do with my life; make films. I met Neil at Film School in our hometown Newcastle and was immediately struck by his passion for movies and his 'interesting' ideas.

On leaving Film School myself and two contempories formed Musketeer Productions and relocated to London where initially we were the usual indie. production company struggling for tv commissions, but we persevered and made several commercials, corporates and pop videos as well as a number of pilot entertainment tv shows for leading independents Mentom and Channel X. After two successful years we mutually agreed to concentrate on our personal goals and parted company.

In August '95 I was hired by Pilgrim Films as Production Manager on the low-budget action thriller 'Killing Time' shooting in and around Newcastle. The experience of making this film, I believe, was invaluable to me as we struggled through and got the film made on a minuscule budget (deferred payment) and on an extremely tight schedule. The production would have run a lot smoother if we had had more time in pre-production preparing all aspects of the principal photography and post production. 'Killing Time' sadly, as in the case of many low budget features, was caught in the distribution trap and has only recently been released in the USA.

Since Killing Time I freelanced as a Producer and Production Manager on award winning commercials and idents working for agencys all over the UK . I have recently parted company with Siriol Scotland in Glasgow where I launched the 2D animation studio for Siriol Productions in Cardiff, one of the UK s leading animation studios. The Scottish studio employed me as Producer/ Studio Manager and for the past eighteen months I have produced numerous animated commercials and shorts as well as managing two broadcast children's series for ITV.

I have for the past year been consulting with Neil over the screenplay of 'DOG SOLDIERS'. I feel we are now at the stage to begin the task of putting the ingredients together to make what we firmly believe to be an exciting and exhilarating feature film. Northmen Productions was formed in January 1998 with the view to doing just that.

OUR AIMS

At present, NORTHMEN PRODUCTIONS exists for just two reasons - to make DOG SOLDIERS to the very best of our ability, and to get as many people as possible into the cinema to experience it. These are the goals. But there are certain self-imposed proviso's attached to our achieving them. They are:

This is a British story about British characters in a British situation, and should be made in Britain, by Britain.

Dog Soldiers will not be made as a deferral film.

This film will be Produced by Keith Bell and Directed by Neil Marshall.

We are always open to suggestions, but the bottom line is that it will be our film, and we would rather stand or fall on our own two feet than have ideas or constraints imposed upon us by people who believe they know what will or will not work. William Goldman once wrote of the film business - "Nobody knows anything." a statement that we believe is as true now as it ever was.

We trust you will have gathered from this document at least an indication of the passion we have for DOG SOLDIERS, and we hope that in reading it you have come to share some of that passion. The British film industry hasn't been quite so buoyant in years and there has never been a better time to make this kind of film; to give audiences the first true British-made roller-coaster ride movie, complete with a couple of shocks, a few scares, a bundle of laughs and a shit-load of action!

AFTERWORD
BY JOHN LANDIS

Some years ago, I was in Vancouver directing an episode of a television series called Psych. By coincidence, my friend Mick Garris was also directing an episode of another television series in Vancouver. We met one Sunday afternoon and walked to the movie theater across the street from the hotel where we were both staying. I knew nothing about the movie and found myself very scared and thoroughly entertained by a clever story well told. I was impressed by the screenplay and direction of an Englishman named Neil Marshall and looked forward to watching more of his films.

Many years later, when I was asked to write the Afterword to this book, I remembered seeing Dog Soldiers with Mick in Vancouver and called him to ensure my memory was correct. It turns out that my memory was not right! Mick remembered our visit to the cinema and how much we enjoyed the Neil Marshall movie playing there, *The Descent*! Let's just call it "Covid Fog." I loved *The Descent* in the theater. It was claustrophobic and intense, with relatable characters and terrific monsters. But this is a book about another Neil Marshall movie, *Dog Soldiers*, which I knew I had seen, but have long forgotten where or when.

I did not see *Dog Soldiers* in a cinema (always the best movie experience), it must have been either on DVD or television. But with the invitation to write this Afterward, I immediately purchased the new Blu-ray and watched *Dog Soldiers* again. Interestingly, I remembered it very well. Neil shared the same problem with all filmmakers of shape-shifter movies; how do you make this old story new? In Joe Dante's *The Howling* (1981, screenplay by John Sayles and Terrence Winkless), Joe did it wonderfully. John Fawcett had a brilliant and fresh approach to lycanthropy with his film *Ginger Snaps* (2000, screenplay by John Fawcett and Karen Waldon, story by John Fawcett). So, what did Neil do to sharpen the approach to his particular tale of wolfmen?

The box office smash *Alien* (1979, directed by Ridley Scott, screenplay by Dan O'Bannon) was a reworking of *It! The Terror from Beyond Space* (1958, directed by Edward L Cahn, screenplay by Jerome Bixby). *Alien* was heavily influenced by Mario Bava's *Planet of The Vampires* (1965, based on the Italian science fiction short story, *One Night of Twenty Four Hours* by Renato Pestriniero). While these two features were low budget "B Pictures," *Alien* was a handsomely designed and brilliantly directed "A" product. Essentially a "Gorilla in a Haunted House" movie, the lavish production design (including the elegant monster by H.R. Giger) and Ridley Scott's direction elevated the film in the eyes of the critics and an appreciative public.

When handed the sequel to *Alien*, director James Cameron decided that instead of competing with the first film as a handsomely mounted monster movie, he would turn it into an action movie. The sequel became the terrific *Aliens* (1986, written and directed by James Cameron). That is precisely what Neil Marshall did with *Dog Soldiers* (2002, written and directed by Neil Marshall). Using all the tropes of a military combat movie (lost patrol, heavy weaponry, the siege of the house, mistrust of the soldiers of one another, running low on ammunition, etc.), Neil fashioned an exciting movie filled with action and werewolves. Instead of trying to keep the seemingly endless numbers of Zulu warriors at bay in Sy Enfield's *Zulu* (1964, screenplay by John Prebble and Sy Enfield) or barricading the house against the zombies in George Romero's *Night of the Living Dead* (1969, screenplay by John Russo and George A. Romero), the soldiers in *Dog Soldiers* are fighting for their lives against insurmountable odds. I enjoyed the hell out of it. Incredibly, it was Neil's first movie. Mr. Marshall has gone on to a long and impressive career and continues to write and direct (including some of the best *Game of Thrones* episodes).

By now, after reading this book, you should be experts on Neil Marshall's *Dog Soldiers*. I can only leave you with this warning; "STAY ON THE ROAD. KEEP CLEAR OF THE MOORS. BEWARE THE MOON."

John Landis
February 11th, 2022
Los Angeles, California

THANKS

Obviously, I would like to thank each and every person I spoke to in the making of this book.

I'm so grateful for people graciously giving up their time, especially Neil who I messaged over and over and over…

I'm honoured to have been able to chat with so many amazing people who love this movie as much as I do. Thank you to everyone who provided me with stories, insights, photos and quotes.

To everyone behind the scenes at Encyclopocalypse, the hugest thanks to you. This book wouldn't exist without Mark, and it looks amazing because of you. I have loved working with you guys and I'm not leaving. You're stuck with me now.

Thank you to Dave Bonneywell for the amazing cover, I love how it's all come full circle now from your first design to this. It was just meant to be.

So much love to Jonathan Janz and Hunter Shea for blurbs that makes me heart all warm and fuzzy.

I have come away from this project with my passion for

horror movies reignited. I want to read more books like this, I want to write more books like this.

And I'd like to thank you dear reader for taking the time to indulge a superfan and come along for the ride. I hope you had even half as much for reading this as I did creating it.

ABOUT THE AUTHOR

Janine Pipe traded in a police badge and classroom for the glamorous life of an indie horror writer. Her debut collection, *Twisted: Tainted Tales*, blurbed by Brian Keene, cemented her love of writing short stories. As well as writing, she co-runs Kandisha Press and is a guest editor with Clash Books. Not limiting herself to fiction, she also spreads her love of genre pieces writing for Fangoria and enjoys interviewing people and talking about horror movies. When she isn't drinking coffee and plotting trips to Disney with her husband and daughter, you'll find her watching Neil Marshall movies or reading Glenn Rolfe books.

Look out for more with Encyclopocalypse Publications as she doesn't want to leave…

You can find her on Twitter @JaninePipe28

Printed in Great Britain
by Amazon